People Places AND Production

SERIES EDITOR: BOB WALTON

Bob Walton and Steve Milner

HODDER AND STOUGHTON
LONDON SYDNEY AUCKLAND TORONTO

British Library Cataloguing in Publication Data

Walton, Bob
People, places and production.—(People and the natural environment)
1. Economic development. Environmental aspects
I. Title II. Milner, Steve
330.9

ISBN 0 340 41301 8

First published 1990

Typeset by Rowland Phototypesetting Limited, Bury St Edmunds, Suffolk
Printed in Great Britain for Hodder and Stoughton Educational a division of Hodder and Stoughton Limited, Mill Road, Dunton Green, Sevenoaks, Kent by Colorcraft Limited, Hong Kong.

CONTENTS

ACKNOWLEDGEMENTS

The authors and publisher wish to thank the following for permission to reproduce material in this book:

E Anderson (9.12, 9.30)
P Atherton (11.13)
Barbados Board of Tourism (5.29)
Barnaby's Picture Library (1.27, 5.1 (f), 9.4, 9.28, 9.36, 10.80)
Bart Hofmeester, Rotterdam (6.9)
CMB Promotional Packaging (10.16)
Canada House (1.12)
Central Electricity Generating Board (PowerGen Division) (10.47)
Chesterfield Town Council (10.40)
Commission for Racial Equality (1.17)
City of Dundee District Council (5.1 (9), 7.34, 7.36, 7.38, 7.49, 10.61)
City of Durham Planning Office (5.23)
French Government Tourist Office (5.27 (a & b))
M J Gleeson Group PLC (11.14)
Godfrey New Photographics (1.19)
GO Transit, Canada (7.12)
Col R Hardie, R.A.M.C. (3.3)
Holiday Club, Pontin's (5.1 (c))
Holt Studios Ltd (9.8 (a & b), 9.40, 10.78)
Hulton Picture Library (6.22 (e))
Hunting Aerofilms (10.50)
Hutchison Library (3.6, 3.17, 4.7, 5.19, 6.2, 6.5, 7.49, 8.9 (a & b), 9.31, 9.45, 10.43, 10.56, 11.16)
ICI Agrochemicals (9.41)
L Kimpton (7.24)
London Borough of Tower Hamlets (1.19)
London Docklands Development Corporation (7.30)
Luchtfoto Aerophoto Eelde (7.44, 7.45)
E Mann (11.77)
Mansfield Brewery (10.28)
Mid Glamorgan County Council (10.19)
G Minshull (3.8)
Museum in Docklands Project, Museum of London (7.29)
Oxfam (4.1)
Peugeot Talbot (10.23)
The Salvation Army (7.8)
Save the Children/Penny Tweedie (4.12)
Sheffield City Council (10.68, 10.69, 10.70, 10.71)
Swindon Town Council (10.21)
Swiss National Tourist Office (3.4, 3.5)
Taylor Richardson Associates (7.9)
Telford Development Corporation (7.46, 7.47)
Torbay Tourist Board (11.20)
City of Toronto Planning and Development Department (6.10)
United Nations (4.15) (UN123, 597)
Volkswagen DO Brasil SA (10.28)

PART ONE PEOPLE

1 CLASSIFYING POPULATION

This British secondary school has 950 students aged 11 to 16. Although the numbers of boys and girls are roughly equal, there are large variations in the male/female ratio between age groups. The average number of students in each age group is 190 but the upper school age groups are larger.

At the end of the school year, 210 fifth year students will leave and an estimated 140 new starters will replace them, giving a drop of 70 in the school population. Most students live in the town as shown by the rural/urban ratio in fig. 1.1 but about one quarter travels in by bus from surrounding rural areas.

Fig. 1.1 *Comprehensive school and its population*

(a) *Age structure*

Age	Number of pupils
15-16	210
14-15	210
13-14	200
12-13	180
11-12	150

(b) *Male-Female ratio*

Age	Boys	Girls
15-16	110	100
14-15	90	120
13-14	90	110
12-13	100	80
11-12	80	70

(c) *Urban-rural ratio*

Age	Urban	Rural
15-16	170	40
14-15	150	60
13-14	140	60
12-13	135	45
11-12	120	30

(d)

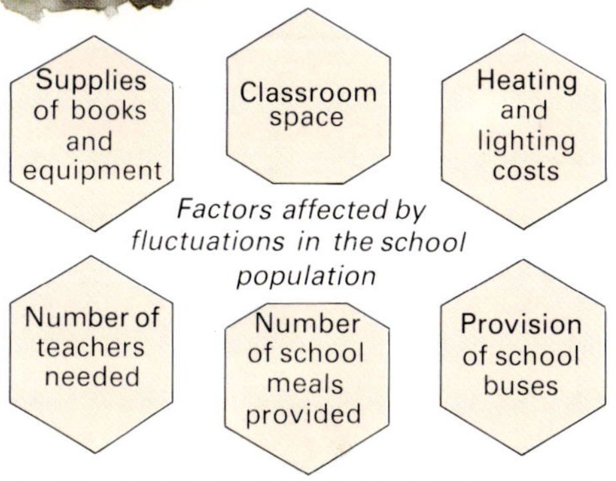

Activities

1 Collect information from your own school to draw charts similar to those in fig. 1.1(a) to (c).
2 Write brief reports about the population of your school, using the following headings: a) Total population. b) Age/sex structures. c) Rural/urban ratio.
3 Interview students from both rural and urban areas to find out their attitudes towards travelling to school, the benefits it has and the disadvantages. Once you have the information, discuss your findings.

Size

You have just studied a small scale example of a population, which introduced a number of key ideas. One of these key ideas is that populations can be classified according to their size. If you live in Britain, you are one of about 56 million people. However, if you live in

Northern Ireland, one of the eleven regions shown in fig. 1.2, you are only one of about 1½ millions. Two regions on this map are similar in area but have very different populations: the North with 3 millions and the South East with 17 millions. These comparisons of size within Britain enable us to classify Northern Ireland as an area with a fairly low population total; the North also as quite low, but the South East as an area with very high population total.

Similar comparisons of size can be made between the 130 or so countries of the world, some of which are shown in rank order in fig. 1.3. Comparisons between continents are made in fig. 1.4.

The size of the population itself may not be a useful way to classify populations. The comparison between Japan and Brazil in fig. 1.5 shows this. These are countries with similar sized populations but their areas are very different.

Fig. 1.2 *Population of British regions*

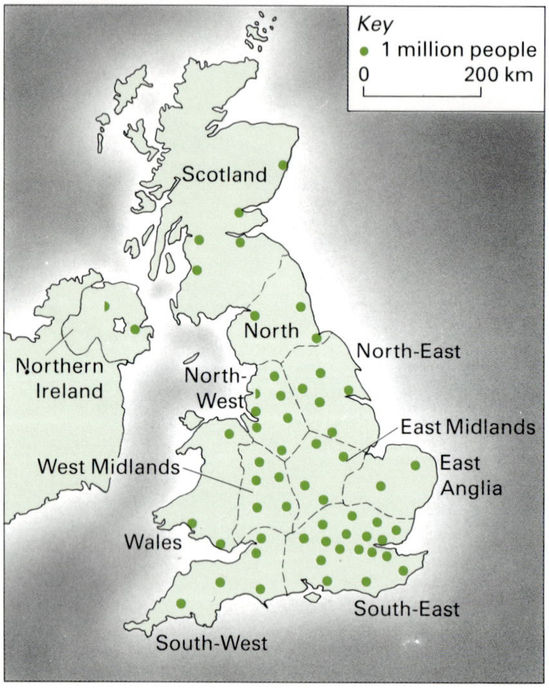

Fig. 1.3 *Population of different countries*

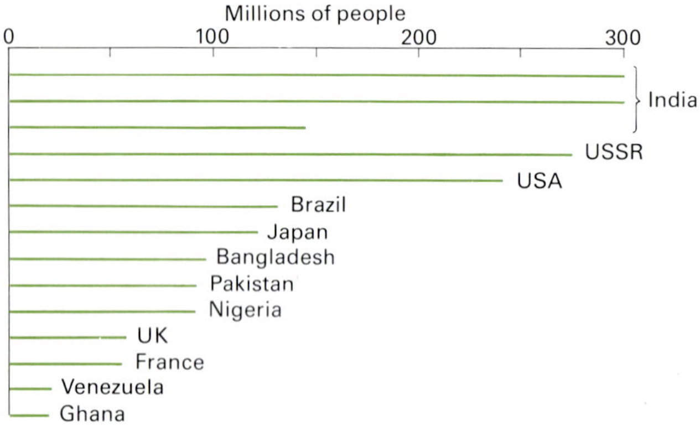

Fig. 1.4 *Population of continents*

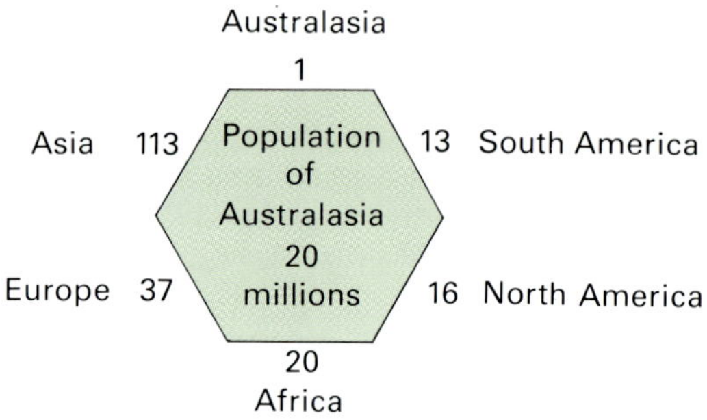

To compare continents, figures show the number of times each continent's population is greater than that of the smallest continent, Australasia.

Fig. 1.5 *Japan and Brazil at the same scale*

Activities

1 Use fig. 1.2 to list the regions of the UK in rank order according to the population total. Make a second list according to the size of region. In both cases, put the largest at the top. Compare the lists.

2 Use fig. 1.3 to choose pairs of countries with similar sized populations. Find out their areas and compare them.

3 In fig. 1.4, have the largest continents in area got the largest populations?

Density

'Density' is a measurement of population per unit area and this is a more useful method of classification than size of population alone. A variety of scales can be used, but there are two which are most common. Figure 1.6 shows the number of people per hectare which is a useful measurement. A hectare is 2.47 acres. In the larger area of Western Europe in fig. 1.7 the number of people per square kilometre is used.

Fig. 1.6 *Population densities of districts in County Durham*

District	*Population density (People per hectare)*
Chester-le-Street	7.7
Derwentside	3.3
Durham	4.6
Easington	7.1
Sedgefield	4.2
Wear Valley	1.1
Teesdale	0.3

Fig. 1.7 *Population densities of Western European countries*

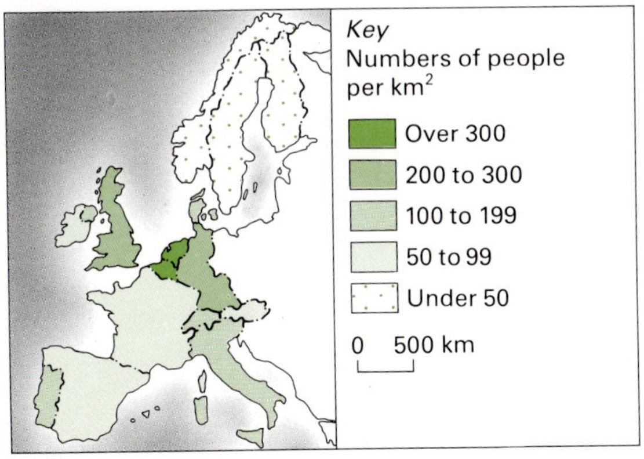

Figure 1.7 is a choropleth map of Western Europe. This sort of map uses shading to show the fall from a high statistic to a small one. The key shows some countries with densities over 300 per km^2. There are also wide variations in density between the countries of West Africa. These are shown in fig. 1.8 by means of bar-graphs for each country. The highest density in the region is Nigeria with just over 80 per km^2. This is quite low in comparison with some European countries. The pattern of densities – high, medium and low-over a region, such as West Africa is called the distribution of population.

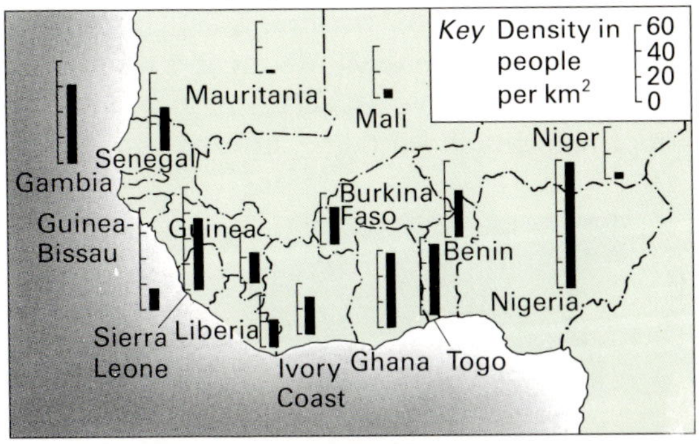

Fig. 1.8 *Population densities of West African countries*

Fig. 1.9 *Districts of County Durham*

Activities

1. Using the information in fig. 1.6 and a copy of the map of Durham Districts in fig. 1.9, draw a choropleth map to show the population density of Durham. Add a key to your map.
2. Using fig. 1.7 and an atlas, list the countries of Western Europe in rank order of population densities. What do you notice about the size of the countries with the highest densities? Describe the location of the countries with the highest densities, then discuss in groups the reasons for this.
3. Using fig. 1.8 and an atlas, list in rank order the three West African countries with the highest and the three with the lowest population densities. Write separate sentences to comment upon the general location of both groups.
4. Write advantages and disadvantages of the two mapping techniques used in figs 1.7 and 1.8 by comparing them.

Age/sex structures

Figure 1.1(b) shows the age and sex of students in a secondary school from age 11 to 16 years. If this school was compared to other British schools, differences would appear between the proportion of the total found in each age group and between the numbers of boys and girls. The numbers in fig. 1.1(b) have been plotted in a graph, fig. 1.10. Such graphs are called 'pyramids' because that is normally their shape. This one shows greater numbers in older age groups, especially of girls. Graphs for other schools would be different.

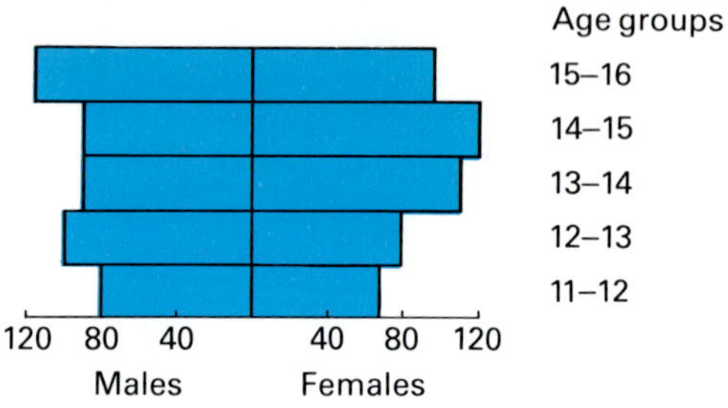

Fig. 1.10 *Age/Sex pyramid for a secondary school*

Age/sex pyramids

Age/sex pyramids can be used in future planning, as illustrated in the following examples. Toronto is the largest city in Canada, and has had rapid population growth in the last fifty years. The growth or decline of numbers of people in different age groups helps to determine the demand for goods and services, such as health, housing and education.

The 'baby boom' in Canada between 1945 and 1964 has been traced in three pyramids in fig. 1.13. People aged between 17 and 36 in 1981 made up 36% of the population. These people, moving out of higher education and forming households, have fuelled demands for housing and have swollen the labour force.

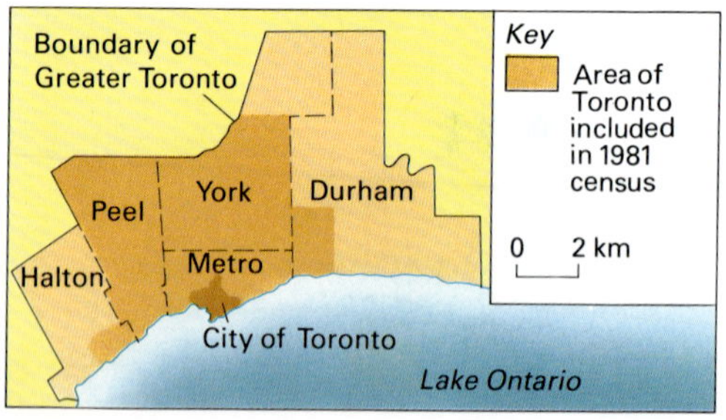

Fig. 1.11 *Municipalities of Toronto, Canada*

Fig. 1.12 *Skyscrapers in Toronto. Do European cities look like this?*

Fig. 1.13 *Age pyramids for Toronto, 1987 to 2021AD*

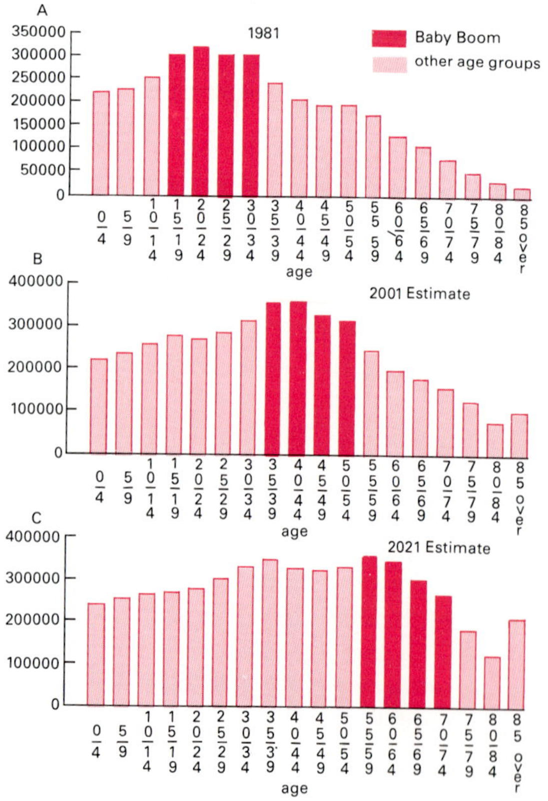

Activities

1 Which services would have had to be expanded for the shaded age groups in fig. 1.13, between 1966 and 1981? Discuss this in groups.
2 Which services are likely to be in great demand after 2001 AD?

Between 1981 and the year 2000 this group, with 528 000 or 62% more people than previously, will make different demands upon services.

Figure 1.15 shows age/sex pyramids for two countries, India and Brazil. Careful study of these pyramids gives the following information:

1. Boys and girls are born in roughly equal numbers
2. The number of people in each age group (5-year blocks) decreases at a steady rate
3. Males and females in each block die at similar rates
4. Half of all people are in the age groups under 20 years
5. The number of people over 60 years is small in proportion to the whole population.

These are ideas or statements which can be made about age/sex pyramids and such ideas can be tested using accurate information. This is called *hypothesis testing*, which is an important geographical skill.

Now study fig. 1.16 which shows pyramids for Britain and Bangladesh. Test each of the hypotheses given above with fig. 1.15 against this information to find out which ones remain positive. Once you are familiar with the use of population pyramids, you will be able to use them to classify population.

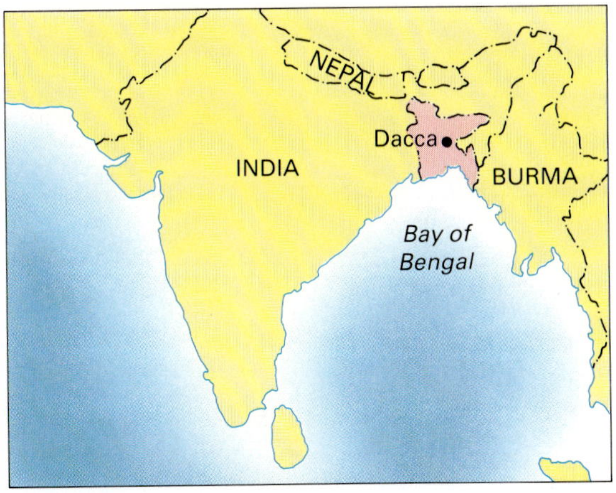

Fig. 1.14 *Location of Bangladesh*

Fig. 1.15 *Age/Sex pyramids for India and Brazil*

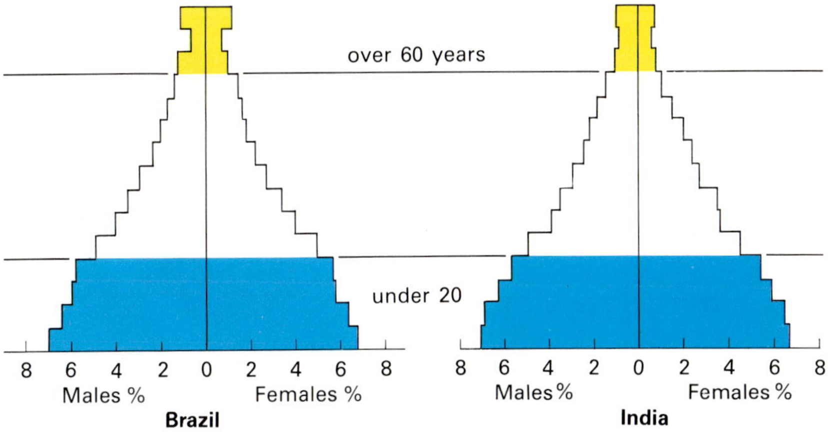

Fig. 1.16 *Age/Sex pyramids for Britain and Bangladesh*

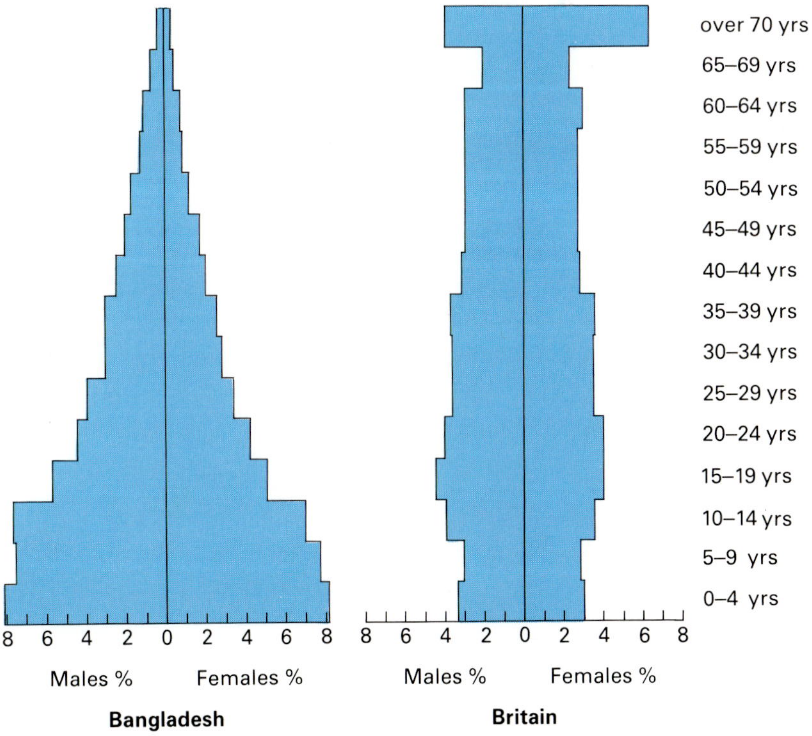

Activities

1 Use the statistics for your school which you collected in the first activity (page 1) and draw a population pyramid (see fig. 1.10).

2 Comment upon the shape of your pyramid. What does it mean as regards your school?

3 Make a list of some of the consequences for your school in two or three years time. Suggest some of the ways that pyramids might help with this planning.

Ethnic origins

Fig. 1.17 *Multiracial Britain*

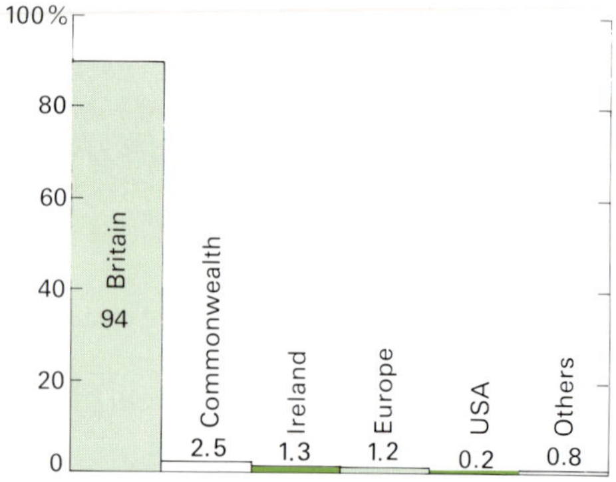

Fig. 1.19 *Population of Britain by birthplace*

Figure 1.17 shows speech day at a girls' school. Such scenes are common in Britain, whose population came from a variety of different countries. This is shown in fig. 1.19.

It is very difficult to classify populations by ethnic origins because of this variety. Britain is a good example. Large numbers of Irish, French Huguenots, European Jews, Latvians and Lithuanians from what is now the USSR have settled in the country, in the last two centuries. Since 1945 West Indians, Indians and Vietnamese have been amongst those people settling in Britain from overseas. They have brought with them a range of cultural, religious and language varieties. Look at fig. 1.18.

Fig. 1.20 *Europeans arriving in Britain in nineteenth century*

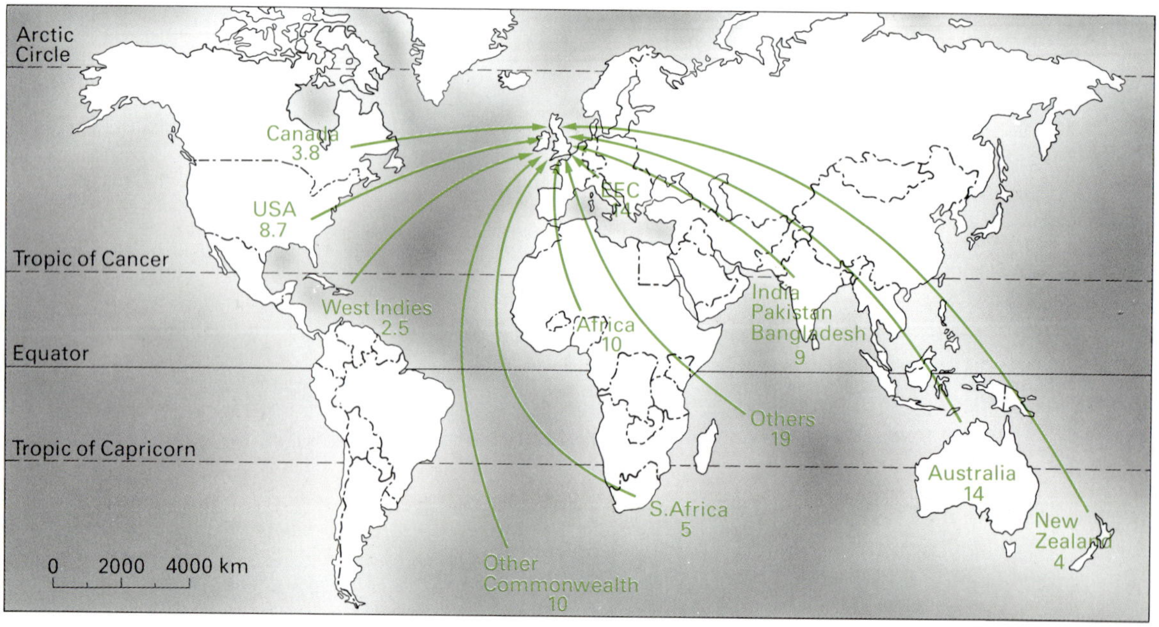

Fig. 1.18 *Origins of immigrants to Britain 1976*

In the City of Birmingham's Inner Area Study of the Handsworth/Soho/Lozells area, very high concentrations of ethnic minorities can be seen. Figure 1.21 shows these ethnic origins.

There are also problems in trying to classify ethnic groups in developing countries. Nigeria in West Africa is typical of many West African countries. It is a highly populated country (see fig. 1.3) and is also the most densely populated

Fig. 1.21 *Countries of birth of people in the Birmingham inner area (1985/86)*

Birthplace	*Census areas* Lozells	*Census areas* Soho
Britain	60.9%	55.3%
Ireland	5.0%	1.6%
Africa	1.6%	2.1%
Caribbean area	7.5%	12.2%
India	8.7%	20.8%
Bangladesh	5.8%	1.7%
Pakistan	8.0%	4.5%
Rest of world	2.5%	1.8%

country in West Africa (fig. 1.8). The present political boundaries were left behind from the days of colonisation by Europeans and make no account of the previous pre-colonial kingdoms which were found in the area. Several different peoples live in Nigeria, as shown in fig. 1.23. Figure 1.24 shows some of the geographical differences between the north and the south of Nigeria. These have been made wider by the influence of Arab peoples from the north and the effects of European colonisation from the south.

The history of Nigeria in recent years has been one of clashes between some of these peoples. In 1967 for example, the Ibo people in the south-east tried to break away from Nigeria to form an independent state of Biafra. Since then attempts have been made by the government to reunite the country. Even the location of a new Federal Capital city in the centre of the country has been planned with national unity in mind (see fig. 1.23).

Fig. 1.22 *Inner Area Study Region of Birmingham*

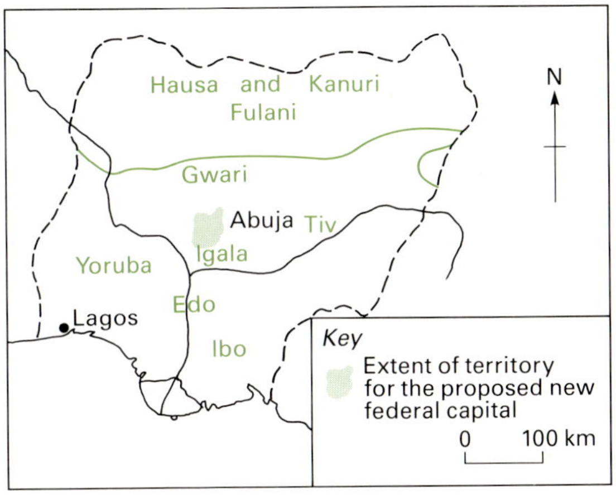

Fig. 1.23 *Ethnic groups in Nigeria*

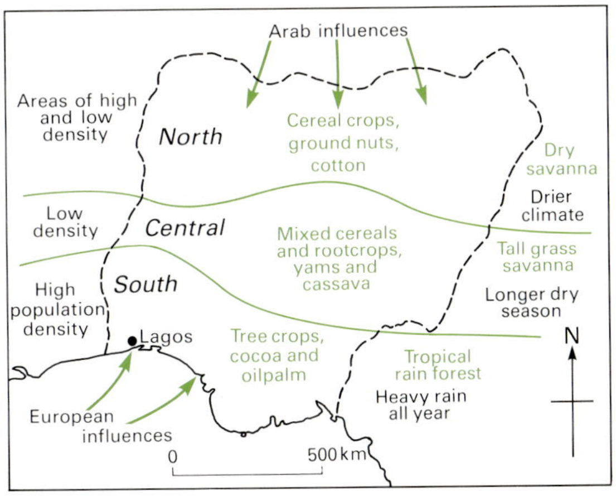

Fig. 1.24 *North-South differences in Nigeria*

Activities

Study fig. 1.19 and fig. 1.21. These show countries of birth of the British population and those who live in part of the Inner Area of Birmingham. Compare the Birmingham area to Britain as a whole and write a paragraph about your findings.

The population of Brazil has a great variety of origins. The first inhabitants were Amerindians, who were believed to have originated in Eastern Asia. There were about 4 millions in the region in 1492 when Europeans discovered it. A population of 100 000 only now remains, mainly living in small groups in Amazonia, the Arawak, Carib and Tupi.

The earliest European, mainly Portuguese, immigrants during the colonial period, up to the late 19th century, were mostly young males. The lack of European females led to marriages between the European males and the native Amerindians. During the slavery period up to 1850, 3½ million people came from Africa. Unions between Portuguese men and Amerindian and African women produced a group known as 'pardos' in Brazil.

Gold rushes, sugar and rubber 'booms' led to further short-lived immigration from Europe in the late 19th century and people from Italy, Spain and Germany replaced Portugal as the main source. Over 200 000 Japanese also entered Brazil between 1900 and 1914. Since 1934, new immigration has been controlled by quotas. These quotas limit total immigration by restricting numbers from individual countries.

Fig. 1.25 *Origin of Brazilian immigrants*

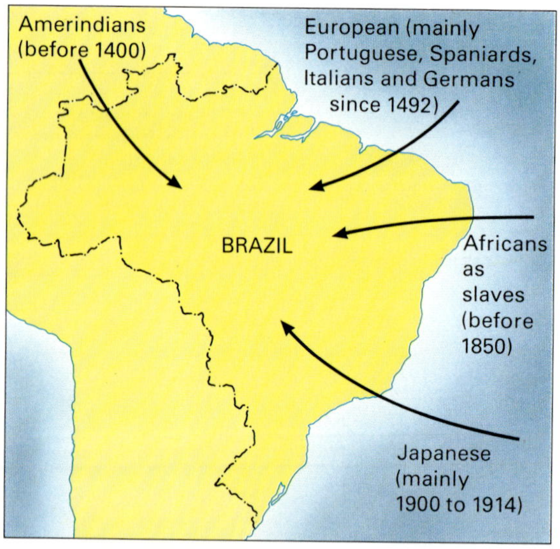

Fig. 1.26 *Distribution of ethnic groups in Brazil*

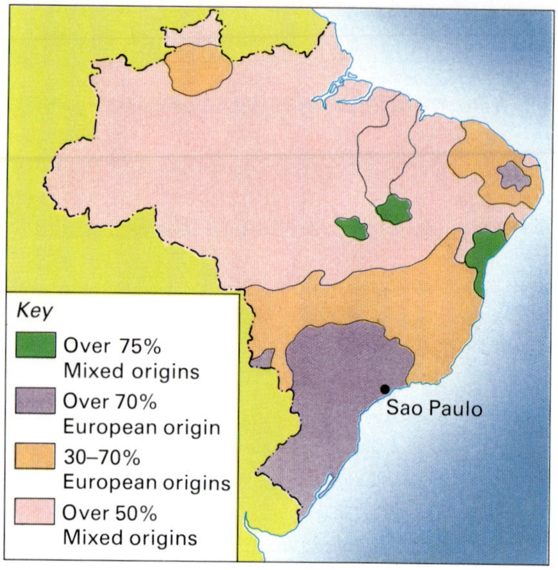

Fig. 1.27 *Multiracial Brazil*

Activities

1 Study fig. 1.18 and fig. 1.25. On a world map showing countries, indicate countries of origin for Brazilian immigrants in one type of shading and those for Britain in another.
2 Compare the two. Are there any similarities? What are the differences?

Urbanisation

Fig. 1.28 *Growth of world population by continent*

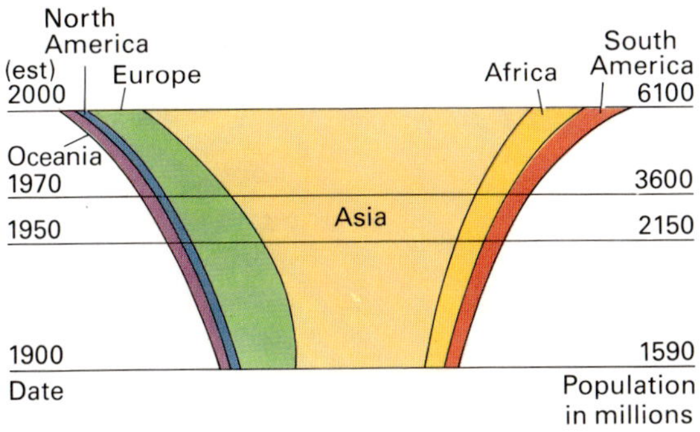

The dramatic growth of world population has been more than matched by the rise in proportion of people living in urban areas. Urban areas can be classified as areas containing towns with 10 000 or more people. This process of growth in number, size and importance of urban areas, and the causes and effects of it, is called *urbanisation*. So, populations can be classified by their rural/urban ratios. People living outside urban areas are classed as rural.

From the time when people first started to develop methods of transporting foods and raw materials from the countryside into villages and towns, the attractions of towns have consistently been greater than those of the countryside. The traditional settlement pattern through the ages has been rural. Farms, hamlets and villages traded their surplus goods at local markets. What towns that did exist were limited in size by the small amounts of surplus food that could be transported from rural areas.

In Britain industrialisation in the 18th and 19th centuries changed all this, as canal, rail and later road transport networks developed. A few towns commanding land and water routeways, called nodal points, could draw supplies from further afield, so they grew larger. By 1900, 80% of Britain's population was urban (See fig. 1.29).

There are various ways in which urban populations can be classified. Figure 1.30 shows the percentage of the population which is urban in several countries, both developed and developing. Another way is to look at the growth of cities in the world. In the 1950s there were only 4 cities with a population of

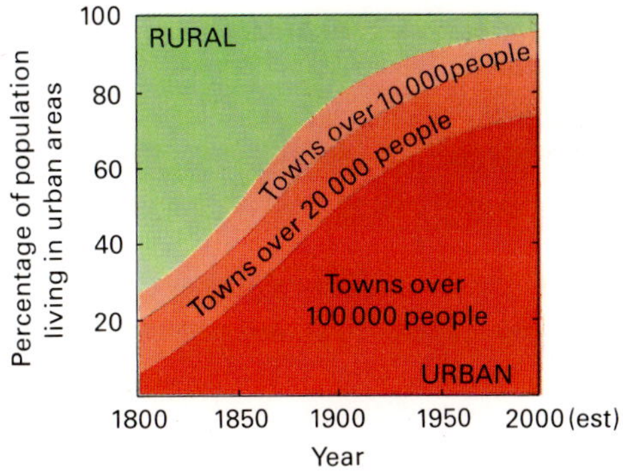

Fig. 1.29 *Growth of urban population in Britain*

Fig. 1.30 *Growth rate and change in percentage of urban populations in 20 countries*

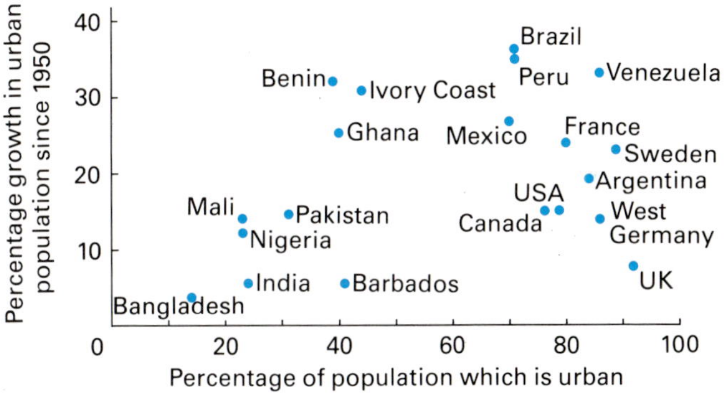

Fig. 1.31 *Growth of million cities since 1930*

Latitude north or south	*1930s 1–5*	*5+*	*1950s 1–5*	*5+*	*1970s 1–5*	*5+*	*1985 1–5*	*5+*
60°	–	–	–	–	–	–	–	–
50°	10	1	12	1	21	2	21	2
40°	11	1	20	1	37	4	50	4
30°	10	1	22	2	39	6	61	9
20°	–	–	11	0	16	2	32	6
10°	–	–	8	0	10	2	16	3
0°	–	–	3	0	10	0	14	1
	31	3	76	4	133	16	194	25

Activities

Study fig. 1.31 and use an atlas to remind yourself of the location of the belts of latitude (eg London is in the 50–60° belt).

1 Complete these statements:
   (a) Belt . . . to . . . shows the greatest growth in the number of million cities since the 1930s.
   (b) Belt . . . to . . . contains most cities over 5 million people today.
2 Write a few sentences to describe rates of growth in number and size of cities in each of the latitude belts shown, since 1930.

over 5 millions. By 1985, there were 25 (see fig. 1.31). 'Million' cities contain populations of a million or more people. Figure 1.31 shows how the numbers of 'million' cities has increased over the last 50 years.

During recent years urban growth in developed countries has slowed down. Congestion and decay of buildings in inner cities, combined with very high land prices and the growth of high-rise office buildings have led to a move back to the suburbs, and often into commuter villages outside towns. Widespread use of cars, commuter trains and rapid transit systems has encouraged this. The story is very different in developing countries.

The greatest urban growth has taken place in developing countries in or near the tropics (see fig. 1.31). Sao Paulo in Brazil has already reached 8.5 million people and is expected to grow to 20 millions by 2000 AD. Mexico City, over 15 millions now, will probably reach 30 millions by then.

The push-pull factors shown in fig. 1.32 help to explain most of this urban growth. There are reasons why many people wish to leave rural areas and these are called push factors. Meanwhile, urban areas provide facilities which attract people and these are called pull-factors. Figure 1.33 shows some of these factors in Brazil.

Fig. 1.32 *Push-Pull factors affecting urban growth*

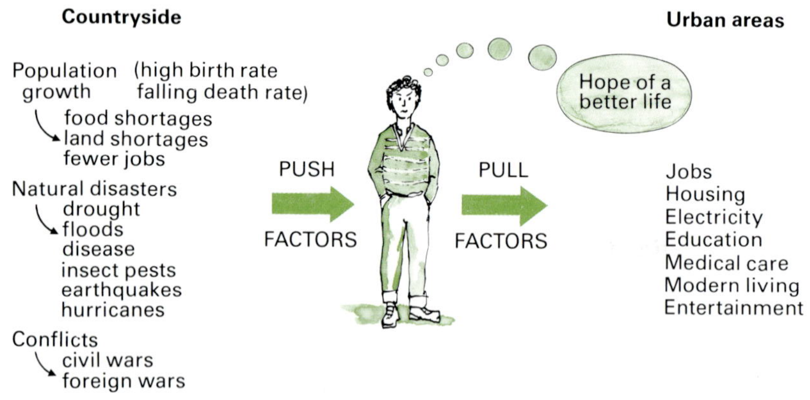

Fig. 1.33 *Basic services and consumer goods in Brazil*

Goods and services	*Percentage of households: urban*	*rural*
Electric light	89	21
Mains water supply	76	3
Mains sewage	38	3
Radio	79	68
Television	73	15
Car	28	9

Such rapid urbanisation creates many problems both in the rural areas from which people have migrated and in the urban areas. In the countryside, the old and very young people are left behind as it is mainly the young adults who are drawn to the towns. Rural living standards deteriorate further and greater frustration sets in. This makes people even more unable to escape the poverty trap.

Brazil's urban growth demonstrated how rapid this urbanisation has been (fig. 1.35).

Fig. 1.34 *Rural poverty trap*

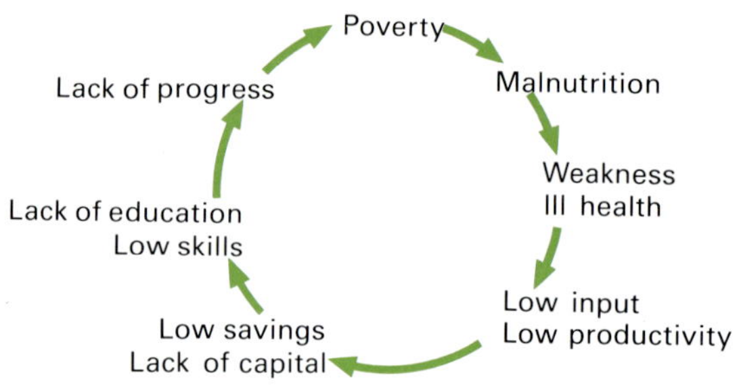

Fig. 1.35 *Urban growth in Brazil*

	Percentage urban	*Percentage rural*	*Total population in millions*
1940	31	69	41.2
1960	45	55	70.9
1985	71	29	132.0

Between 1940 and 1985 Brazil's total population rose by 322% or 91 million people. At the same time, the urban part of this population rose by 731% or 81 million people.

This urban growth is also reflected in the expansion of Brazilian cities. In 1940 there were only two 'million' cities. Figure 1.36 shows the situation today.

Fig. 1.36 *Size and location of Brazilian cities*

Occupational structures

Primary, Secondary and Tertiary employment sectors can be used to classify populations.

Figure 1.37 shows how people are employed in three towns. Their jobs are divided into 24 occupational groups. 1 and 2 are primary, that is they produce foodstuffs and raw materials from the land and sea. Processing these goods and making other goods from them is the secondary sector, groups 3 to 17. All other occupations are grouped as tertiary, mainly services.

Town A in fig. 1.37 has over 50% of its people in the secondary sector so it can be called an industrial town. Town B has over 70% tertiary and could be called an important service centre. Town C has an important mining section, 15%, but it could not be called a mining town since over 50% of workers are still in the tertiary sector.

Stages 1 and 2 in fig. 1.38 include almost all developing countries. They have very high percentages of workers in primary occupations, especially agriculture. The proportion of workers in agriculture is often used to classify populations. Figure 1.39 shows the dates at which the agricultural percentage of countries' populations drops below 50%. Countries which industrialised early, developed very efficient agricultural systems

Fig. 1.37 *Occupational groups in three towns*

Name of group		*Towns – Percentage of total*		
		A	*B*	*C*
Primary	1 Agriculture, forestry, fishing	0.7	0.6	0.1
	2 Mining and quarrying			15.2
Secondary	3 Food, drink, tobacco	9.4	1.1	1.1
	4 Chemical industries	5.2	0.1	0.4
	5 Metal manufactures	3.8		0.1
	6 Engineering, electrical	20.3	6.0	5.6
	7 Shipbuilding, marine engineering			
	8 Vehicles	4.2		
	9 Other metal goods	4.2	1.6	2.1
	10 Textiles	2.4		0.9
	11 Leather and furs			
	12 Clothing and footwear	0.9	1.5	3.0
	13 Bricks, pottery, glass	0.3	0.4	8.1
	14 Timber, furniture	0.8	0.8	0.6
	15 Paper, publishing, printing	2.4	2.4	2.1
	16 Other manufacturing	5.2	1.6	1.4
	17 Construction	5.4	11.3	5.1
Tertiary	18 Gas, electricity, water	1.5	3.9	2.1
	19 Transport and communication	3.9	6.8	5.1
	20 Distributive trades	9.7	19.1	19.6
	21 Insurance, banking, finance	1.6	2.4	1.6
	22 Professional and scientific	7.7	14.8	11.1
	23 Miscellaneous services	6.9	18.2	11.0
	24 Public administration and defence	3.5	7.4	3.7

Fig. 1.38 *Four stages of economic development*

1 Traditional or pre-industrial

Most people are dependent upon farming, growing mainly subsistance crops. Land is often owned by the community and tasks shared. This led to a strong social organisation. Energy supplies are mainly human and transport systems poorly developed.

2 Transition to industrial

Gradual changes occur, often the result of outside influences. Some crops are grown for sale and raw materials are exported. Transport systems develop. The country is often dependent on primary products. Urbanisation begins.

3 Industrial

Industries are small at first and dependent on cheap labour. A wider range develops and the secondary sector grows. Higher energy use begins and transport systems are well developed. A strong tertiary sector appears. Living standards rise and capital is generated for use elsewhere.

4 Post industrial

Some industrialised countries undergo a further change. Industry automates and specialises in high-skill products. Increasing numbers of people take jobs in the tertiary sector, often high-tech industries. These workers are often classed as quaternary. The size of the secondary sector decreases.

Fig. 1.39 *Dates at which agricultural labour force fell below 50%*

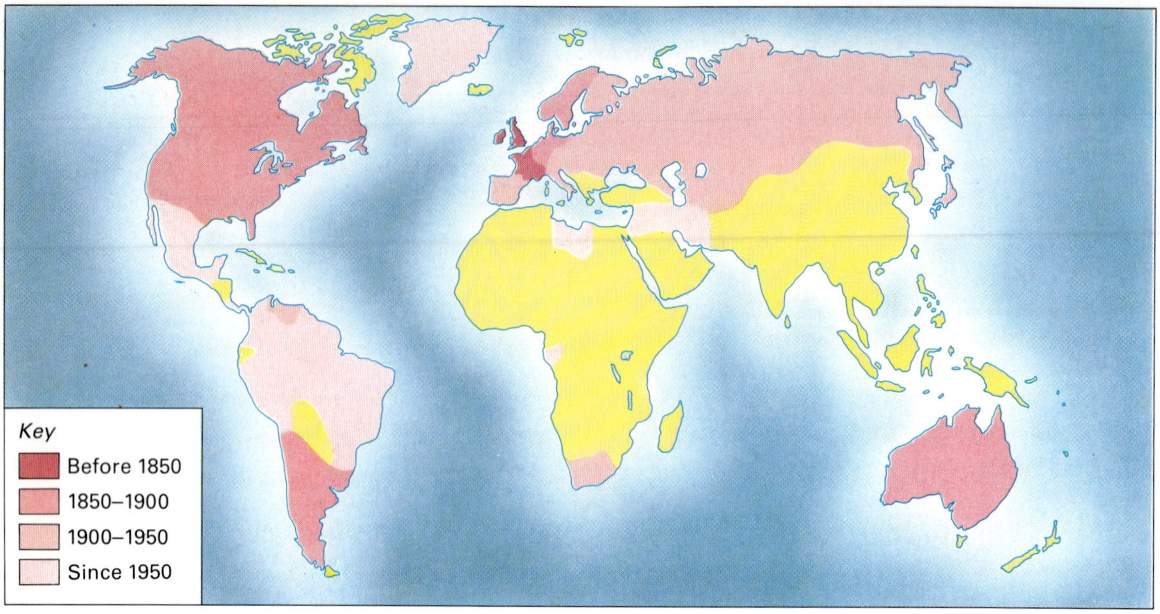

Fig. 1.40 *Percentage of working population in agriculture in 16 countries*

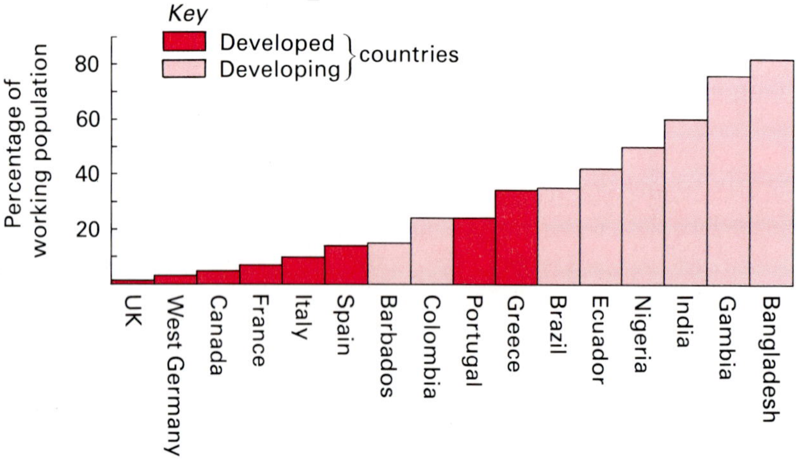

Activities

1 Study fig. 1.37. Discuss in groups why Town B is likely to be a coastal resort in South East England. Make notes for yourself about the group's findings.
2 Study fig. 1.39. For all the countries in fig. 1.42 make a list of when their agricultural workforces fell below 50%.
3 In fig. 1.40 the developed countries, Canada, West Germany, France and Italy, are all exporters of agricultural products. Find out about these products. For one of the countries, carry out a group enquiry to find out why there is such a small agricultural workforce.
4 Study fig. 1.41. Test the hypothesis that wealthy (developed) countries have the lowest percentage of primary workers (hypothesis testing – see fig. 1.15).
5 Compare the similarities and differences in employment structures of developed and developing countries in fig. 1.42.
6 Extended writing: Explain how populations can be classified with reference to both developed and developing countries.

which were based upon machinery, efficient transport and high capital investment. As fig. 1.40 shows, their labour inputs to agriculture are relatively low.

Fig. 1.41 *Relationship GNP and size of primary sector employment*

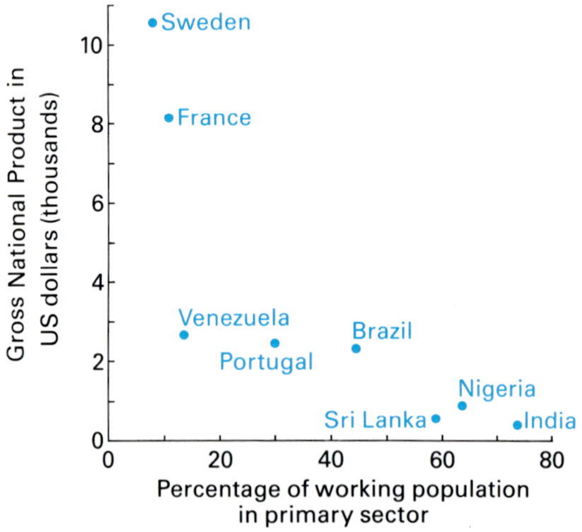

Fig. 1.42 *Employment structures*

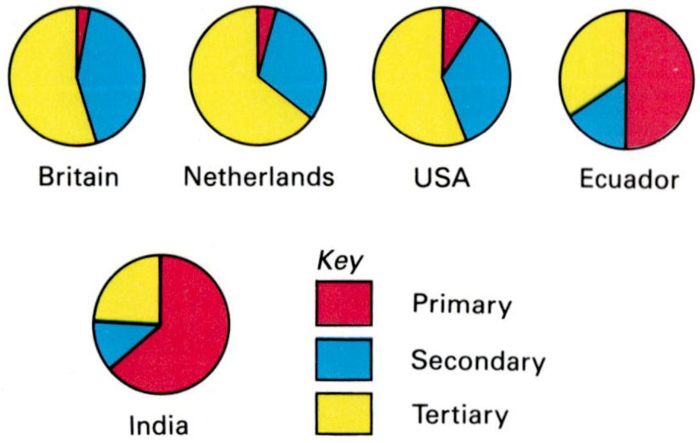

2 POPULATION CHANGE

Birth rates

Populations change at varying rates and are rarely stable at any level, local, national or global. Many social and economic factors, and some environmental factors, are at work all the time, producing increases in population in some areas and decreases in others.

In 1985, in three small towns a few miles apart, there were six comprehensive schools with a total 11 to 16 population of 4830. If the population of these schools was stable, 960 fifth years would leave each year to be replaced by 960 first years. Figure 2.1 shows the real situation, with a changing school population. A decline has been taking place for several years and will continue to at least 1990.

Fig. 2.1 *Number of students in six secondary schools*

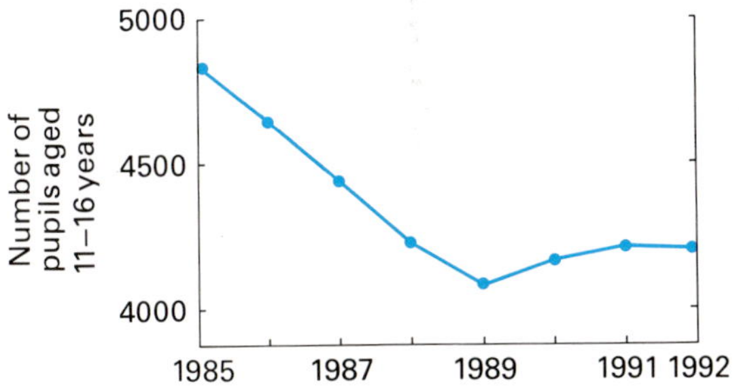

Fig. 2.2 *Birth rates in Britain, 1851–1991*

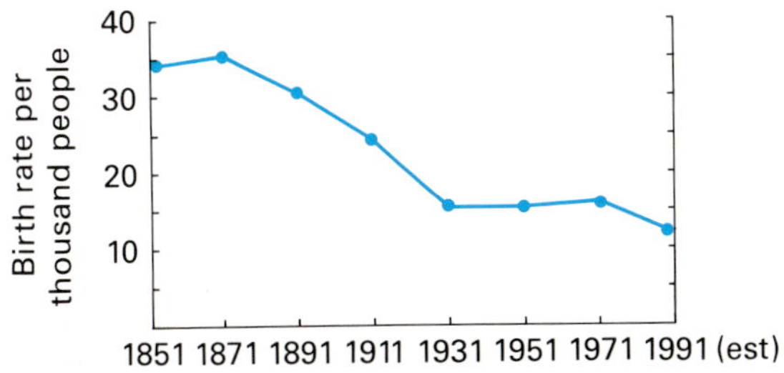

By 1992 there will be 620 fewer students, about 13%, than there were in 1985.

The main reason for the changing numbers of school students is the fall in the birth rate. This is the number of live births per 1000 people per year. For a variety of reasons, there have been fewer children born each year since about 1875 in Britain (fig. 2.2).

Fig. 2.3 *Sir Alan Herbert voiced some reasons for declining birth-rates in a debate in Parliament in 1937*

In 1937 was a rumour going around
That income tax was soon to be six shillings in the pound;
The cost of education every season seemed to swell,
And to everyone's surprise the population fell.*

They pulled down all the houses where the children used to crowd,
And built delightful blocks of flats where children weren't allowed;
And if father got a job there wasn't anywhere to dwell,
But to everyone's astonishment the population fell.*

Five hundred brand new motor cars each morning rode the roads
And flashed about like comets or sat motionless as toads;
Whichever course they took they made the public highway hell,
And to everyone's astonishment the population fell.*

The laws were very comical; to bet was voted lax,
But your betting was the only thing that nobody would tax;
You couldn't have a wine unless you'd sandwiches as well,
But to Parliament's astonishment the population fell.*

Abroad to show that everyone was passionate for peace,
All children under seven joined the army or police;
The babies studied musketry while mother filled a shell,
And all the nations wondered why the population fell.*

The world, in short, which never was extravagently sane,
Developed all the signs of inflammation of the brain;
The past was not encouraging, the future none could tell,
And some of us were not surprised the population fell.*

* *It was the birth rate that fell.*

Activities

The six schools in 1986, in fig 2.1, in these three towns could provide places for 5000 students, so, clearly, some important decisions would have to be taken. The Local Education Authority (LEA) had a great problem because one of the towns was smaller than the others, with only one school. If this school was closed, students would have to travel to another town. As in all school closures, a variety of different attitudes would appear:

a) The LEA (b) The councillors in each town.
c) The governors of each school. d) The students in each school. e) The parents and people in each town.

Divide your class into five groups representing each of these five attitudes. Each group should decide by discussion the attitude it would take in a public enquiry about school closures – one school has to be closed. Each group should have a speaker to represent them in an enquiry with the whole class.

Death rates

A stable population has a death rate, that is the number of deaths per thousand people per year, which is very similar to the birth rate. Death rates have actually varied greatly over time. Before about 1700 AD, the population of the world was fairly stable, as fig. 2.4 shows. Birth rates were high, but so were death rates. As a result, the natural change in population, the difference between the birth rate and the death rate, was very small.

Fig. 2.4 *Estimated growth of world population*

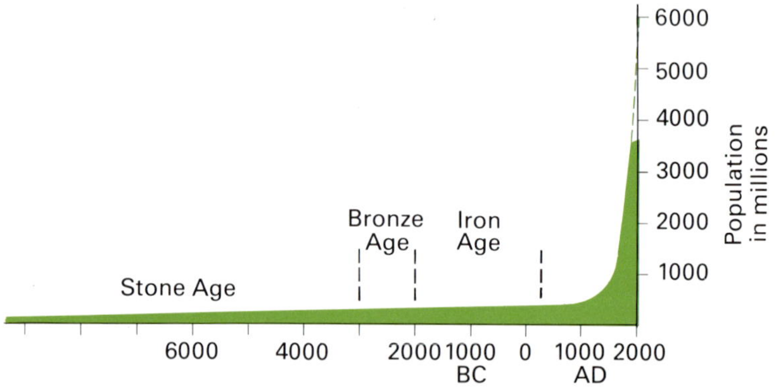

After about 1800 AD, the death rate began to fall in Britain. As with the birth rate, there were many reasons for this. Some were slow, steady changes which had no dramatic effects at the time. Others were more noticeable. Dr William Budd wrote in 1858–9 that smells from the River Thames in London, mainly from untreated sewage, were so bad that 'for many weeks, the atmosphere of Parliamentary Committee Rooms was rendered only tolerable by the suspension before every window of blinds saturated with chloride of lime and by the lavish use of this and other disinfectants' (see fig. 2.6).

A greater public awareness of the problems of sanitation, housing, medical health and education came at regular intervals. This played a large part in improving an environment in which death rates, especially infant mortality rates, began to fall.

Fig. 2.5 *Death rates in Britain 1851–1991*

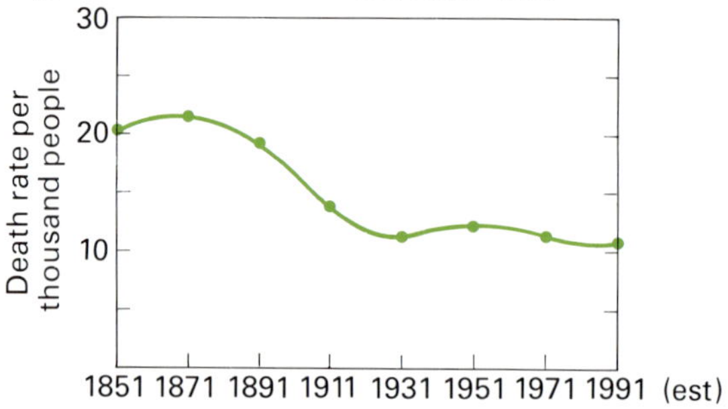

Fig. 2.6 *Poem found after a joint Mersey and Irwell Committee meeting, 1901*

'If with a stick you stir well,
The poor old River Irwell,
Very sick of the amusement
You will very soon become;
For foetid bubbles rise and burst
But that is really not the worst
For little birds can hop about
Dry-footed on the scum.'

Activities

1 Study the poem (fig. 2.3) then carry out a brainstorm, an activity designed to stimulate ideas. One member of the class acts as recorder on the blackboard. Members of the class call out words or phrases which they think affected the number of births. All ideas must be recorded in a brief but random way. Then a discussion should take place about each one, to refine or validate it. Some ideas will explain more births and some less. The class should then divide into groups. Each group should try to place the ideas in rank order of importance. Comparing these rank orders later should demonstrate how different people will have different attitudes towards an issue.

2 Carry out a similar brainstorm, this time for the causes of a fall in the death rate.
Figure 2.7 shows the effects of one brainstorm, for question 1 (above).

Fig. 2.7 *Brainstorm on birth rate changes*

Natural change

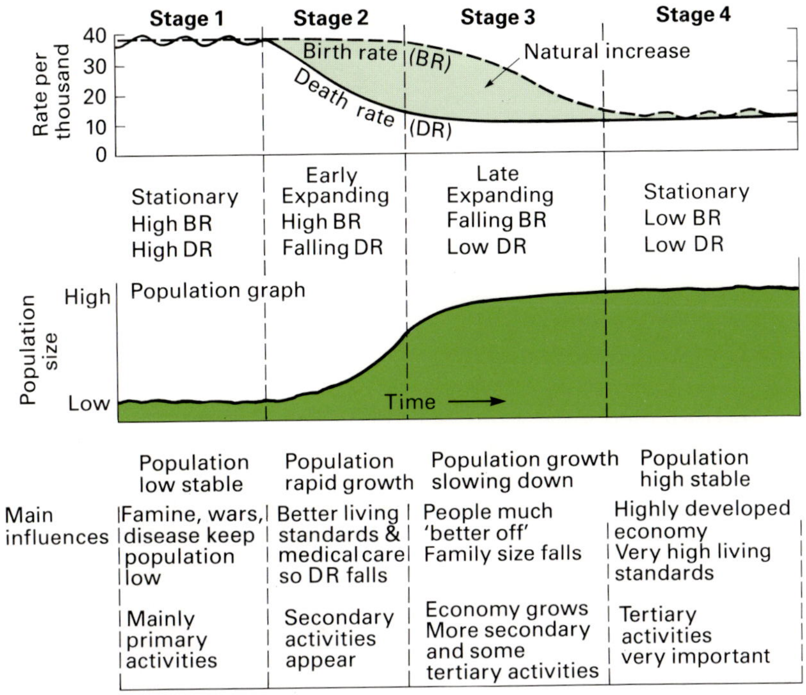

Fig. 2.8 *Demographic transition model*

The natural change of populations is the difference between the birth rate and the death rate. This also varies in time. Changes in the birth rate and death rate produce fluctuations in the natural change of populations. Demographers, people who study populations, have suggested that countries, as they develop economically, go through four stages or demographic transitions. Developed countries like Britain have passed through stages 1 to 3 and are now in stage 4. Most developing countries are still in stage 2, or perhaps stage 3. The demographic transition for an imaginary country is shown in fig. 2.8.

The natural change also varies in space. Most developing countries have a high natural increase in population. Although some have managed to reduce death rates, and the statistics for Sri Lanka and Brazil in fig. 2.10 show this, it has been less easy to reduce birth rates.

One of the greatest changes in population has occurred in Brazil, which has reached stage 3 of the transition model (see fig. 2.10). In 1872, Brazil's population was only 10 millions and even this owed much to immigration. Yet, by 1905 the population had doubled and, since then, the rate at which it doubled has quickened (see fig. 2.11).

Country	*Birth rate %*	*Death rate %*	*Natural change %*	*Population increase %*
Sweden	12	11	+ 1	0.1
France	14	10	+ 4	0.4
Spain	18	8	+10	1.0
India	35	16	+19	1.9
Sri Lanka	30	8	+22	2.2
Nigeria	49	23	+26	2.6
Brazil	37	9	+28	2.8

Fig. 2.9 *Population statistics*

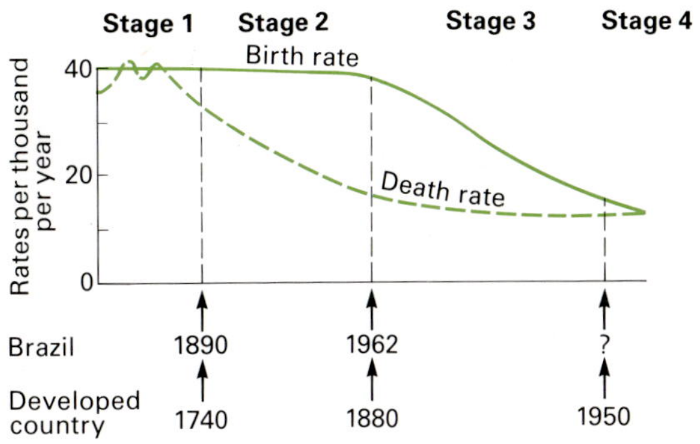

Fig. 2.10 *Demographic transition model for Brazil*

The speed of population growth and the rapid movement through the demographic transition was much faster than that of European countries in the 19th century. Greatly improved medical care, which was available to over 80% of Brazilians, together with high immigration, caused this rapid growth. Between 1874 and 1957 over 5 million people entered the country.

Fig. 2.11 *Rate of doubling of Brazil's population*

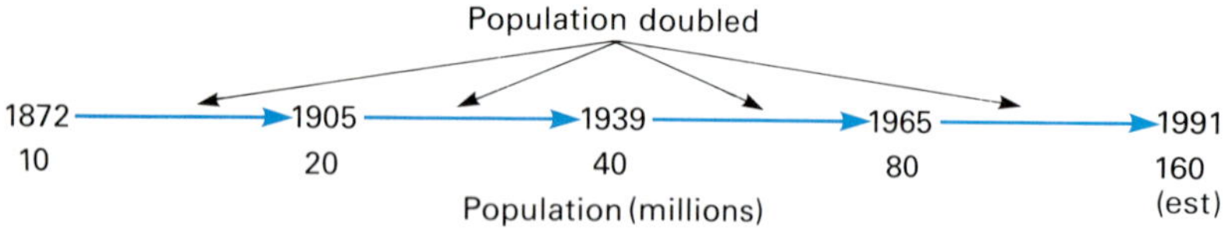

During this period of falling death rates, the birth rate remained stable, as in stage 2. It was not until 1962 that Brazil entered stage 3 and the birth rate began to fall.

Activities

Analysing data.

1 Figure 2.9 shows the population statistics for several countries some developed and others developing. Using the demographic transition in fig. 2.8 suggest which stage each country has reached.

2 Work in small groups and try to reach agreement.
   (a) Use fig. 2.12 and an atlas and, in each continent, name countries
      i) with the highest natural change.
      ii) with the lowest natural change.
   (b) From this information, which is the most developed continent?
   (c) Which continent has the widest variety of natural change?

3 Use fig. 2.8.
   (a) What is the birth rate in stage 1?
   (b) What is the birth rate in stage 4?
   (c) What do you notice about the natural increase in stages 1 and 4?
   (d) What is the difference in natural increase between stages 2/3 and 1/4?
   (e) In which stages is population stable?
   (f) Why does the death rate fluctuate so much in stage 1?

4 Use fig. 2.8.
   How does the demographic transition model explain
   a) population growth in stage 2?
   b) slow down in population growth at the end of stage 3?

5 Use Fig. 2.9.
   (a) What is the annual population change in i) France ii) Nigeria?
   (b) Which is the most developed country?
   (c) Which European country is least developed?

The rapid growth of population had produced large families and people began to realise that there were advantages in reducing family size. As birth control methods and information became more easily available, the natural increase in Brazil's population slowed down from the high figure of 35 per thousand (3.5% per year) to under 28 per thousand (2.8% per year). However, the absolute growth of the population continues because the population base is now so large, at about 132 millions. A growth rate even as low as 2% per year which might be achievable, will still mean an extra 26 million mouths to feed each ten years.

Fig. 2.12 *Natural change of population in three developing countries, 1980*

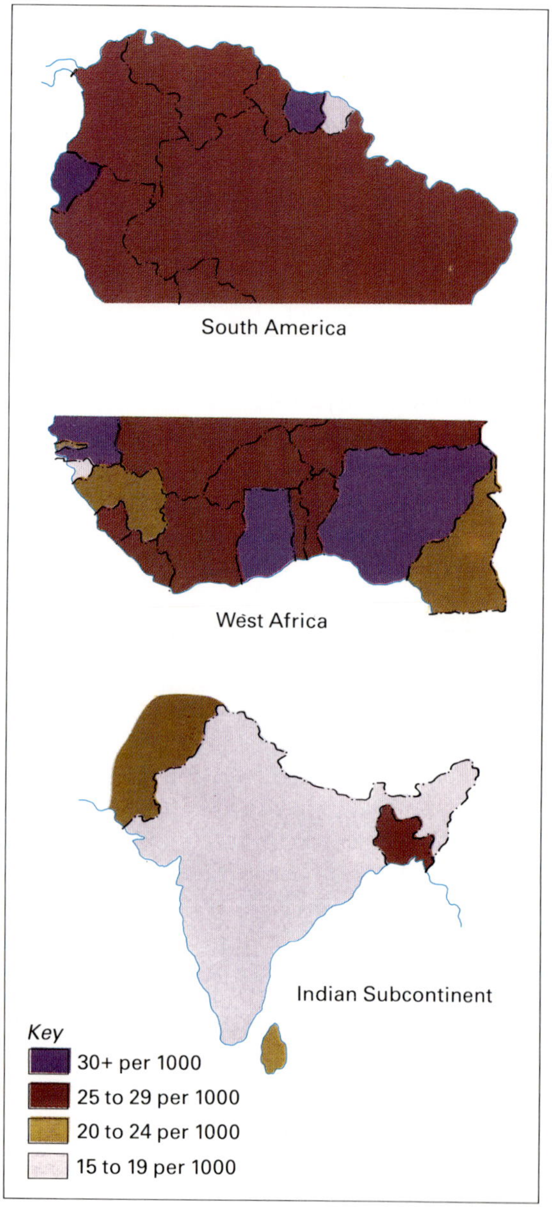

Migrations

Population changes are also brought about by movements of people. The natural change of populations is decided by the difference between the birth rate and the death rate. The overall change is the natural change modified by migration, the movement of people from one place to another, permanently.

Fig. 2.13 *Reasons for population change*

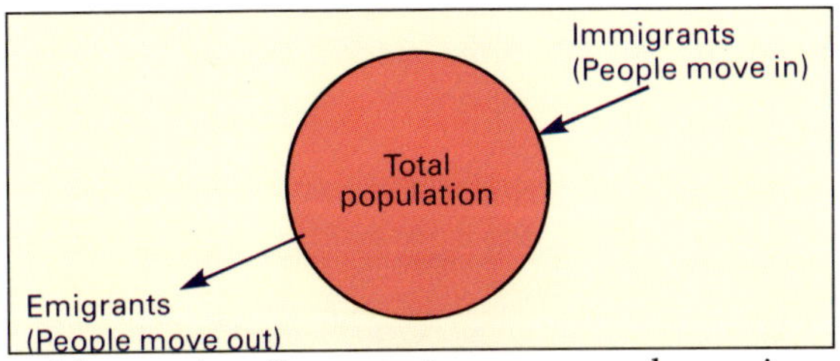

Many migrations are temporary, shown in fig. 2.15, but some are permanent and on a large scale. As changes in population can be related to the demographic transition model (fig. 2.8), so the same four stages can be identified in the mobility transition, the changes brought about by migrations (fig. 2.14).

Fig. 2.14 *The mobility transition*

Stage 1

In very undeveloped societies today and in European countries before 1700 AD, few people had reasons to move. They depended largely upon the local land for necessities and rarely left the village of their birth.

Stage 2

During this period of rapid population growth, more people found reasons to move. Trading between settlements began and the land in villages could no longer support the growing population. Some moved to relatively empty land in their own country. Others moved to new jobs in towns or emigrated to other countries.

Stage 3

As population growth slowed down, so emigration to other countries slowed down, very often because the receiving country could no longer absorb large numbers. Quota laws were introduced.

Stage 4

In advanced countries where transport systems are very developed, mobility grew even more. People can travel long distances to work. Even commuting between London and New York is possible using Concorde. Emigration is less widespread as governments became concerned about 'brain drains', the attraction of highly skilled expensively trained workers to other countries.

Today, in Britain, internal migration of people is actively encouraged by the government. The economic growth of the South-east has not been matched by similar growth in other regions. As a result, people are drawn towards areas with employment opportunities. Figure 2.16 shows the overall change in the population of English counties which includes migration.

Fig. 2.15 *Migrations (temporary and permanent)*

Temporary	**Permanent**
Transhumance – seasonal movement of people and their animals in Norway	*Millions of Africans forcibly transported to North and South America.*
Pastoral nomadism – tribal groups in West Africa move to find better pastures	*Over 40 million Europeans emigrated to USA before 1914.*
Fruit pickers in Britain move to places like Kent and East Anglia in summer	*One million European Jews left Europe for Israel after 1945*
Daily commuter movements in advanced countries where transport systems are well developed.	*Five million Europeans entered Brazil before 1939*
Summer holiday movements to seaside towns	*Over 20 million people left Italy between 1870 and 1914, mainly to North and South America.*

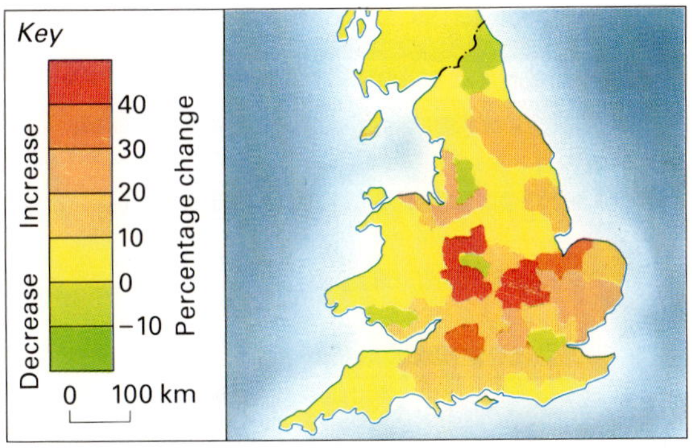

Fig. 2.16 *Population changes in England and Wales, 1968–1981*

Activities

Permanent movement of people in Britain may vary from a change of house in the same street to a move of many hundreds of miles. Choose ten of the following, putting them in rank order of importance to you. Then write briefly to explain how each heading provides a reason for a permanent movement.

marriage new job inheritance social unrest better house employer moves premises medical reasons promotion inside your company bought a car first child 4 years old new motorway built nearby retirement

Toronto is the largest urban area in Canada. It has a population of 3.4 millions, in an area of 7000 km^2 and can truly be called a conurbation. For census purposes, it is divided into five municipalities, shown in fig. 2.17. They are Metropolitan Toronto and four regional municipalities. Although population growth has slowed since 1976, the growth from 1950s 1.4 to today's 3.4 millions has been rapid.

The main reasons for this growth were a high natural increase and an equally high immigration rate, shown in fig. 2.18. The global scale of this immigration is shown in fig. 2.20 for Ontario, the Canadian Province in which Toronto is the main town.

Taking place at the same time as these international movements of people has been movement inside Greater Toronto. In 1951 most of Toronto's people lived inside the City of Toronto and the three municipalities inside Metropolitan Toronto (The Inner Three). The outer three metropolitan municipalities, Etobicoke, North York and Scarborough had only 16% of the population. Outside Metro, the 'fringe region' (now the regional municipalities) was mainly rural with a few small towns (fig. 2.19).

Fig. 2.17 *Toronto region, Canada*

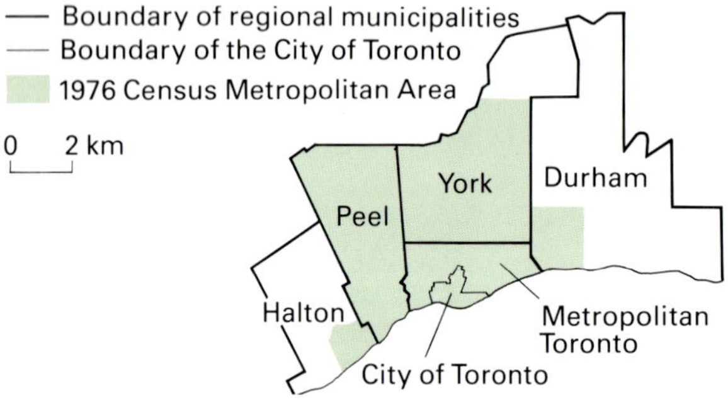

Fig. 2.18 *Components of population growth, Toronto region, 1956–1981*

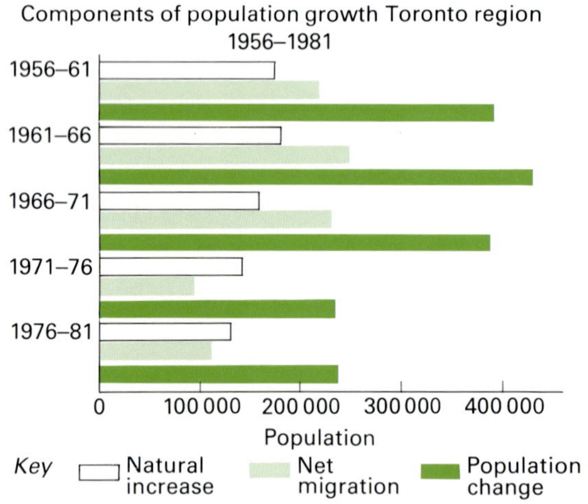

Fig. 2.19 *Population growth (in thousands), Toronto*

	1951	%	1951–1961	1961	%	1961–1971	1971	%
City of Toronto	699	(50)	4	703	(33)	10	713	(24)
Inner Three	890	(64)	43	933	(44)	32	965	(33)
Outer Three	227	(16)	459	686	(32)	435	1 121	(38)
Metro Total	1 117	(80)	501	1 169	(76)	467	2 086	(71)
Fringe	276	(20)	233	509	(24)	325	833	(29)
Toronto Region	1 394	(100)	734	2 127	(100)	792	2 919	(100)

Inner Three includes Toronto, York and East York.
Outer Three includes Etobicoke, North York and Scarborough.
Metro includes the Inner Three and the Outer Three.
Fringe includes Durham, York, Peel and Halton Regions.

Source: Census of Canada

Fig. 2.20 *Immigration to Ontario, Canada*

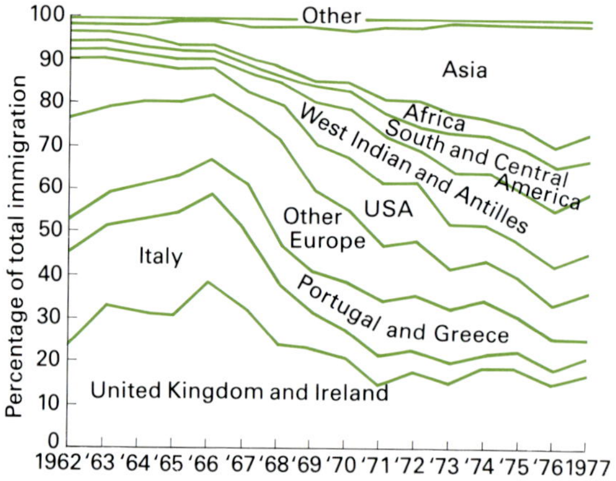

During the last thirty years, the City of Toronto and the Inner Three have grown slowly in comparison with the rest of Toronto. The City, with a central location and a large stock of small rental homes, continues to attract young adults. Once these young people age a little and form their own families, they leave the City to occupy larger houses elsewhere. This pattern of movement is shown in fig. 2.21.

Activities

Study figs. 2.17 to 2.21.

1. Identify two types of migration which affected the population of Toronto.
2. Comment upon the growth of population in the 'fringe region' since 1951.
3. Explain the slow growth of the Metropolitan Toronto compared to the 'fringe region'.

Fig. 2.21 *Population movement, Toronto*

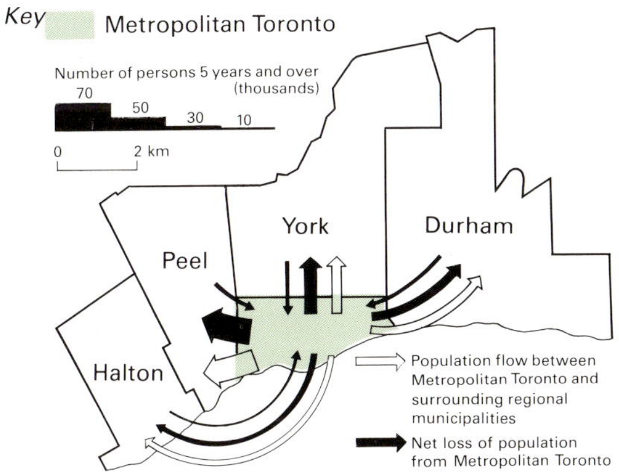

Fig. 2.23 *Simplified age/sex pyramids for Brazil since 1940*

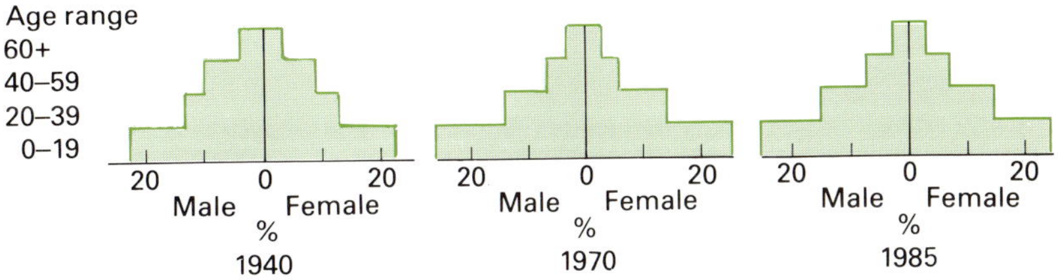

Population pyramids

Population pyramids show changes in birth and death rates. Figure 2.10 shows that Brazil's death rate had fallen by 1940, but the birth rate was still high. This high birth rate is reflected in the pyramids by the high percentage of people in the young age groups, well over 50% in 1940. What had happened to the birth rate by 1960? (use fig 2.10 again). The death rate fell even further by 1960 and more people were living longer. How does the 1960 pyramid show this? By 1980, the death rate was quite low and the birth rate was falling. What are the main changes in the 1980 pyramid?

The effects of a changing birth rate have also been traced in the population pyramids for Toronto, Canada, in fig. 1.13. The 'baby boom' of the post-war period is still having effects upon demands for services in Toronto.

Population pyramids show the effects of migrations. Push-pull factors have produced rapid population growth in many cities in the developing world. Calcutta, in India, is a good example.

Fig. 2.22 *Location of Calcutta, India*

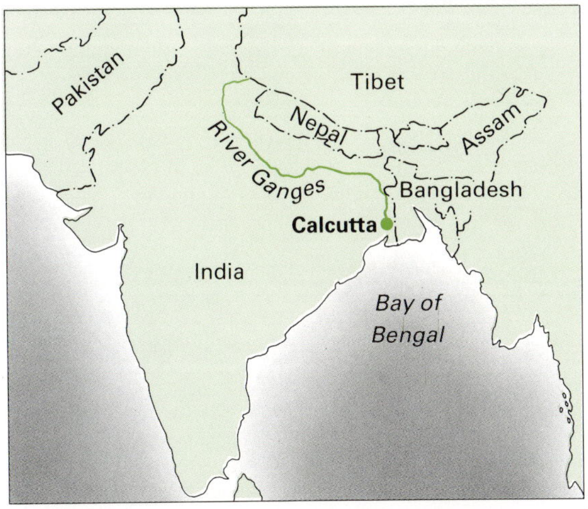

Fig. 2.24 *Age/Sex pyramid for Calcutta*

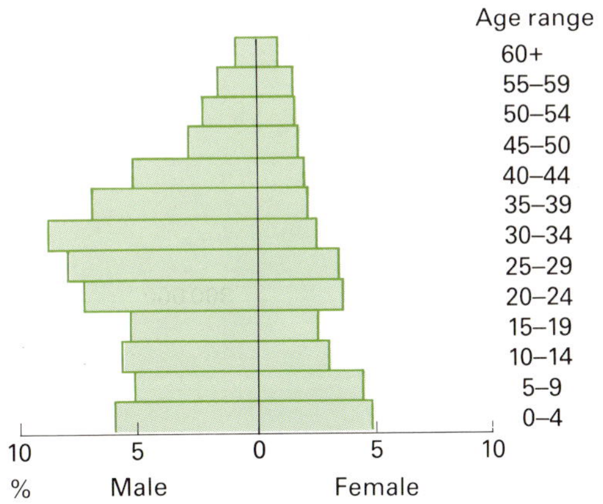

Activities

1. Use fig. 1.15 for all of India and fig. 2.24 for Calcutta. Make a list of the differences between the two pyramids.
2. What proportion of the population of Calcutta is male? How can immigration explain this?
3. In which age groups are there higher numbers of people in Calcutta? Can this be explained by immigration? Give your reasons.
4. Write a paragraph to explain some of the possible effects of having a population structure such as that of Calcutta.

3 POPULATION DISTRIBUTION

What is distribution?

Distribution of population describes the variations in density, the number of people per unit area, over the land area of the world. Areas of high, medium and low density can be identified, because the population is spread unevenly.

The world map in fig. 3.1 shows that large areas of the world have very low density of population, under 10 people per km^2. In fact, about 80% of the 4.3 million people of the world lives in about 20% of the land area.

The map shows four major concentrations of population:

1. Indian subcontinent – mainly the Punjab and the Ganges Valley of Bengal.
2. The Far East – mainly Eastern China and Japan.
3. Western Europe – mainly the Northern Plain from France to Poland.
4. North America – mainly Eastern USA.

Population density can vary dramatically at regional and national level and can be seen by looking in detail at smaller areas than are shown in fig. 3.1. There are many reasons for the unequal distributions throughout the world and within specific regions. Both environmental influences and human activity affect this distribution.

Fig. 3.1 *World population distribution*

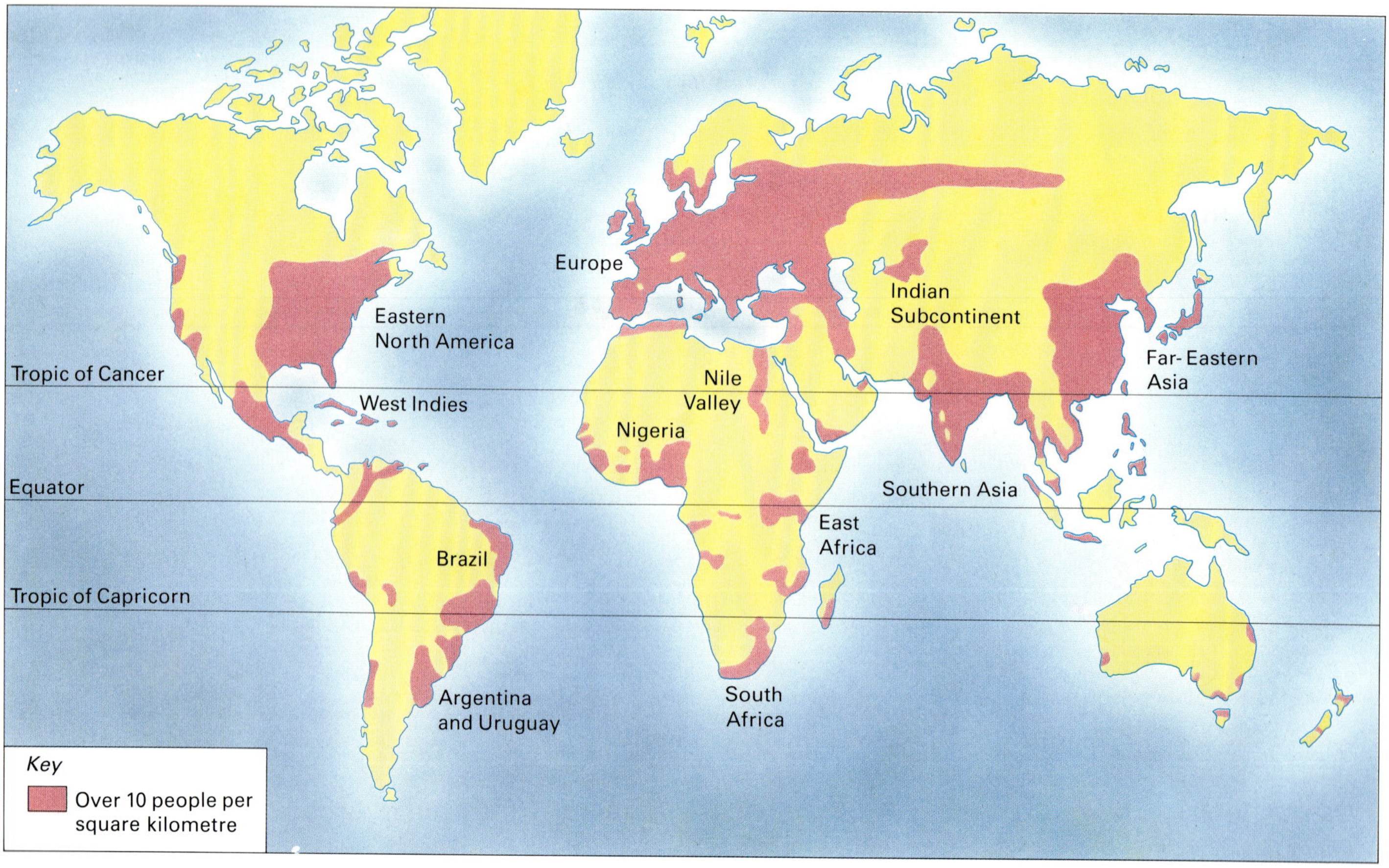

Environmental influences

Altitude

The main mountain systems of the world are shown in fig. 3.2. The largest mountain region is in Central Asia around the Plateau of Tibet and the Himalayas. If you should attempt to climb Mt Everest, over 9000 metres above sea level, breathing equipment would be needed. The amount of oxygen in the air decreases with altitude until a point is reached where people need to use oxygen. For this reason, the highest parts of mountain regions remain uninhabited, although in the Himalayas and parts of the Andes, people have managed to eke out a living and adapt to 'thin air' at an altitude of 5000 metres.

It is not just 'thin air' which makes living at high altitudes unattractive. Large areas of bare rock, very steep slopes and thin soils make any form of crop growing difficult. Even where it is possible, accessibility is so poor that movement of people, animals and goods is very difficult. Road building is expensive and rarely can be justified (see fig 3.4).

The altitude also has a climatic effect. Temperatures decrease with altitude at an average rate of 1°C per 200 metres. This means that even near the Equator, temperatures at 5000 metres are about 25°C below equivalent areas at sea level. As a result, many mountain regions are permanently covered with snow (fig. 3.5).

Lowland areas on the other hand, attract people because they provide opportunities for human activities. Given a suitable climate and fertile soils, large numbers of people concentrate on lowlands to earn a living from the land. In older populated regions such as the Ganges Valley of India, farmers cultivate every available hectare of land. Even in more recently populated regions such as the Canadian Prairies, level land encourages large scale use of machinery and road and rail access is better. It is not surprising that populations concentrate on lowlands.

Fig. 3.2 *World mountain regions*

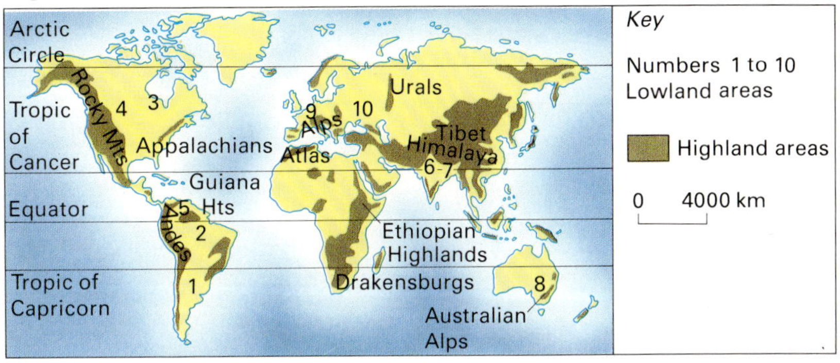

Fig. 3.3 *Himalayan climber*
Fig. 3.4 *Alpine landscape*
Fig. 3.5 *Permanent snow in the Alps*
Fig. 3.6 *Paddy fields in India*

Activities

1 Study figs 3.1 and 3.2 with an atlas. Draw and complete a chart like the one below. Name each lowland area numbered 1 to 10 on fig. 3.2. State whether population density is high or low: for low density areas, suggest one important reason for the low density.

No.	Name of lowland area	Density	Reason

2 Discuss in groups the phrase 'suitable climate for encouraging the growth of population'.
3 Study fig. 3.4. Write a paragraph to describe the difficulties for human settlement in this area. What evidence is there of human activity? What might be the main human use of such areas?
4 What information does fig. 3.6 show to suggest that this area attracts population?

Fig. 3.7 *Climatic factors influencing world population distribution*

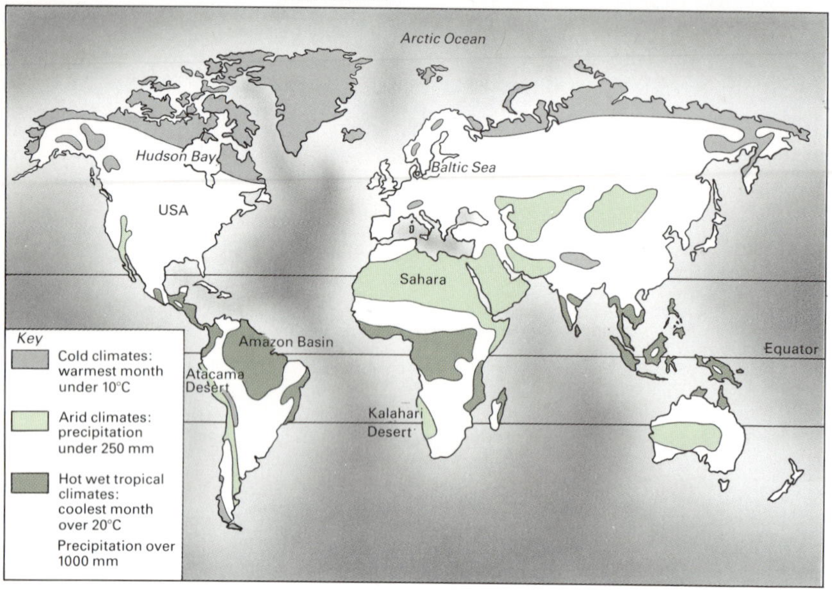

Climate

Figure 3.7 shows some of the main climatic factors that affect distribution of population. Few people live where there are extremes of climate, where it is very hot or very cold, very wet or very dry. Where these factors combine, population may be entirely absent as in the hot dry regions of the world such as the Sahara, Kalahari and Atacama Deserts. Heat and drought make any kind of human activity very difficult.

Fig. 3.8 *How have people changed the natural vegetation of these Mediterranean lands?*

Lands in warm and cool regions are called temperate regions and attract farmers. Temperatures are above 6°C for enough months in the year for crops to grow. Where precipitation is adequate, well above 300mm per year, crops can grow without irrigation.

Figure 3.1 also shows that there are major populations in tropical lands where temperatures are very high. The controlling factor here is water supply. Even deserts can flourish if water is available. The high population density in the Nile Valley of Egypt proves this. On the northern edge of temperate lands in the northern hemisphere, the growing season shortens and crop growing becomes more difficult. These areas are less attractive to population.

Vegetation

Some types of natural vegetation present opportunities to people because, unlike relief and climate, plant life can be removed or altered by people's efforts. The Mediterranean lands of southern Europe, shown in fig. 3.8 have vegetation today which is almost entirely the result of human effort over at least 30 centuries. Similarly in Britain, the great tracts of natural broad-leaf forests have been removed since the Middle Ages for house-building, ship-building, fuel, etc. The impact of people upon vegetation has not been so marked until recently in the equatorial forests of the Amazon Basin of South America. The climate there produces a lavish growth of plants all year round. Until government policies such as those in Brazil, to 'open up' and colonise these regions, appeared, there had been very little human impact. Prior to this recent development 'slash and burn' farming methods of the Amerindian people of Amazonia had produced small clearings which were soon abandoned by settlers, over which secondary forest quickly grew.

Activities

Use your library to investigate the nomadic 'slash and burn' farming activities in Amazonia. What sorts of settlements develop? Are there any limits to population growth?

Human influences

Stages of development

Most British people are concentrated on land below 200 metres above sea level. There are great variations within this area. Figure 1.39 shows four stages of development for an advanced country like Britain. Before the 18th century, it was in Stage 1 when most people were dependent upon the land and settlements were scattered. Figure 3.9 shows the estimated population distribution in 1701.

During the 18th century, Britain entered Stage 2 and became an industrial country. The industrial revolution took place and products like textiles were made in factories instead of the home. Water power then steam power led to a demand for coal to drive steam engines and to smelt iron in furnaces and many jobs appeared on coalfields. As a result, as fig. 3.10 shows, by 1801 a major change had occurred in the population distribution.

In Stage 3 a wider range of industries developed as technology improved. When electricity replaced steam power, the need to locate industries on coalfields disappeared and improved transport let people travel greater distances to work. So population moved away from coalfields. This process was well under way by 1911, shown in fig. 3.11.

Britain is now in the post-industrial stage where tertiary occupations take up larger proportions of the population. People have been drawn increasingly to the South-East where job opportunities are good thus changing the distribution of population again. Figure 3.12 shows the 1971 situation, the last year before changes in county boundaries.

Fig. 3.9 *Population distribution in Britain 1701*

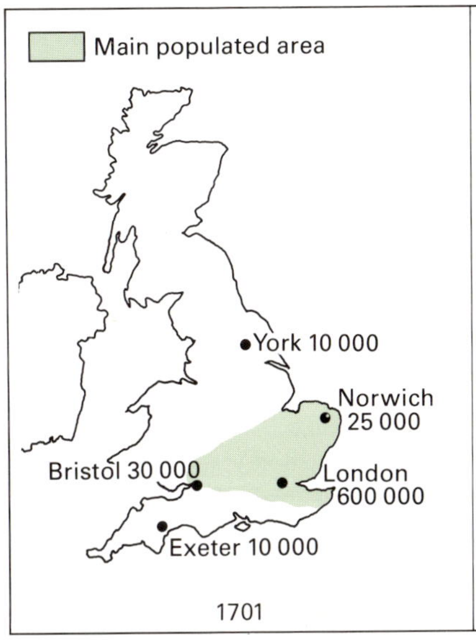

Fig. 3.10 *Population distribution in Britain 1801*

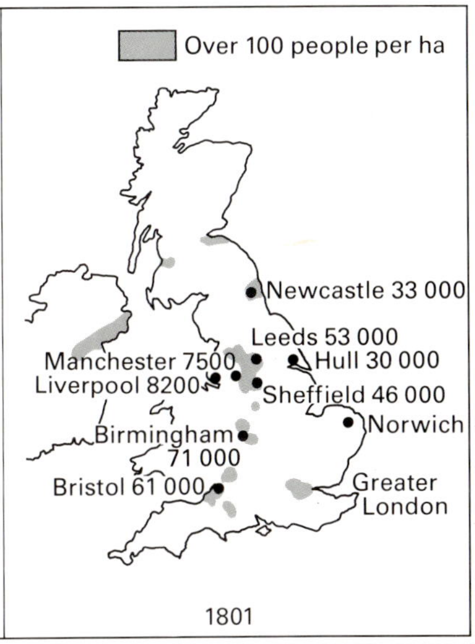

Fig. 3.11 *Population distribution in Britain 1911*

Fig. 3.12 *Population distribution in Britain 1971*

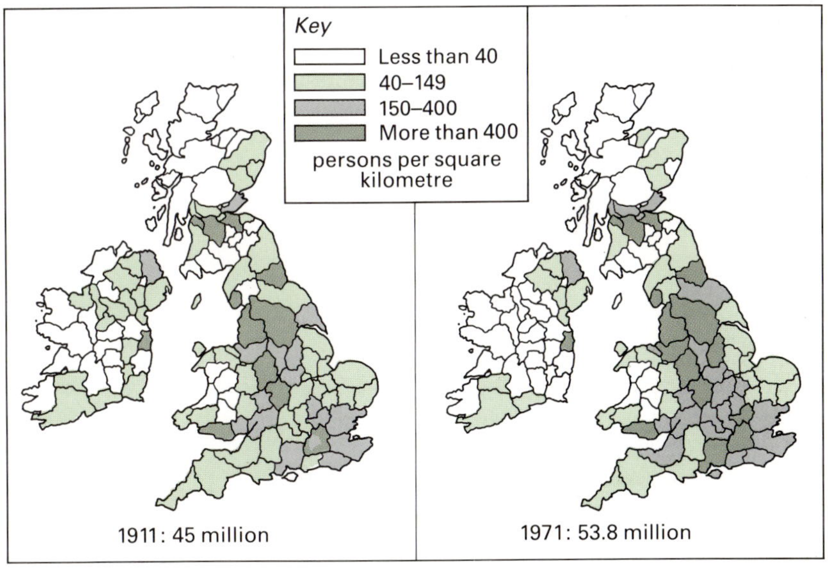

Activities

1 Study an atlas of Northern Scotland. Find out about the altitude, relief and accessibility of the region. Write a paragraph to explain why you think there is a low population density.
2 Discuss in small groups why people continue to live in such an area. Then compare them with the attitudes of those who leave.
3 What should governments do about such a region?

Colonial period

A period of colonial rule can affect population distribution. The environment has strongly influenced population distribution in Nigeria. Before the mid-19th century, the country was at the pre-industrial stage of development. The next 100 years saw it develop economically as a result of outside influence and this produced changes in population distribution. Nigeria's present boundaries are a result of the period of British colonial rule which lasted from 1861 to 1960.

In 1860, the population distribution was typical of most of West Africa. Northern Nigeria, the Sudan area, was part of three Arab kingdoms, Sokoto, Gwandu and Bornu, which stretched along the southern edge of the Sahara. This was the most developed part of Africa at the time because the trade links and cultural contacts with other Arab states, north of the Sahara, brought economic advance. Although the population was mainly rural, there were some large cities, Sokoto having about 120 000 people and Kano, 100 000.

Central Nigeria was a transition zone between the Sudan and the equatorial coast in the south. Population was sparse because of the slave trade run by Arabs to the north and Europeans from the south. Southern Nigeria was quite densely populated and there were several large towns, Ibadan, Oyo and Calabar which were centres of defence against slavers.

After 1861 the main political and administrative influences came from the south where Britain took effective control. National and provincial boundaries were set with no regard for existing ethnic and cultural groups or to past history. Some of the pre-colonial cities declined, for example Sokoto's population fell to 52 000 by 1952. Other cities, favoured by the colonial rulers flourished.

An important influence upon population distribution was the building of railways, between 1890 and about 1930. These became the framework around which the country was developed, economically. Cities like Port Harcourt, Enugu, Onitsha and Kaduna grew from nothing. As these 'British' cities were centres of administration as well as trade, investment in the infrastructure was made here but denied other cities. The main purpose was to organise the export of tropical foodstuffs and raw materials to Britain. Hence, population was attracted to the ports and towns along the railway. The only reliable census took place in Nigeria in 1963 and the distribution then is shown in fig. 3.14. Since independence, the main changes have been a result of rural-urban migration, many more people moving to towns. Lagos, for example, had only one million people in 1963.

Fig. 3.13 *Nigeria*

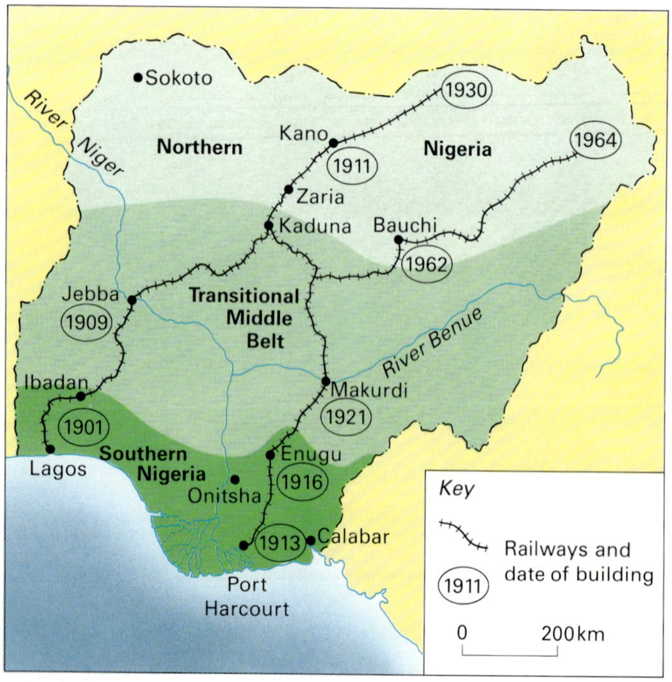

Fig. 3.14 *Population distribution in Nigeria*

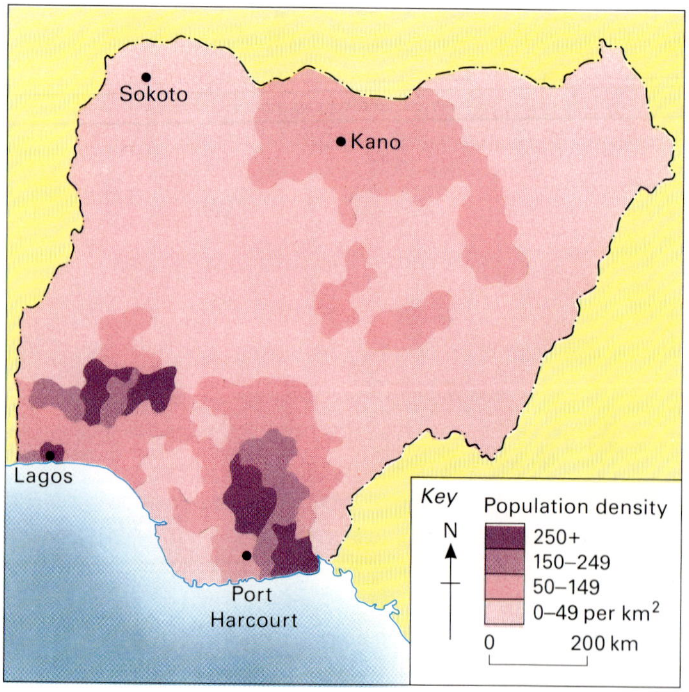

Core regions

Economic development tends to produce the growth of a 'core'. It is rarely spread evenly across a country. It tends to become concentrated in certain areas, which can be called 'core regions'. These regions are very attractive to populations which migrate from the surrounding less developed regions, known as 'the periphery'. Look carefully at fig. 3.15 which is a flow chart explaining core growth.

The development of a core region begins with a new activity such as the building of a port, or a major industrial complex like an oil refinery. The new activity has 'spin-offs' locally which provide markets for other industries. Local service industries like banks, insurance and so on are stimulated. Jobs appear in the core and people are attracted. The increased population and general rise in wealth lead to road and rail improvements and perhaps the need for an airport. New housing, schools, hospitals and the like are needed and construction industries grow. More labour and capital are attracted from outside the region and the process begins all over again. This process and its effects upon population distribution has happened in several South American countries, especially in Venezuela. The opening up of oilfields in the 1920s provided the stimulus for new activities. Although oil is still produced in the eastern Llanos of Venezuela, the lowlands around Maracaibo in the north-west are the main source of oil today. Oil revenues make up as much as 90% of the country's foreign currency.

These finances have provided for a great variety of activities in the area between Maracaibo and the capital city, Caracas. The core region has developed around these two cities with the result that people have migrated from the poorer agricultural areas of Venezuela to the core. The 14 million people of Venezuela are concentrated in the core with nearly three millions in Caracas and a million in Maracaibo.

Fig. 3.15 *Core development*

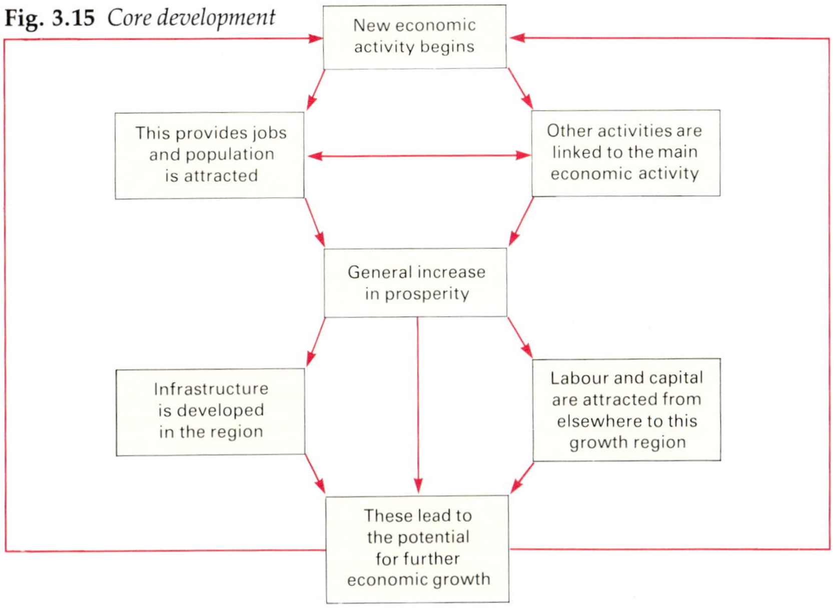

Fig. 3.16 *Core region of Venezuela*

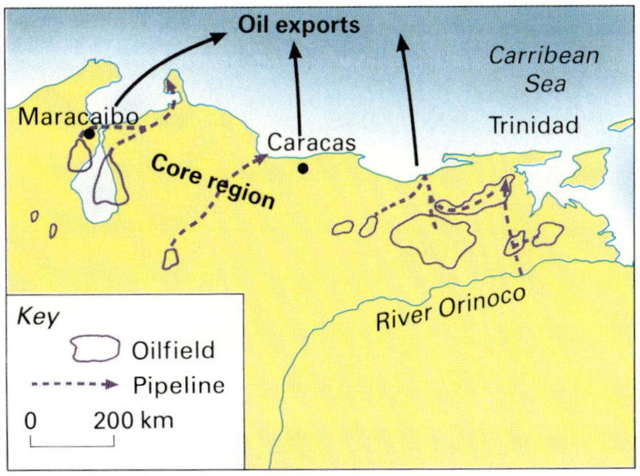

Fig. 3.17 *Does economic development alone explain the growth of Caracas?*

Activities

1 Study 'core development'. Draw a map of Nigeria to identify 'a core region'. Make a list of the reasons for your choice of area.
2 How did British colonial rule in Nigeria lead to the formation of 'a core region'?
3 Choose one other developing country where a core region has formed. Find out the reasons why it did.

Core development tends to lead to uneven population distribution. The effects in developed countries like Britain are not just simple contrasts between the core and the periphery. The South-East of England from Dover through London and Birmingham has the highest levels of prosperity in Britain. From an axis formed by the M2, M1 and M6 motorways, running south east to north west, prosperity generally decreases west towards Cornwall and Wales and northwards into Scotland (see fig. 3.18).

Fig. 3.18 *Simplified map of prosperity in Britain*

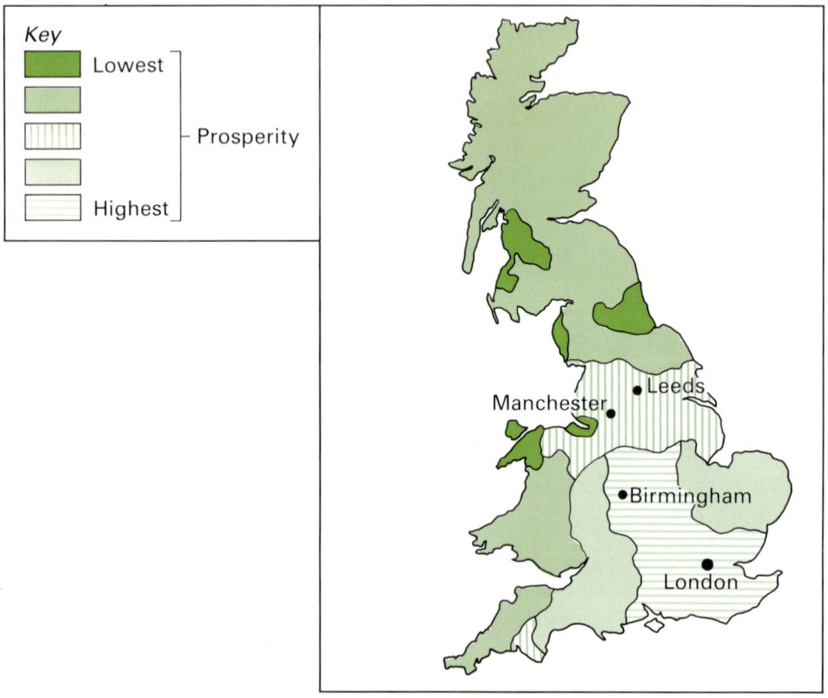

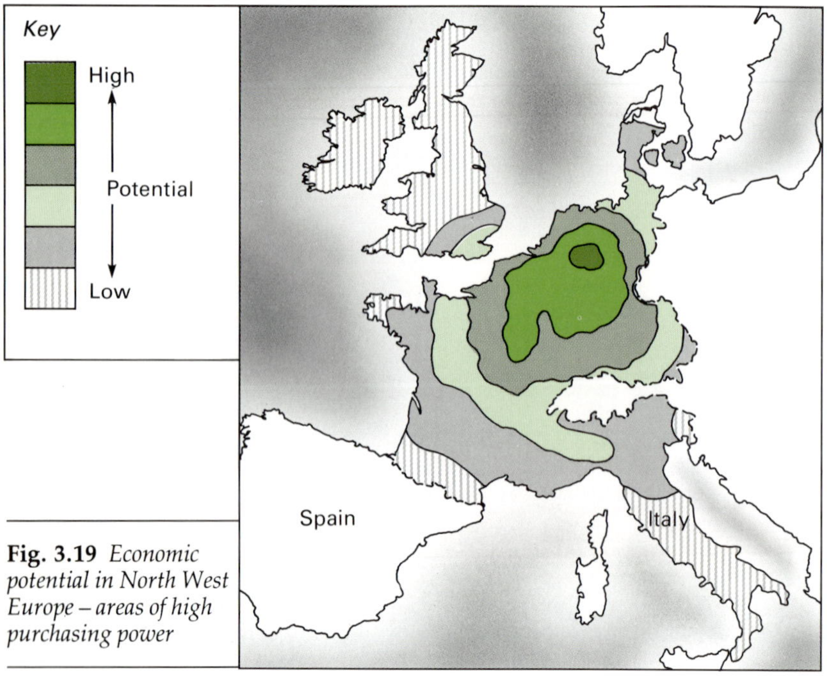

Fig. 3.19 *Economic potential in North West Europe – areas of high purchasing power*

In the peripheral regions the relatively low standards of prosperity are reflected in high unemployment, lower standards of health services, more inadequate housing and lower numbers of students staying on at school beyond 16 years. These are some of the 'push factors' aiding steady migration south and eastwards.

In the 20th century, manufacturers have been increasingly attracted to markets, the areas of higher population density and higher prosperity, instead of towards sources of raw materials. The decline of heavy industry in the periphery was matched by increasing attractiveness of the South-East. The capital city and the large population of Greater London has provided both a labour supply and a market for goods. Vehicles industries, electrical and electronic industries especially have been attracted to the region.

When Britain joined the EEC in 1970, a further stimulus was given to development in the South East. Its geographical location put it very close to the core region of the EEC (fig. 3.19). The growth of tertiary occupations at the expense of secondary, to a point where over half of all employees in Britain are tertiary, has benefited the South East mainly. For example, over half of all office workers in England and Wales work in London.

Government policies

Government policies affect population distribution. The growth of population in the south east of England has been a target of government policies for many years. In general, these policies were directed to helping the peripheral regions. At the same time, they merely accentuated the importance of the core. For example, motorway building policies show the advantages that economic activity bring to the South East.

Attempts to assist the regions took a variety of forms. Grants, loans and tax concessions have been used to attract employers to the periphery. The later phases of New Town building were in the hardest hit regions of South Wales, Merseyside, the North east and Scotland. They were even given the names of 'development areas' (see fig. 3.21).

In the 1960s and 1970s in Britain, the government moved some of its own departments into these regions. The DVLC went to Swansea; the Royal Mint also to South Wales; large departments of the DHSS and

Fig. 3.20 *Britain's motorway system*

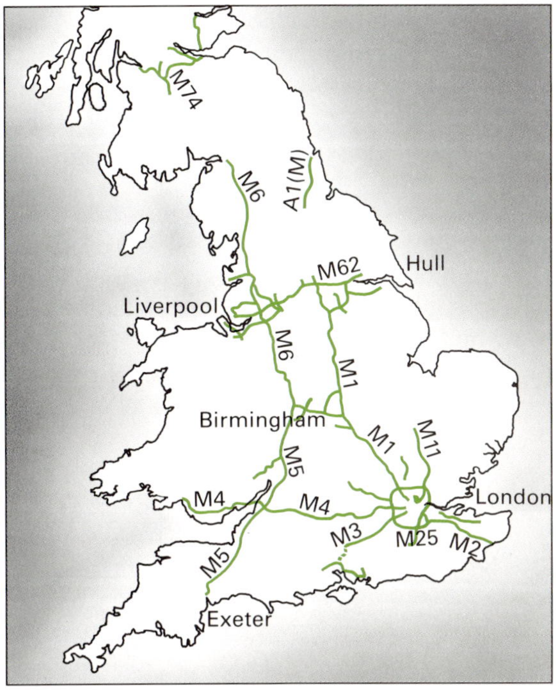

Fig. 3.21 *New Towns and Development Areas*

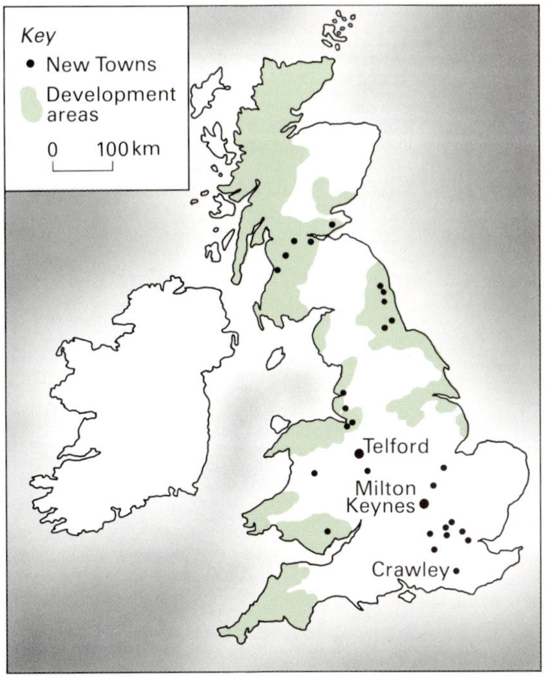

DES were opened in North east England. The hope was that they would not only reduce the urban pressures in the core region of the South East, but would assist with unemployment problems in the periphery. When large investors such as the Japanese companies, Sony and Nissan, wished to open factories in Britain, to give access to the EEC markets, they were guided to the development areas, by attractive cheap sites and a variety of grants.

Human factors are also important at the local scale. Generally the smaller the scale, the less important the effects of environmental factors. Figure 3.22 shows the growth of a city which was typical of many in Britain. At the 1981 Census, Leicester was the ninth largest in England, with a population of 280 324. The main growth of population had occurred in the 19th century as fig. 3.23 shows. The development of industries like boot, shoe and textile manufacturing attracted people from the surrounding areas.

The distribution of people inside the city was relatively unplanned before 1939. Industrial sites and high density housing for workers expanded along the roads out of the existing town. Some wards such as Belgrave and Westcotes, shown in fig. 3.24, were occupied by large numbers of working families in cheap, high-density housing.

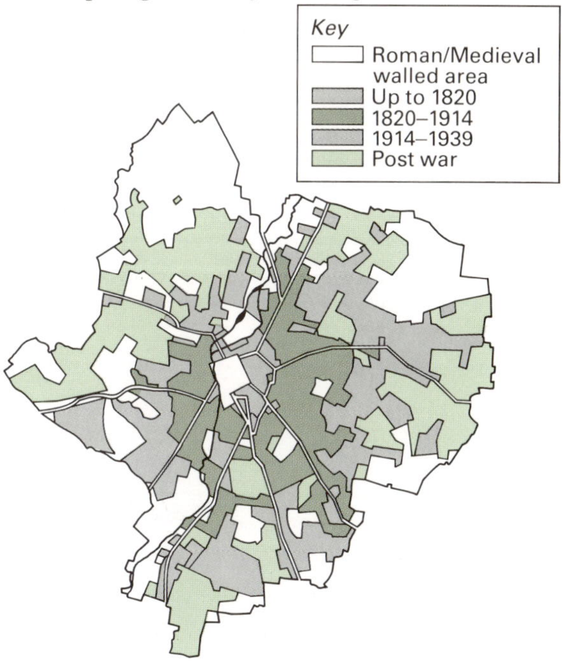

Fig. 3.22 *The growth of Leicester*

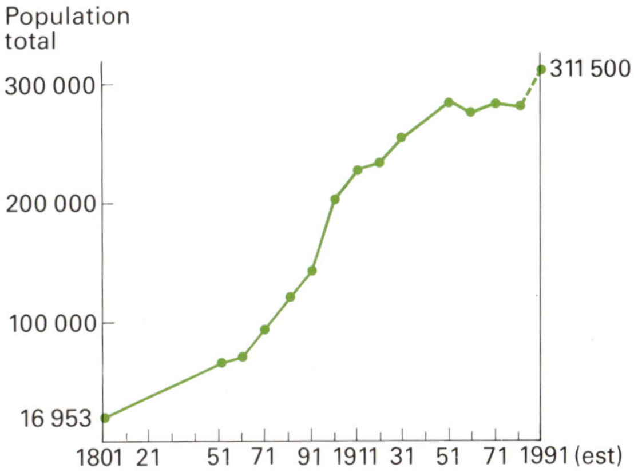

Fig. 3.23 *Growth of Leicester's population*

Fig. 3.24 *Population changes in some Leicester wards*

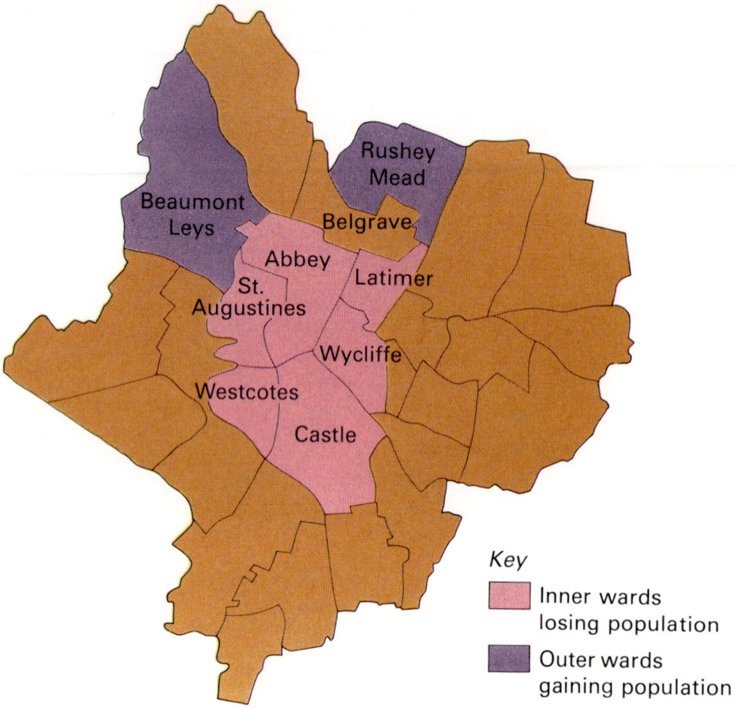

In the 20th century, the distribution was increasingly affected by human factors especially plans by the local government. The planning authorities have had two main approaches. They have carried out large scale urban renewal programmes in the inner city and developed new residential neighbourhoods in the suburbs.

Inner wards have had large demolition programmes since 1971 and some have lost large numbers of people. Westcotes has 27% fewer people today and Castle, 22%. At the same time, suburban developments have increased population in other wards. Bushey Mead in the north of the city, has had a 62% population increase since 1971. An even bigger change is planned for Beaumont Leys in the north west, a 432% increase. This area will have a comprehensive neighbourhood development.

Activities

1 Study fig. 3.19. Make a list of the main population centres in the core region of the EEC. Find out why these centres have attracted so many people.
2 In small groups, discuss fig. 3.18 and the differences in prosperity between core and peripheral regions in Britain. What attitudes would your groups take towards a strong government policy to improve living standards in the periphery at the expense of the core region? Write a report about the findings of the group.
3 Imagine you live in a street in the Inner Area of Leicester which is designated for demolition. Your family has been offered a new home in Beaumont Leys. The opportunity is still there to move to another part of the Inner Area. What is your own attitude towards the move? Will the other members of your family have similar values to you? Describe them.
4 Choose a peripheral area of Great Britain. Describe some of the advantages of living there. Are these greater than the disadvantages?

4 POPULATION AND DEVELOPMENT

What is development?

Careful study of advertising on television points out to us that, if material possessions are indicators of standards of living, then there are many well off people in Britain. The photograph in fig. 4.1, however, reminds us that not all people are well off. Many are without the basic necessities of life such as shelter, food and good health. So, the idea of development is a relative one.

Fig. 4.1 *What does an advertisement like this tell us about development?*

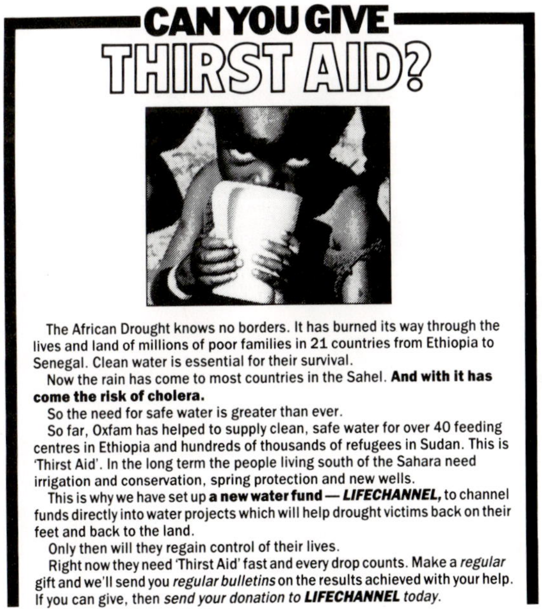

The wealth of the world is not shared equally between people or between countries. There is a gap between the wealthy minority and the less wealthy majority. To a certain extent the wealthy have become rich at the expense of the less well off majority. It was the main theme of the Brandt Report in 1980 that the developed and developing countries should act together to face the worldwide threats of poverty and hunger. The Report went further to state that there was a moral responsibility to help developing countries and to remove the injustices which prevented their development in the past.

Levels of development change in time and space. The ancient Greeks, 1000 years before Christ, had produced a highly developed way of life. Yet, today, as fig. 4.11 shows, Greece is well down the development scale. Development also changes spatially, between groups of people and countries. Figure 4.3 shows that even inside developed countries like Britain there are areas of lower development. The EEC Development Fund is specifically used to help such areas. On the other hand, inside developing countries like Brazil there are pockets of very high development. Hence, we use relative terms to describe it, less-developed, developing or developed.

Fig. 4.3 *EEC Regional Development sign*

Fig. 4.2 *Indicators of development 1984*

Indicators	Peru	Nigeria	Britain
GNP per person per year in US dollars	595	730	6514
Calories per day (average food intake per person)	2141	2444	3210
Adult literacy rate %	72	not available	99
Energy used in tonnes per person per year of coal equivalent	0.65	0.19	4.67
Newsprint per person per year in kg	4.8	0.2	29.5

Measuring development

Geographers should try to measure development but when attempts are made to do this problems arise. For instance, is an area where people have large, owner-occupied houses, with an average of two cars per family, more highly developed than an area without them? Or is it just that people living there place a high value on material possessions? Is personal wealth alone a satisfactory measure of development? Can the term 'development' even be applied to individuals or small groups of people? Indeed, can it be measured with any accuracy at all? Perhaps it should be stated that levels of development can only be judged rather than measured since the attitudes of those doing the measuring are very important.

There is no single method of measuring levels of development accurately. What can be done is to use a number of indicators to make broad, general comparisons of areas, groups of people and countries. Also, the reasons why some countries and people are called developed and others developing should be carefully explored.

One indicator used to compare countries is the Gross National Product per person (study fig. 4.4). This is calculated by dividing the value of all goods and services produced in a country in one year by the number of people. An indicator such as this allows us to make comparisons on a global scale.

Other indicators measure people's well-being. Use fig. 4.2 to compare the food intake of people in Britain with those in Peru and Nigeria. Similarly, if people in Britain are ill, how do their chances of treatment compare?

Fig. 4.4 *Contrasts in development, 1984*

Activities

1 Carry out a brainstorm similar to that in fig. 2.2. Find out what types of indicator could be used to measure levels of development.
2 Use fig. 4.2. Write brief comments to explain the meaning of each of the indicators used and compare the countries for each indicator.
3 The line on the map in fig. 4.4 shows the North-South division used in the Brandt Report. How does this line help to indicate levels of development?

Indicators can be used in a small area to show differences in levels of development. At the time of the 1981 Census in Britain, Leicester was the ninth largest city in England with a population over 280 000. Although its origins date back to before Norman times, 1066 AD, and it was an important market town in the Middle Ages, its main growth took place during the Industrial Revolution of the 18th and 19th centuries. The population grew from 19 953 in 1801 to 211 579 in 1901. Figure 3.22 shows the growth of the city.

The Inner Area of Leicester today is a ring of buildings around the city centre, the CBD, built before 1914. The houses, shops and factories in this area are old, and built to a high density, with narrow roads and little space between them. In addition, modern problems of traffic congestion and car-parking have made it a less than desirable place in which to live.

A process of selective migration has taken place in Leicester in that people who could afford to move to newer, better housing in the suburbs have chosen to do so. Others, usually those who could least afford to choose, have remained in the Inner Area. In the area, the city council has indicated seven priority areas for urban renewal. To justify its decision, it produced a number of indicators. These were used to compare the Inner Area with the rest of Leicester. Some of them are shown in fig. 4.5.

Fig. 4.5 *Indicators of living standards in the Inner Area of Leicester*

Indicator	*City average (%)*	*One inner ward (%)*
Unemployment overall	12.5	19.7
Unemployment, 16 to 19 age	22.0	24.0
Householders–no inside WC	7.0	18.4
Household with no car	51.7	61.2
Households with no bath	1.9	8.4
Households – more than 1.5 persons per room	1.2	3.5

The differences between areas of high and low development in a country like Britain are usually less noticeable than in a developing country like Brazil.

Three facts about variations in development in Brazil are quite clear.

Fig. 4.6 *Regions of Brazil*

1. During the last 25 years, the wealthiest one quarter of the Brazilian population has become even wealthier. It has increased its share of national income to over one third. At the same time, the least wealthy 40% has got an even lower share of national income, as low as 9%.
2. The south east region with 42% of the population of Brazil, has 63% of the national income.
3. Levels of development are higher in urban areas than in rural areas, which encourages even more people to move into the towns.

From these three statements, it can be said that relatively small numbers of people in the cities of south east Brazil have reached higher levels of development than the rest of the country.

However it is in the cities of the south east region that one also finds the lowest levels of development in the country. In Rio de Janeiro, for example, favelas or shanty towns, are built on the steep slopes overlooking the city (fig. 4.7). These slopes are considered too dangerous for normal building and, as a result, people flocking to Rio de Janeiro from rural areas, unable to find housing, end up there. The actual number of such people is hard to estimate, but it is thought to be between one half and one million in Rio alone.

Fig. 4.7 *Favelas in Rio de Janeiro*

People living in favelas represent the extreme case of urban deprivation. Their houses, shanties, are a ramshackle collection of huts made from whatever materials are at hand. Virtually all services such as water supply, drainage, sewage, etc. are absent. This leads to many people living in squalor, with abandoned children being a particular problem. Many are forced to steal and commit other offences just to survive. It is very ironic that these favelas are located above one of the most beautiful cities in the world. A city where, within a few hundred metres of favelas, there are examples of great wealth.

Fig. 4.8 *Number of people per doctor in Brazil*

Number per doctor	*Region*
1226	Whole of Brazil (average)
531	Rio de Janeiro
879	South east region
1359	South region
1394	Centre west region
2145	North east region
2268	North region

Fig. 4.9 *Indicators of development in South-east Brazil*

Percentage of national total	*Indicator*
63	National income
55	Industrial production of Brazil
70	Industrial employment of Brazil
75	Higher educational establishments of Brazil
82	Urban population

Activities

1 Study the photograph in fig. 4.7. Make a list of all the indicators of development shown in the photograph.

2 Use figs 4.8 and 4.9. Test the hypothesis that a small number of people in South-east Brazil have higher levels of development than people elsewhere in Brazil.

3 Study figs 4.5 and 4.7. In small groups, discuss the differences in living standards between the average population of Leicester and one Inner Area ward of Leicester. How do they compare with the differences for Brazil?

4 Image that there is a shanty settlement located about 50 metres from your home.

a) What problems do you think would arise in your neighbourhood?

b) What would be the attitudes of your parents, neighbours and yourself towards the shanty dwellers? What might be the responses of the shanty dwellers?

c) In discussion groups, decide what could be done about such settlements.

Population and development

Information about populations can be used to indicate development levels. Several indicators have already been used to help you to make judgements about levels of development. They showed that development is not simply a matter of wealth. They cover a wide range of factors, health, education, housing and employment. Population information is very helpful in making these judgements but statistics should be treated carefully as they are not always reliable.

Maps or diagrams such as fig. 4.11 can be used to compare sets of facts which show relationships. Such relationships which can be tested by other methods are called hypotheses.

Fig. 4.10 *Death rates for the 18 countries in fig. 4.11 (per 1000 people)*

Country	*Rate*	*Country*	*Rate*
Venezuela	6	India	15
Sweden	8	W. Germany	15
Barbados	9	Spain	15
USA	9	Nigeria	18
Argentina	9	Ghana	19
Brazil	9	Cameroon	19
France	11	Bangladesh	19
Peru	12	Greece	20
UK	14	Mali	22

Activities

1 Use fig. 4.11 for 18 countries. Test the hypothesis that the wealthier a country is, the lower its birth rate. Write a paragraph about your findings.
2 Use the table in fig. 4.10 and fig. 4.11. For the same 18 countries, test the hypothesis that wealthier countries usually have lower death rates.
3 Study the statistics in fig. 4.10 carefully. In some cases, they are the latest estimates made by the United Nations. Which do you find surprising? Give your reasons for this.
4 What does fig. 4.12 show about development in India?

Fig. 4.11 *GNP and birth rates for 18 countries*

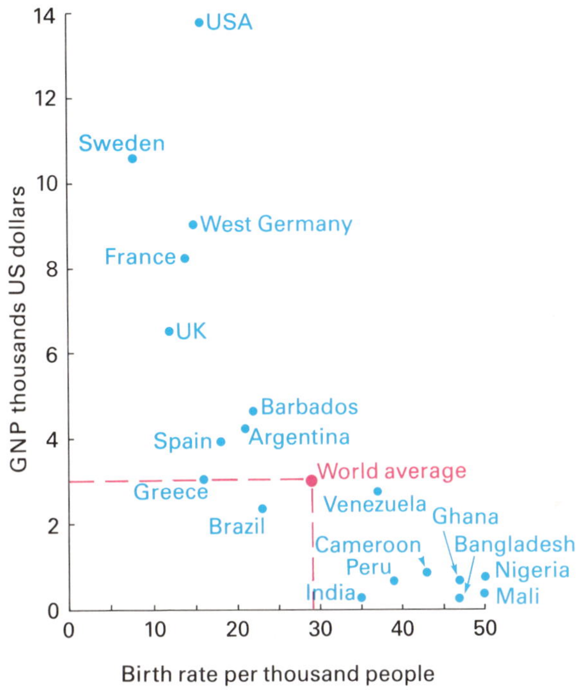

Fig. 4.12 *'The number of newspapers bought is an accurate measure of development'. Discuss this statement using the photograph here*

Fig. 4.13 *Natural increase in population*

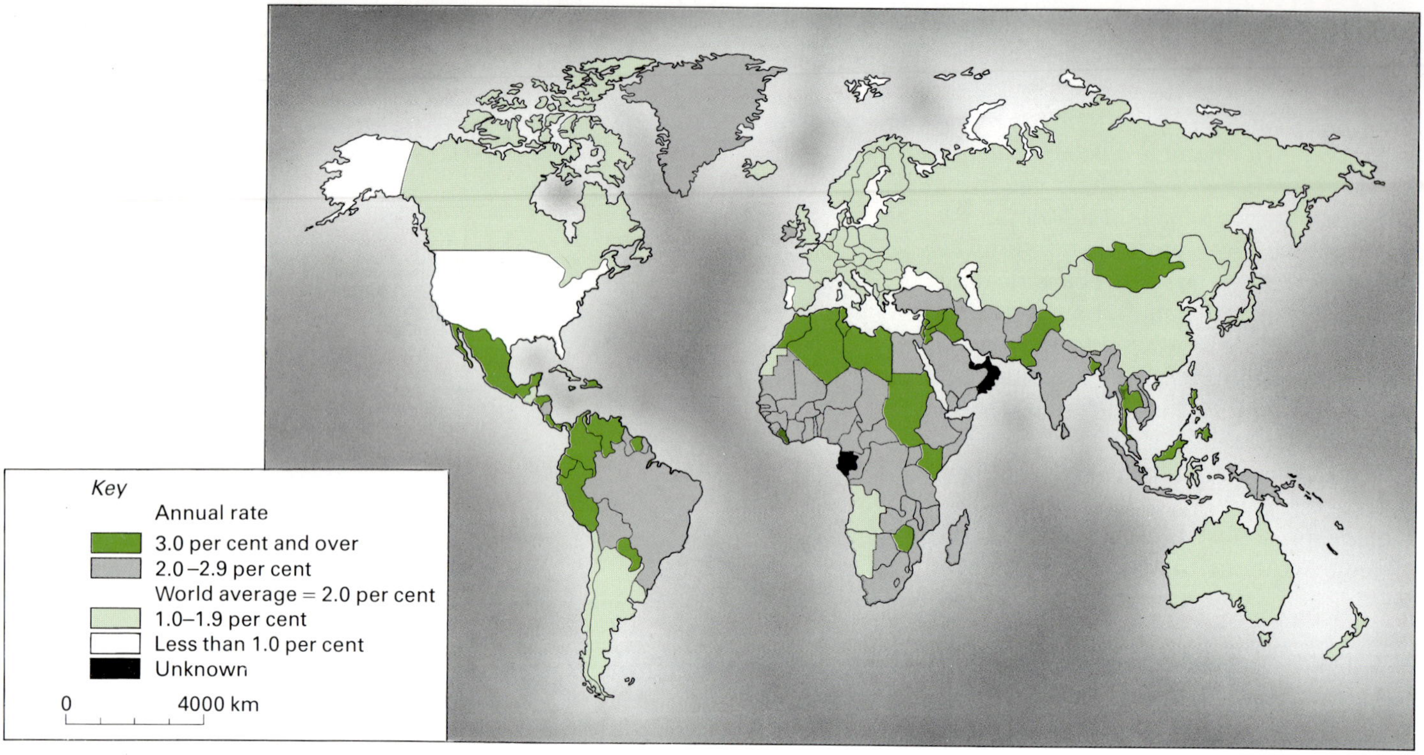

Fig. 4.14 *States of southern India*

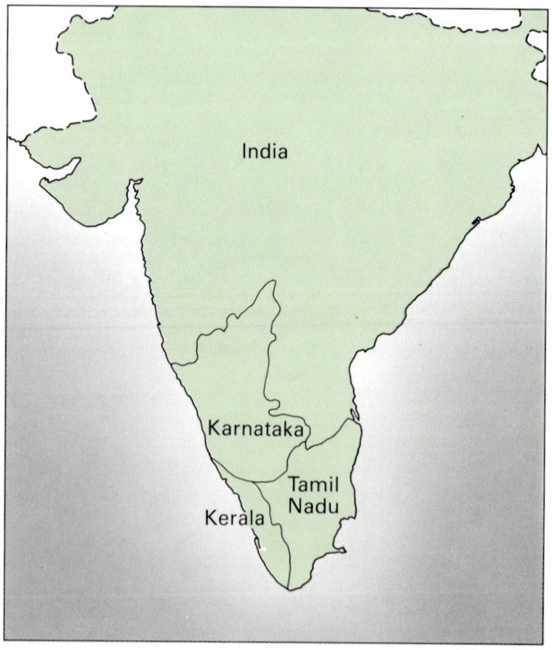

Careful study of fig. 2.10, which shows the demographic transition, shows that countries in Stages 2 and 3 have falling death rates and, although they are also falling, still quite high birth rates. As a result, these countries have quite high natural increases in population. Figure 4.13 shows natural increases for the countries of the world.

India has the second largest population in the world, after China. The latest Indian Census in 1981 showed 684 million people, an increase of over 100 millions since the previous Census in 1971. The main reason for this rapid growth was the fact that the death rate has fallen sharply but the birth rate has remained quite high.

During the last 40 years, the government of India has been faced with the possibility of overwhelming increases in the number of people, partly as a result of its own successes in reducing death rates. National programmes since the country was formed in 1947 have greatly reduced the effects of diseases such as malaria, leprosy, cholera, etc.

Activities

Test the hypothesis, using fig. 4.13, that developing countries have high natural increases in population and developed countries have low ones. Write a paragraph about your findings.

Fig. 4.15 *Birth control education in India (United Nations/ILO 123,597)*

Improved quality of drinking water and better methods of storing and distributing food have also helped to lower death rates.

Meanwhile, the birth rate remained high (see fig. 4.11). Family planning has been used for over 50 years but, after 1960, it became a major item in government policy. However, methods of contraception alone had little effect upon the birth rate. Low educational standards and religious opposition were two reasons for this. The government between 1970 and 1977 found itself forced to concentrate upon sterilisation as a form of birth control. A fairly simple operation on males, they hoped, would have a major effect upon the number of births.

After a publicity campaign involving gifts and cash payments to volunteers, there were some successes. In one year, 1972–3, over 3 million people volunteered to be sterilised. But by 1975, the supply of volunteers dried up. The government then went one stage further and tried to coerce people into sterilisation. This built up so much resentment that it was one of the reasons why the Indian government lost the 1977 election. Thus birth control policies became less effective.

Although India's national policies and the overall population growth continue to cause anxiety, some provinces in India have had great success in reducing birth rates. This has been very true in the southern part of India shown in fig. 4.14. In Karnataka, Tamil Nadu and above all in Kerala the birth rate has fallen to levels very similar to that of developed countries. The areas have been carefully studied in recent years to try and explain this trend. Most of the answers may be found in fig. 4.16. They had less to do with deliberate policies to reduce births than with success in raising the general standards of living. In Kerala, families have found it in their own interests to reduce the numbers of children in order to raise living standards.

Fig. 4.16 *Falling birth rates in Kerala*

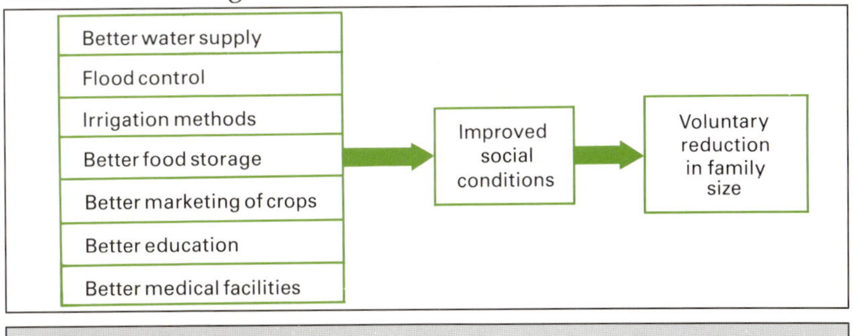

Activities

Discuss in groups whether it is realistic to introduce and carry out birth control policies in a compulsory way. After the discussion, write a paragraph about the problem, referring to:

a) the needs of the country.
b) the practical problems
c) the attitudes and values of the people towards such policies.

Population pyramids

Population pyramids are a very useful way of showing levels of development. Figure 2.10 shows the demographic transition for Brazil. The country moved out of Stage 2 in the early 1960s into Stage 3. This means that the high birth rate and falling death rate have given way to a low death rate and falling birth rate. In fact, the difference between birth and death rates in Brazil before 1962 gave a natural increase as high as 3.5% per year. This was an extra 1.8 million people to feed each year. Since the birth rate began to fall in 1962, the natural increase has dropped to about 2.0%. At the same time, life expectancy rose from 51 years in 1951 to 63 years today.

The shapes of population pyramids for Brazil are shown in fig. 4.17. The effect of falling death rates by 1970 can be seen in the pyramid because the base of the pyramid widened as more babies survived. Indeed, by 1970, 52.4% of the population was under 20 years old. However, the birth rate began to slow down during the late 1960s and the base of the pyramid stopped widening. By the late 1970s, it began to narrow. In 1985, only 49.5% of the population was under 20 years old. If the birth rate continues to fall, the base of the pyramid will narrow even further.

Fig. 4.17 *Age/Sex pyramids for Brazil*

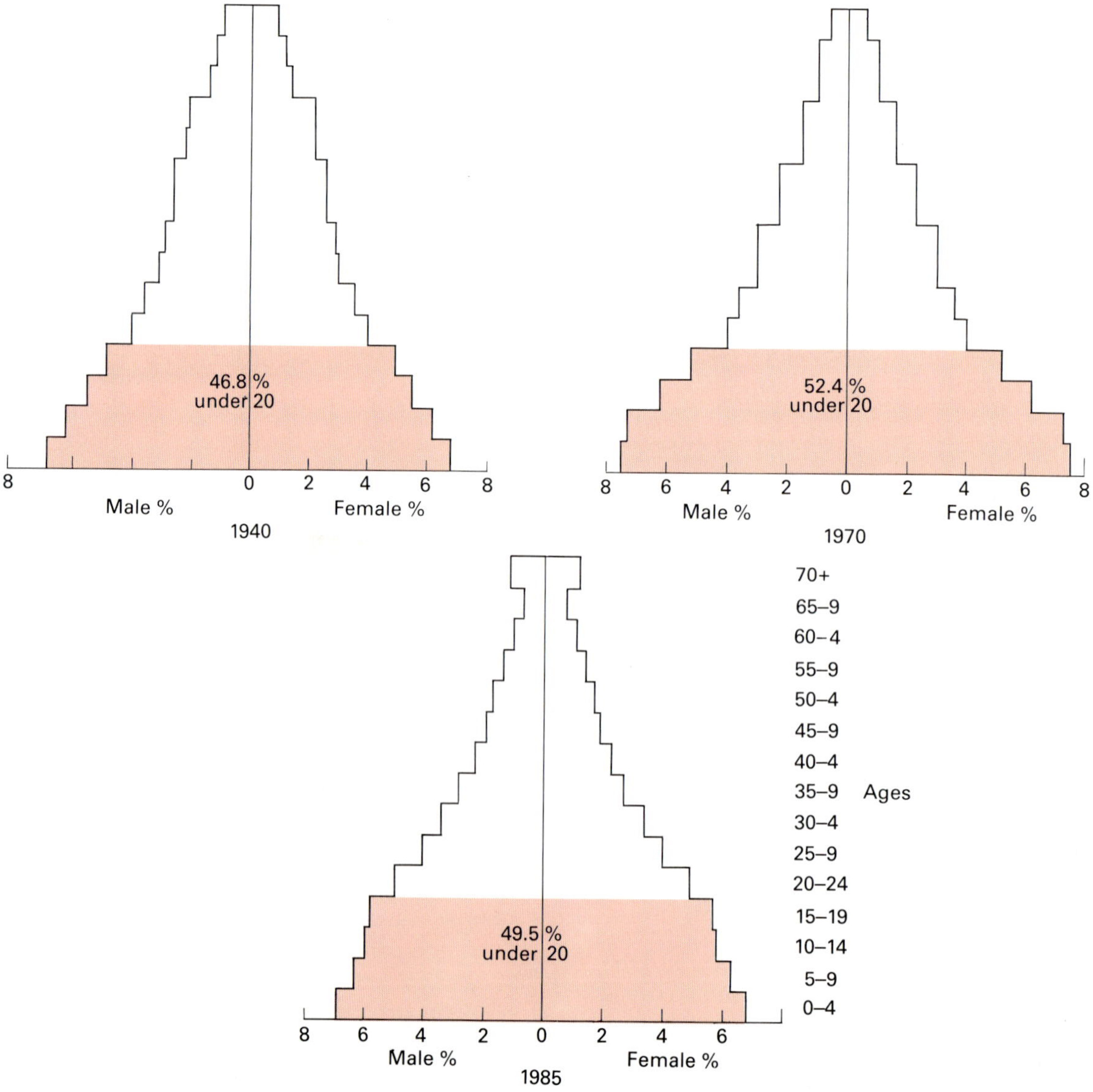

PART TWO PLACES

5 CLASSIFYING SETTLEMENTS

Settlements can be classified in a number of ways. These classifications look at different characteristics of settlements and can all be used in describing settlements.

Fig. 5.1 *Types of settlement*

1

2

3

4

5

6

7

8

Size

Activities

Study fig. 5.1. To illustrate the problems of classifying settlements, put ticks in the columns on a copy of fig. 5.2. Your ticks should best describe each type of settlement in the photographs.

Fig. 5.2 *Methods of classifying settlements*

	Classification photographs in Figure 5.1							
	1	2	3	4	5	6	7	8
Large size								
Medium size								
Small size								
Temporary								
Permanent								
Agricultural								
Industrial								
Commercial								
Individual								
Hamlet								
Village								
Town								
City								
Conurbation								
Megalopolis								

One way to put settlements into some form of order is to classify them according to size, using a hierarchy of settlements (fig. 5.3).

Fig. 5.3 *Hierarchy of settlements*

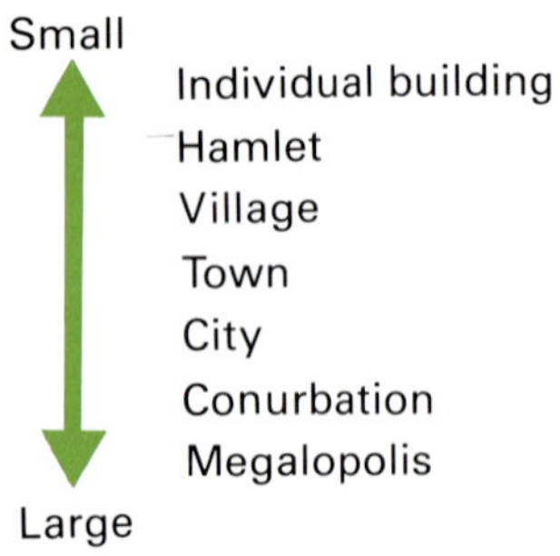

Settlements vary in size from an individual house to large conurbations where several towns have merged and to a megalopolis where conurbations have merged. An example of a megalopolis is the built-up area of north

Fig. 5.4 *Rank size rule*

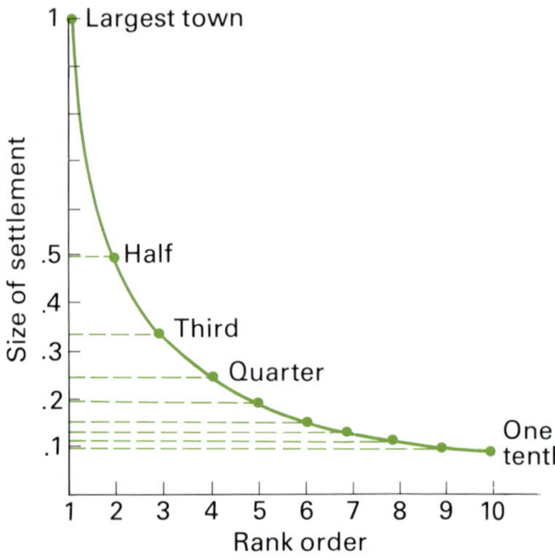

east USA from Washington DC to Boston in New England.

Settlements in many countries show a regular decrease in size from the largest to the smallest. The rank size rule in fig. 5.4 states that in a country, the second largest town will be half the size of the largest, the third largest will be one third the size of the largest, and so on.

This rule is a hypothesis which can be tested using actual examples. Figure 5.5 shows the rule for the ten largest towns in West Germany, a developed country, and Nigeria, a developing country. How far do these examples show the rank size rule to be effective?

Rank size ordering of the settlements in some countries shows them to have a 'primate' pattern. In such a pattern the largest settlement is very much larger than all other settlements in the country. Copenhagen in Denmark for example is over five times larger than the next largest town. In some cases, it may be a double primate pattern where two towns dominate the rank order (see fig. 5.6).

Fig. 5.5 *Rank size of cities in West Germany and Nigeria*

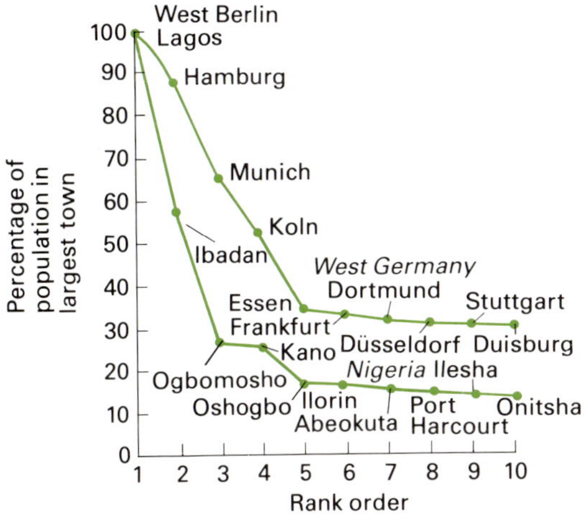

Fig. 5.6 *Rank size for the ten largest towns in France and Brazil*

France		*Brazil*	
Town	*Percentage of largest town*	*Town*	*Percentage of largest town*
Paris		Sao Paulo	
Lyons	14	Rio de Janeiro	60
Marseilles	13	Belo Horizonte	21
Lille	11	Salvador	18
Bordeaux	7.5	Fortaleza	15
Toulouse	6	Recife	14
Nantes	5	Brasilia	14
Nice	5	Port Alegre	13
Toulon	4.8	Nova Iguacu	13
Grenoble	4.5	Curitiba	12

Activities

Use the statistics in fig. 5.6 to draw rank size graphs similar to those in fig. 5.5.

Service provision

Most settlements, from the size of a village upwards, provide a number of services for the people in and around them. Middridge is a small County Durham village, about ten miles from Darlington. The only services in the village, apart from a community hall, are one village shop, a pub and milk and vegetables supplied from a local farm (see fig. 5.9).

The village shop and the farm provide low order services. These are services which are needed regularly or often and people prefer not to travel too far for them. This distance of travel is called the 'range' of the service or goods. Figure 5.7 shows the range of service for five low order goods needed by people in the village.

Some goods or services require a minimum number of customers for them to stay in business. This is called the threshold of the goods or service. The threshold is the minimum number. For electrical goods, clothing or furniture, for example, the threshold is much higher than for bread and milk. These articles, for which people are willing to travel longer distances in order to find a greater choice, are called high order goods or services.

Another way of describing these shopping habits is to think of them as convenience or comparison shopping. Low order services need to be provided close at hand, in order words, to be convenient. High order services where people need to compare between the choices offered, are called comparison goods. It should be remembered that large towns

Fig. 5.7 *Shopping patterns in the small village of Middridge, County Durham*

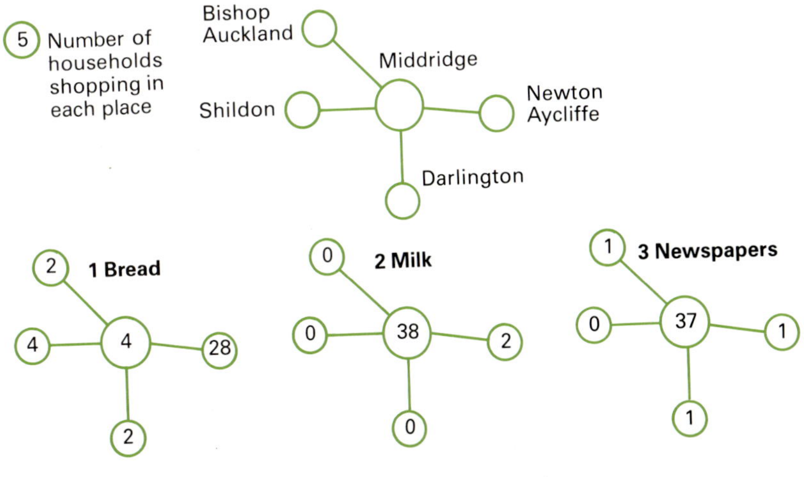

include almost all of the low order services and goods. Smaller settlements may only provide a few low order goods and services and rarely any high order goods. Figure 5.8 compares services provided by four different types of settlement in South west Durham.

Fig. 5.8 *Services provided by four settlements in south-west Durham*

Settlement	*Type*	*School-Sec*	*School-Primary*	*Hospital*	*Rail station*	*Bus station*	*Bus stop*	*Garage (petrol)*	*Pub*	*Health centre*	*Insurance Co*	*Estate agent*	*Library*	*Bank*	*Post Office*	*Travel Agent*	*Clothing*	*Hardware*	*Butcher*	*Shoe shop*	*Baker*	*Chemist*	*Supermarket*	*General store*
Middridge	Small village						*		*															
Heighington	Large village		*		*		*	*	*						*								*	
Shildon	Small town	*	*		*	*	*	*	*	*	*	*	*	*	*	*	*	*	*	*	*	*	*	*
Bishop Auckland	Medium-sized town	*	*	*	*	*	*	*	*	*	*	*	*	*	*	*	*	*	*	*	*	*	*	*

Fig. 5.9 *Village shop*

People living in a small village like Middridge, normally shop locally for their low order goods but are prepared to travel quite long distances for high order goods. Figure 5.10 and 5.11 illustrate the patterns of shopping in Middridge.

Fig. 5.11 *Comparison shopping for higher order goods in Middridge*

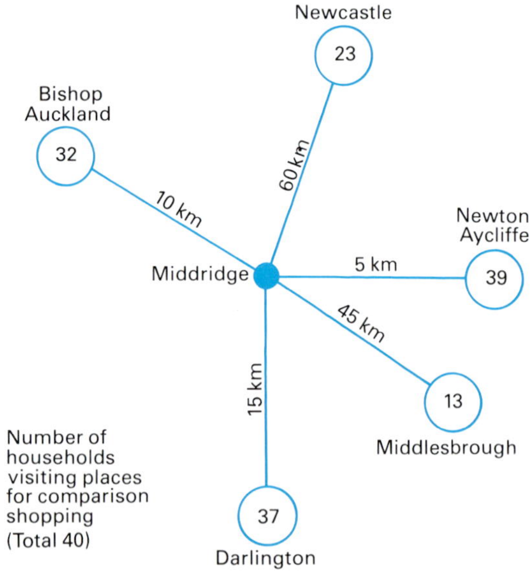

Activities

What services does the shop in fig. 5.9 offer?

Fig. 5.10 *Shopping habits of one household in Middridge*

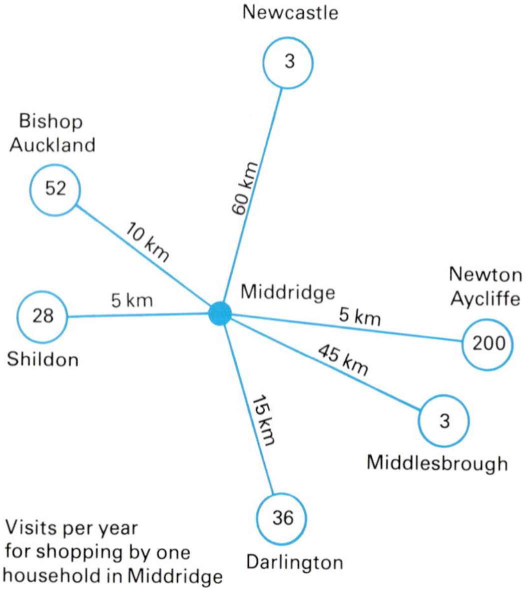

The area around a settlement from which people come to shop is called the 'sphere of influence', or market area. Figure 5.12 shows the sphere of influence for Bishop Auckland, a market town in Durham. Because it provides most high as well as low order services, it provides comparison shopping for people in a largely rural area of the county.

Market towns and high order centres compete with each other for trade. Figure 5.11 shows the choices open to people in

Fig. 5.12 *Sphere of influence of Bishop Auckland*

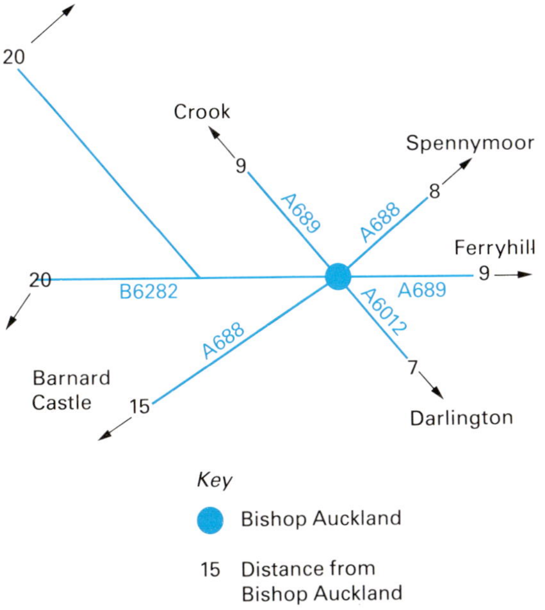

Middridge. The point between two towns which divides people travelling one way for services from those going the other way is called the 'breaking point'. Linking up these breaking points around a settlement on a map helps you to locate the sphere of influence of that settlement, or its market area.

Another method used by geographers to compare the services offered by different settlements is to look at a number of major retail companies, especialy large multiples such as Marks and Spencer, Woolworths, Boots, etc. Since many of these companies have policies to ensure that they have premises in most areas of the country or region, their presence can be used to classify settlements. Some, like Marks and Spencer, go so far as to grade their stores according to the size or market importance of towns. Figure 5.13 shows this method applied to the same four towns in County Durham.

Fig. 5.14 *Large multiple retailer*

Fig. 5.13 *Location of retail shops in towns in south-west Durham*

Settlement	*Type*	*Marks & Spencer*	*Woolworth*	*Boots*	*W. H. Smith*	*Gateway*	*Morrisons (Superstore)*	*MFI*	*Elec. Show Room*	*Gas Show Room*	*Sec. Schools*	*Further Ed Coll*	*Hospital*
Shildon	Small town										1		
Newton Aycliffe	New Town		1	1		1			1	1	*		
Bishop Auckland	Market town	1	1	1	1	1	1		1	1	*	1	1
Darlington	Large regional centre	1	1	*	1	1	1	1	1	1	*	1	1

* = more than 1

Activities

1 Carry out a shopping survey for the place or street where you live. Draw up a questionnaire to obtain the information you need. This information can then be used to draw diagrams similar to those in figs 5.10, 5.11 and 5.12.

2 For towns or shopping centres in your area, complete a table similar to that in fig. 5.13. You may need to use different retailers.

Pattern

In the 1930s, Walter Christaller in West Germany developed a theory that the location and pattern of settlements, and the size of their spheres of influence, were related to the types of services they provided for the area around them. The 'serviced area' can be called the hinterland. This became known as 'Central Place Theory'.

Ideally, settlements in rural areas would be spread evenly across the landscape, as shown in fig. 5.15(a). Each settlement would provide services and goods for a roughly circular area around it. This was because the people living inside that circular area would find this settlement to be the most convenient for them. They would collect their low order goods there. Figure 5.15(b) shows these circles.

Fig. 5.15 *Central Place Theory, according to Christaller*

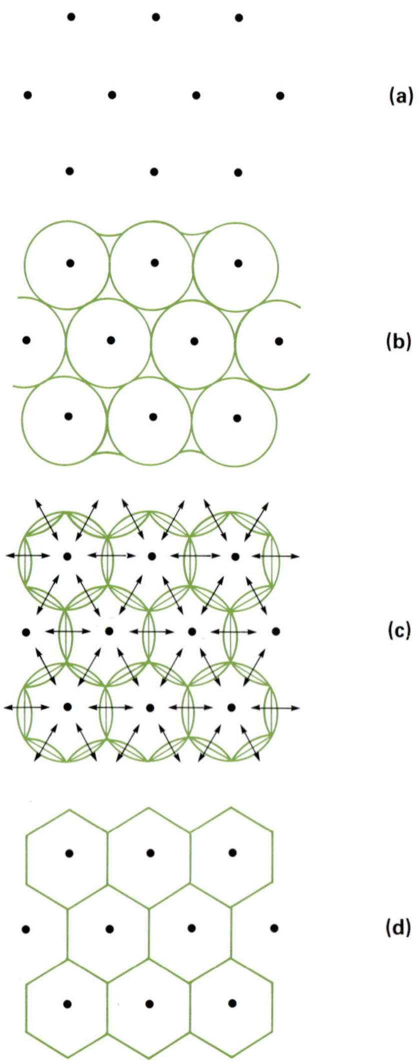

Christaller stated that these circular areas were not efficient because some areas were left outside the spheres of influence of the settlements. Hence, he suggested a pattern of overlapping circles which would include all areas of land. This is shown in fig. 5.15(c). This produced, when the circles were joined together, as in fig. (c), a pattern of hexagons. Removing the circles from the diagram in fig. 5.15(d) produced hexagonal spheres of influence.

The hexagonal arrangement was taken further by Christaller who identified high, medium and low order central places. In fig. 5.16, Settlement A is a central place for one of the hexagonal areas. It also provided higher order services for a larger hexagonal area indicated on the diagram by Line 1. An even larger area, Line 2, obtained high order services from the settlement.

Fig. 5.16 *Centrality*

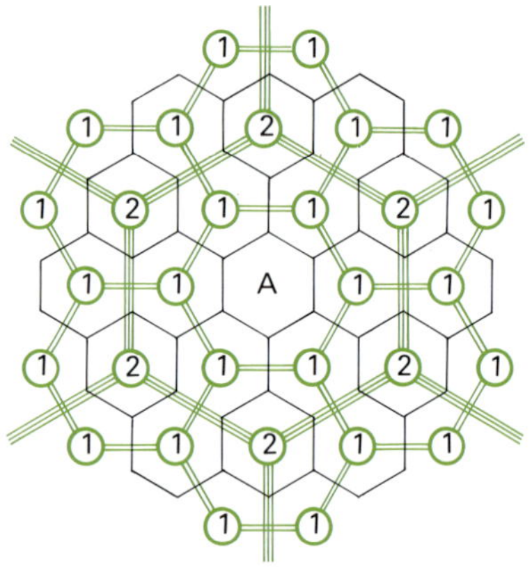

People living in the area between Lines 1 and 2 would obtain their low order services from the settlement in the centre of their small hexagon, that is bread, milk, newspapers, etc. They would travel to Settlement A for higher order services such as clothing, furniture and electrical goods. This came about, according to Christaller, because of the centrality of Settlement A in the central place for this pattern of hexagonal spheres of influence.

Christaller developed these theories in West Germany where he lived, but they have been applied to many parts of the world. The rural area of Norfolk in East Anglia and the Great Plains of USA show these features.

Site and situation

The site of a settlement is the actual ground on which it is built. When agriculture was the main way of life, those settling in new areas had several basic needs which had to be satisfied. These included fresh drinking water, farmland where crops could be grown and animals fed, and a supply of building materials, either timber or stone. In the past, defence was also a consideration. So, the physical environment played an important part in the decision as to where a settlement should be sited.

Fig. 5.17 *Sites of settlements*

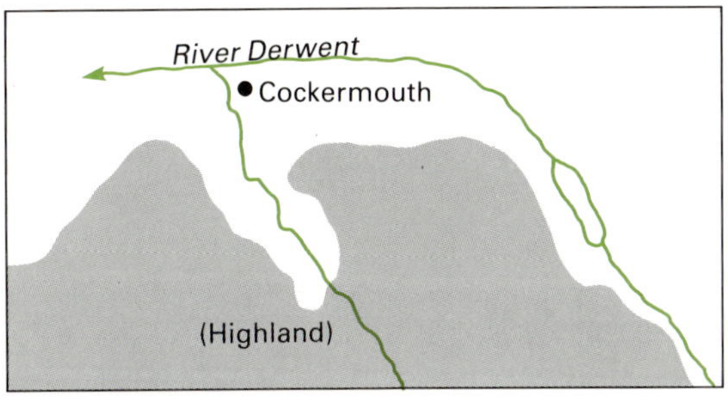

(a) *Confluence Site*

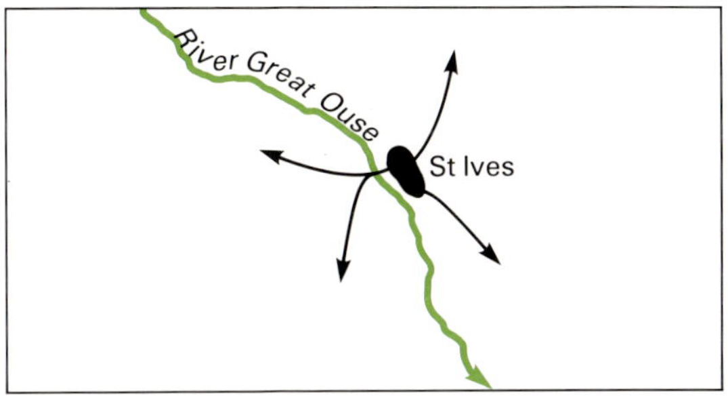

(b) *Bridging Point*

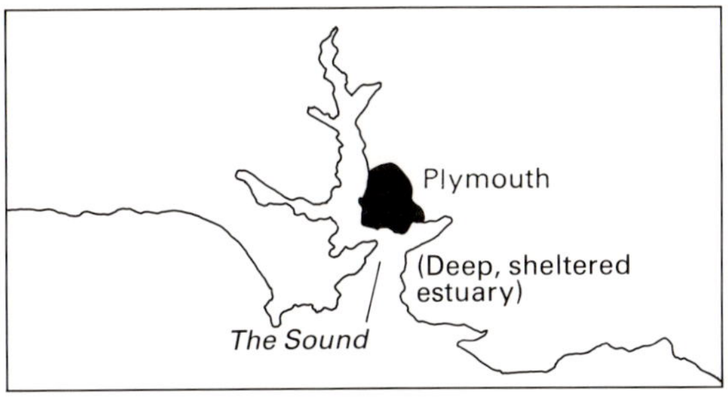

(c) *Natural Harbour*

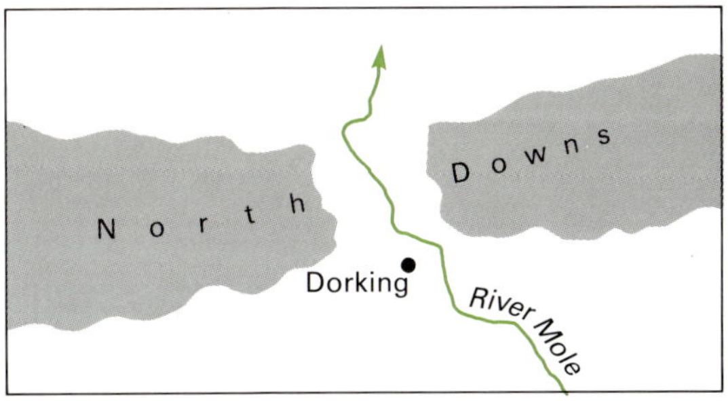

(d) *Gap Settlement*

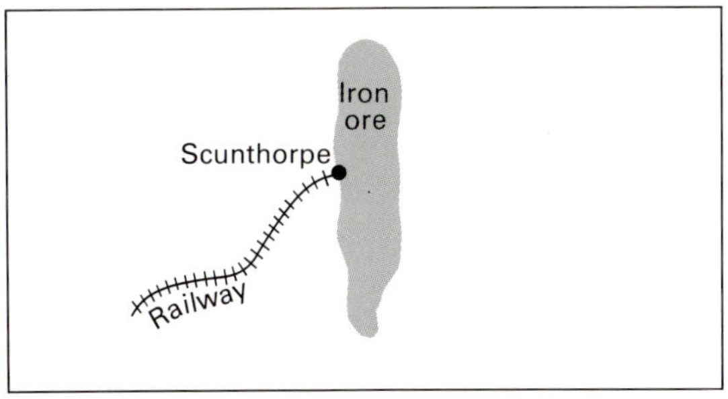

(e) *Mineral Site*

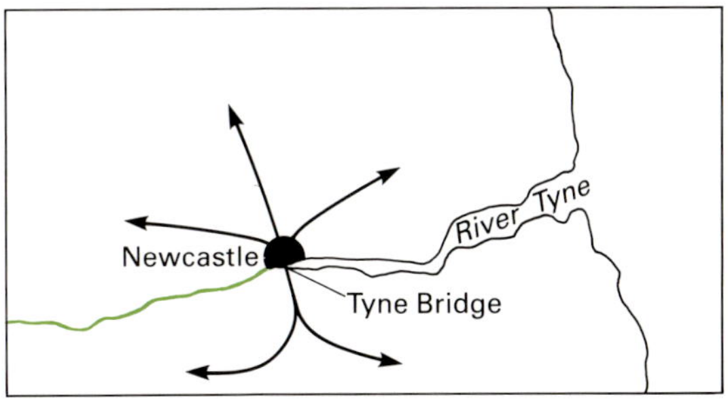

(f) *Lowest Bridging Point*

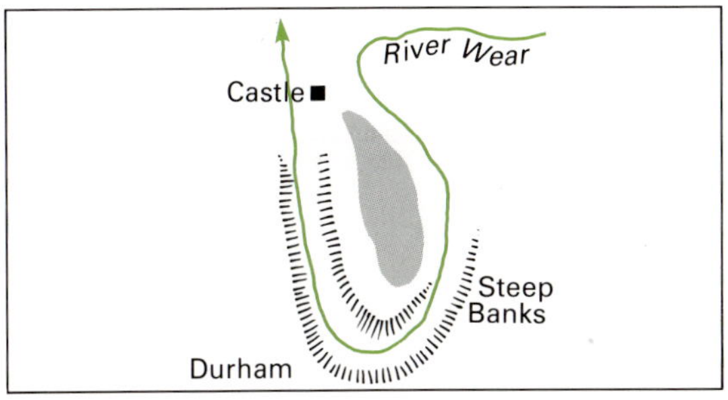

(g) *Defensive Site*

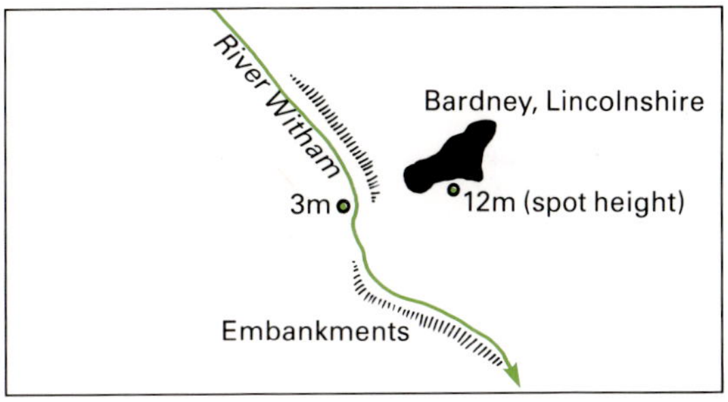

(h) *Dry Point Site*

Whether a settlement grew into an important town, often had more to do with its situation than its site. Situation is the position or location of a settlement in relation to its surrounding area. For example, the region behind a port which the port serves, may be unproductive. This limits port development.

Fig. 5.18 *Milford Haven, southwest Wales*

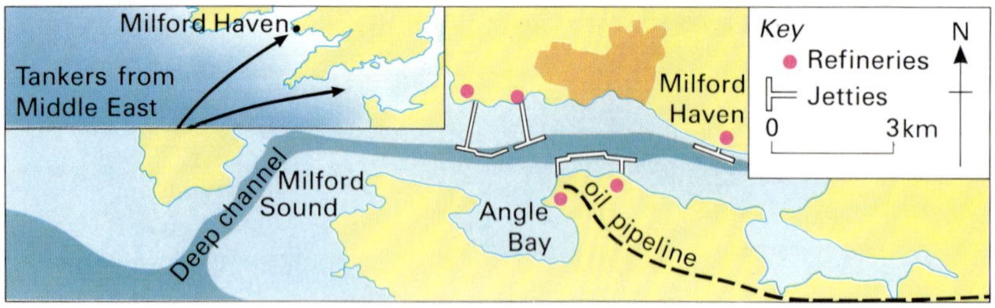

Milford Haven in south west Wales is located on a deep, ria estuary called Milford Sound. It had only local importance as a fishing port until its port development was expanded after the closure of the Suez Canal in 1967. Tankers were forced to go round South Africa and oil companies quickly invested in larger ships. To handle these giants, new, deep-water ports were needed in Britain.

Fig. 5.19 *Lagos in Nigeria has many advantages for port development*

Despite its distance from the main population centres, and its former poor hinterland, Milford Haven proved ideal and quickly became the largest oil importing port in Britain. The need for deep water was greater than the problems of poor accessibility to the port.

Lagos, in Nigeria, was a port whose situation helped to make it by far the most important settlement in the country. During the 19th century, Nigeria was developed as a colony to provide tropical products for the home country, Britain. These products were grown inland in Nigeria so railways were built to transport them to the coast. The site advantages of Lagos' port were strengthened by it becoming the focus of inland

Fig. 5.20 *Location of Lagos*

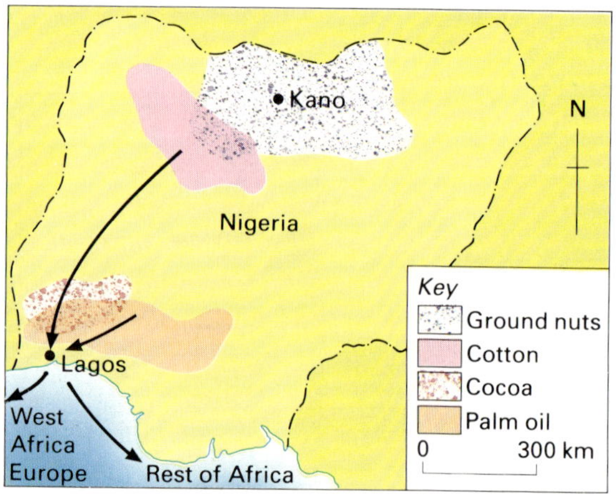

communications. Palm oil, rubber and cocoa were brought to Lagos for export.

Although its shares of world production of these commodities have fallen since independence, Nigeria is still West Africa's biggest producer of palm oil (10% of world production) and second largest world producer of cocoa (10%). The trade and industries which have developed in Lagos as a result of its situation, have made it twice as big as any other Nigerian town (see fig. 5.5).

Function

We have seen already that settlements provide services for surrounding populations. Also, the sites of some settlements allow them to develop into more important towns. Whether or not they do is often largely determined by the range and size of their functions (see fig. 5.21).

All settlements provide homes for their

Fig. 5.21 *Functions of settlements*

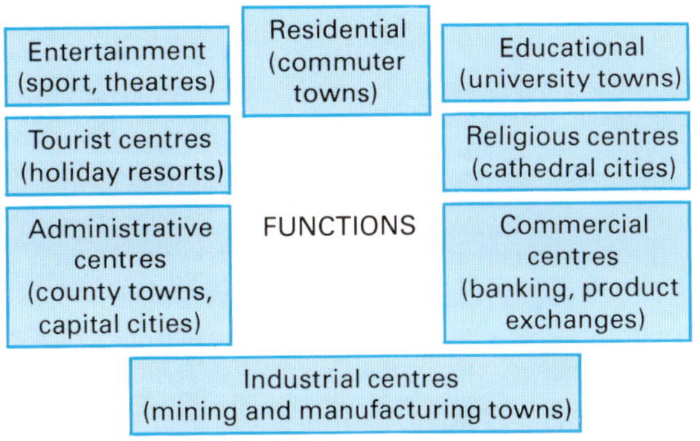

inhabitants and in doing so they are performing a residential function. Some settlements specialise in this function more than others. For example, a place where there are few occupations and where most people work elsewhere can be called a commuter settlement. In developed countries where transport systems in and around towns are extensive, many settlements become 'dormitory towns', so called because the people work elsewhere but return to sleep. Figure 5.22 shows dormitory towns around London.

Fig. 5.22 *Dormitory towns around London*

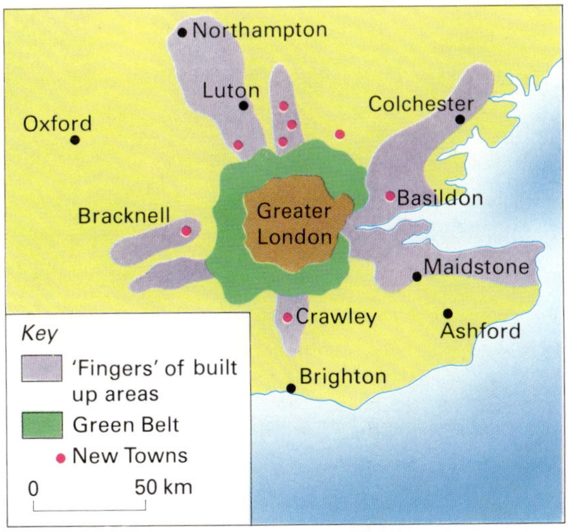

An industrial town is so-called when a fairly high proportion of its workers, usually about 50% or more, are employed in industries. In Luton, for example, over 40% of workers are employed in vehicle manufacturing and other important employers are engineering and clothing companies. In Scunthorpe, over 40% work in metal manufacturing. Both these examples can be called industrial towns.

Durham City in north east England is a good example of a town with administrative, religious and educational functions. These three have been closely related over the centuries. In the Kingdom of Northumbria, before 1066 AD, there was an important religious shrine on the high land inside a peninsula formed by the River Wear at Durham. The Normans recognised the value of this site for defence and built their massive cathedral. The Bishop, who was also the administrator of this northern region of Britain, strengthened the site by building a castle at the entrance to the peninsula (see fig. 5.23).

Fig. 5.23 *Durham city. How many functions can you identify?*

In the 19th century, the Church extended its religious function by setting up a University College in the castle which formed the basis of the later University of Durham. The university caters for about 4000 students today. Durham meanwhile had become the county town of Durham County and its large County Hall is a major local employer.

Fig. 5.24 *County Hall, Durham*

The presence of these ancient but well preserved buildings has allowed Durham City to develop another function, that of tourist centre. Some settlements, however, specialise in tourism. One of these is Blackpool. In the late 19th and early 20th centuries, the growth of railways made it possible for people living in the densely populated industrial areas inland to travel to the seaside. All over Britain, small seaside towns with sandy beaches attracted day-trippers from the industrial areas (fig. 5.25).

Fig. 5.25 *Coastal resorts in England and Wales*

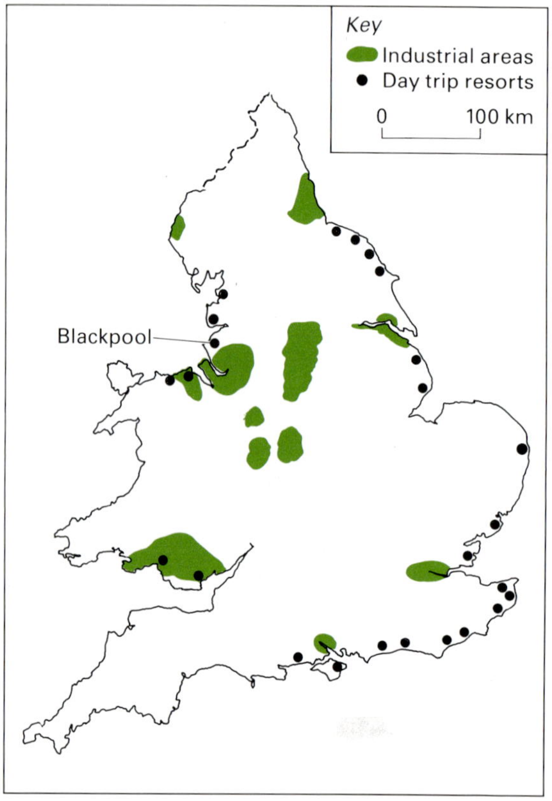

The annual week or fortnight holiday at the seaside became a regular feature for workers in Britain's industrial regions. Some of the holiday towns, like Blackpool, began to provide a great variety of entertainments to attract even more holiday-makers.

The 20th century saw the arrival of fast road, rail and air transport and the mass-movement of holiday-makers in summer. Some governments in both developed and developing countries realised the advantages of creating employment for people in less developed regions by investing money in tourism. One such region was the coast of Languedoc in southern France.

Activities

1. List the main functions of Durham City.
2. Find out about the functions of the county town where you live.

This area of France before 1960 was an area of low development in a very developed country. Although it enjoyed the same 3000 hours of sunshine per year as the Riviera, the coastline across the Rhone, it had some disadvantages. Summers were hotter and strong Tramontane winds blew off the Massif Central. Winters were colder and wetter than the Riviera. Also, unlike the picturesque mountainous coast of the Cote d'Azur, Languedoc was more of a flat, monotonous plain. The many marshy lagoons or etangs were an attraction to malaria carrying mosquitoes.

Fig. 5.26 *Why has this stretch of Languedoc coastline been developed for tourism?*

In 1961, the French Government began to buy land to provide for a development plan. The flagging economy of the region, based upon monoculture of vines, needed to be diversified. So the plan had to have many parts. Irrigation was provided by the Rhone-Sete Canal. The marshes were drained and malaria wiped out. Large-scale production of fruits and vegetables began.

The largest part of the plan was to develop the tourist potential along the coast as at the time many French people were taking cheaper holidays in Spain. Six areas were designated for tourist development, one of which was the earliest and largest, La Grande Motte. Four hundred and fifty hectares of land was purchased and a 43 000-bed holiday resort opened up. Camping grounds and holiday villages were built first, followed by hotels. It was such a success that not only did French people take holidays there but, increasingly, La Grande Motte has attracted foreigners. Many temporary jobs in construction industries, and permanent jobs in service industries were provided by the scheme. The government soon got its original investment money back. However, the overall unemployment problem in Languedoc has not been solved. Too many jobs are of a seasonal nature and La Grande Motte has not developed any functions other than those of a tourist centre.

Fig. 5.27 *La Grande Motte before and after development*

Some developing countries have taken advantage of the tourist boom to change their economies. Barbados is one. A small island dependent upon the sugar trade until recently, its government invested heavily in tourism after 1960. Figure 5.28 shows some of its advantages. Because the island was becoming so heavily dependent upon imports of foods and manufactured goods, tourism offered not only employment, but the chance to earn foreign currency. The west coast of Barbados, 'the platinum coast', has become world famous as a result.

Fig. 5.28 *Advantages of Barbados for tourists*

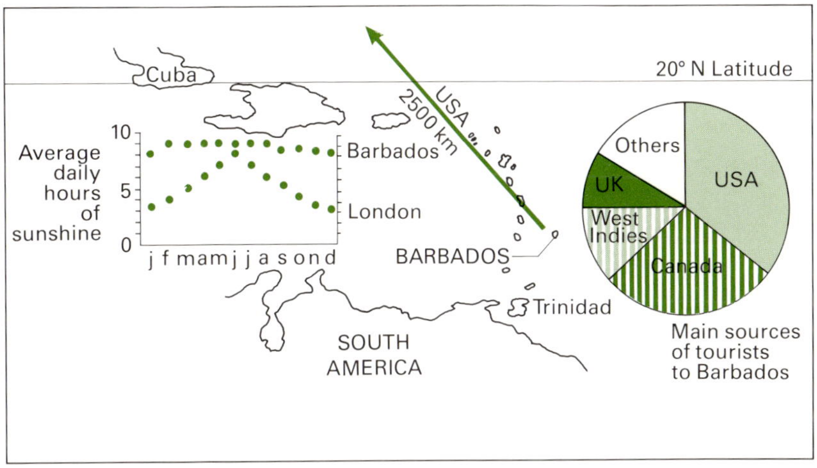

Fig. 5.29 *If you lived in a developing country like Barbados, how would you feel about tourist developments like this?*

Activities

1. Make a list of the disadvantages of the Languedoc coast for tourist developments.
2. Make another list of the advantages of the coast for tourist developments.
3. Suggest why the 'new settlements' in Languedoc have rarely developed into permanent settlements.
4. Explain the pattern of tourists visiting Barbados, using fig. 5.28.

6 FUNCTIONAL ZONES IN TOWNS

Fig. 6.1 *Functional zones in London's West End*

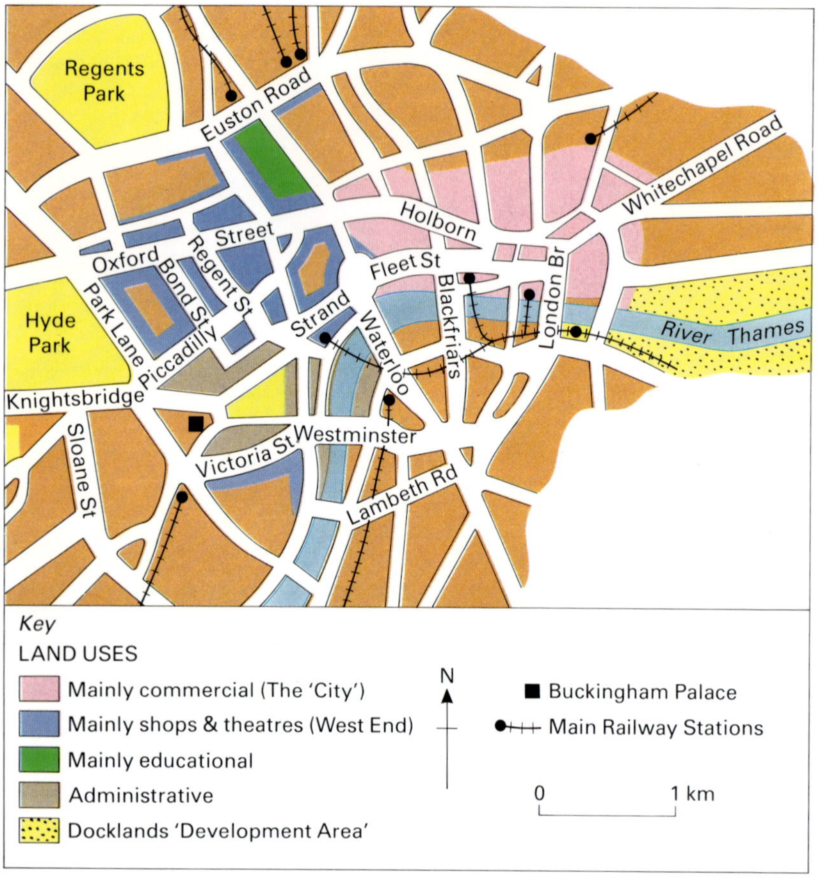

Chapter 5 showed that settlements develop certain functions and that larger settlements may develop many functions. Although some of these functions are found side by side in settlements, they are usually separated into distinct areas, called land-use zones. Some of them can be seen in fig. 6.1 of London.

Fig. 6.2 *Central London. How can you recognise this as a CBD?*

Central Business Districts

London has the largest Central Business District (CBD) in Britain, reflecting the importance as the capital city (see fig. 6.1). Within the CBD the administrative function of capital city can be seen in the large area of buildings between the Thames and Piccadilly. The 'City' of London is the commercial zone, containing the Bank of England and the Stock Exchange. Educational functions are spread all over London but there is a concentration around the University of London, south of the Euston Road, including museums and teaching hospitals.

Why should certain zones be used for particular functions? Town centres or CBDs as they are known, are very attractive to some users of land because of their good access by road and rail. Also, they are central for most people. The CBD is often the oldest established part of the town. In fact, in very old towns, what is now the CBD was, at one stage, the whole of the town. So, there was a tradition of business, shops and even industries in town centres.

In the CBD there is competition for land between people and businesses that try to acquire particular parcels of land for their own purposes. This competition often develops between different types of land use. Look at the site of the MFI store in Darlington, shown in fig. 6.3. This piece of land became available in the late 1970s and was located near the main bus station and the market place, and within walking distance of the main railway station.

Which of the three land-uses in fig. 6.4 would have been most or least willing to bid for this site? The land had plenty of space for building and storage, as well as possible car-parking. It was near the main shopping centre where large numbers of people came to do their comparison shopping. Figure 6.3 shows it had good access by road – a new inner ring-road in Darlington. These circumstances were very attractive to a company wishing to open a large store and it was eventually taken by the multiple furniture company, MFI.

House builders were less attracted to the site. Only a small number of dwellings could be built unless high-rise buildings were considered. The noise and congestion in the shopping centre would deter many house-buyers. This means that the builder of houses could probably not afford to bid as highly as the shop owner. The financial return to the house builder would be less than to the shop owner, over a period of years.

For an industrial user of land, nearness to the shopping centre was less of an attraction. In addition, it was unlikely that town planners would have viewed an industrial development so near to the shopping centre with favour. Planners try to keep factory noise and pollution away from people.

Figure 6.4 shows that as distance from the town centre increases shop-owners compete less and less for land. The price of land therefore usually falls to a level where house builders can compete. However, industrial land users will compete strongly where sites are near main roads because they need access for cars and heavy lorries. So, even in suburban areas, house builders still have competition.

In the CBD itself, there is often strong competition for sites between businesses of the same type, and so land prices can be very high. It is often possible for a business to make best use of a site only if it builds upwards. Hence, an important feature of many CBDs are high-rise buildings. See fig 5.1 of Toronto. Sometimes, the upward surge has less to do with land prices than competition for prestige amongst businesses. Building a landmark higher than that of a close competitor is a strong motive in many cities.

Fig. 6.3 *MFI store in Darlington. Discuss the advantages of this site*

Fig. 6.4 *Competition for land in towns*

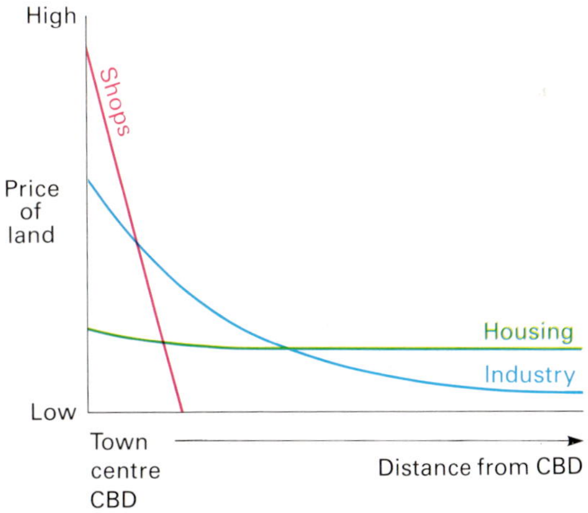

Activities

1 What sort of work would you expect to find in the buildings in the administrative area on fig. 6.1?
2 Describe the location of London's main railway stations in relation to the CBD. Can you explain this?
3 Why have so many commercial functions become concentrated in the area of 'the City'?

Residential areas

Figure 6.4 shows that away from the CBD, housing increases in importance as a land use. The residential function takes up the largest area of land in almost all towns. Since it does not produce such a high return upon an investment, it is mainly found on the cheaper land. Only the most expensive housing is usually located on dearer land.

Sao Paulo in Brazil was founded by Jesuit pioneers in 1554, at the confluence of the Rio Tiete, 760 metres above sea level. Throughout Brazil's colonial era, with its defensive site and pioneer function, it remained a small market town. Its population as late as 1874 was only 25 000. But, during the coffee-growing boom in the late 19th century, especially after the rail link to the port of Santos was built in 1867, it grew rapidly.

The CBD of Sao Paulo was formed in the small 19th century town and became known as the Triangulo. In the early 20th century, a high-class residential area developed round the Triangulo and lower class housing beyond it. Industrial growth came after the opening of the Cubatao hydro-electric power station in 1901 and investment in the infrastructure of the region was associated with another coffee boom.

By 1950, the population had reached 2 millions and a further boost was given when the government developed manufacturing industry, especially vehicles, in Sao Paulo. The urban structure of the town by then was chaotic. The Triangulo had expanded rapidly, like the CBD in developed countries and new housing spread outwards. Large areas of land, much of it poor land, the deep, dangerous ravines of the Rio Tiete, were left empty. These soon became sites for shanty towns (favelas). Higher quality housing spread beyond these and by the 1960s, attempts were made to remove the 'worst' of the favelas from the central area of Sao Paulo. It was not until 1974 that a Metropolitan Planning System was introduced and the growth of the city and its conurbation came under any form of planning.

Today, Sao Paulo is a sprawling city of 8½ million people and likely to be the largest city in the world by 2000 AD.

Fig. 6.5 *The Triangulo – CBD in Sao Paulo, Brazil*

Activities

Your classroom groups should play the roles of some residents living in a quiet area of a town where a hypermarket is to be built on the site of a playing field. You oppose the plan. What sort of facts would you use and how would you make your case to the local council?

Industrial zones

Fig. 6.6 *Location of industrial zones in towns*

1 Near or in the CBD where industries originally began during the early growth of the town.
2 Along transport routes such as rivers, canals, railways and roads, as well as in seaports.
3 In suburban areas where there is easy access for vehicles and where there is a labour supply.

The growth models which will be explained later show that industry has a variety of different locations (see fig. 6.6). Industrial zones tend to be located according to the period of time when they originally developed. The example of London in fig. 6.7 illustrates the pattern.

The importance of routeways is also clearly illustrated in Rotterdam/Europoort which has an industrial sector along the New Waterway. Look carefully at the land use map in fig. 6.8 and the photograph of Rotterdam in fig. 6.9.

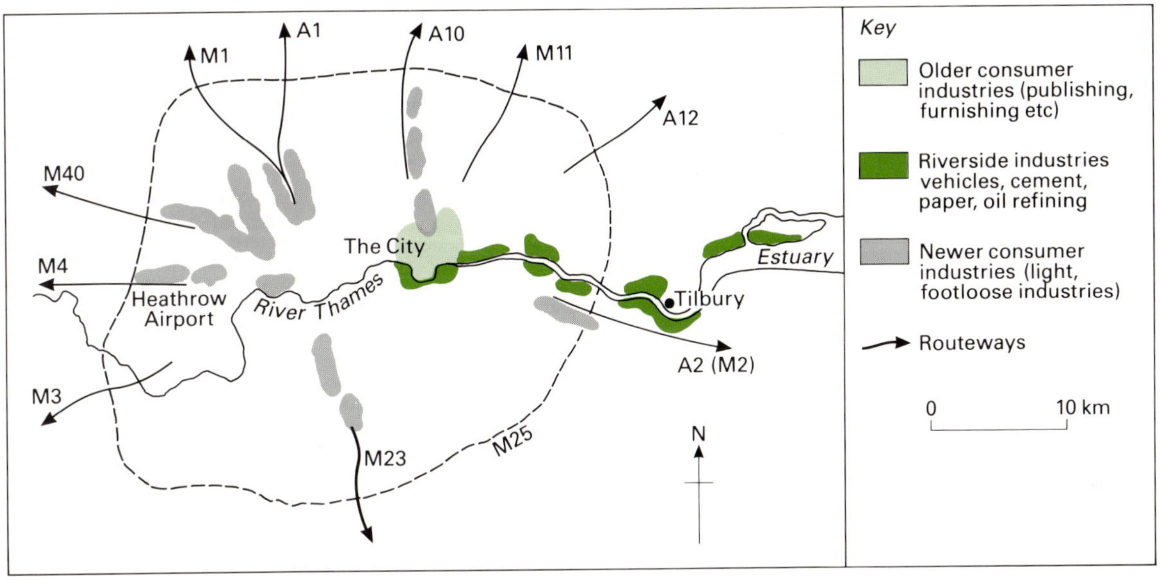

Fig. 6.7 *Industrial zones in London*

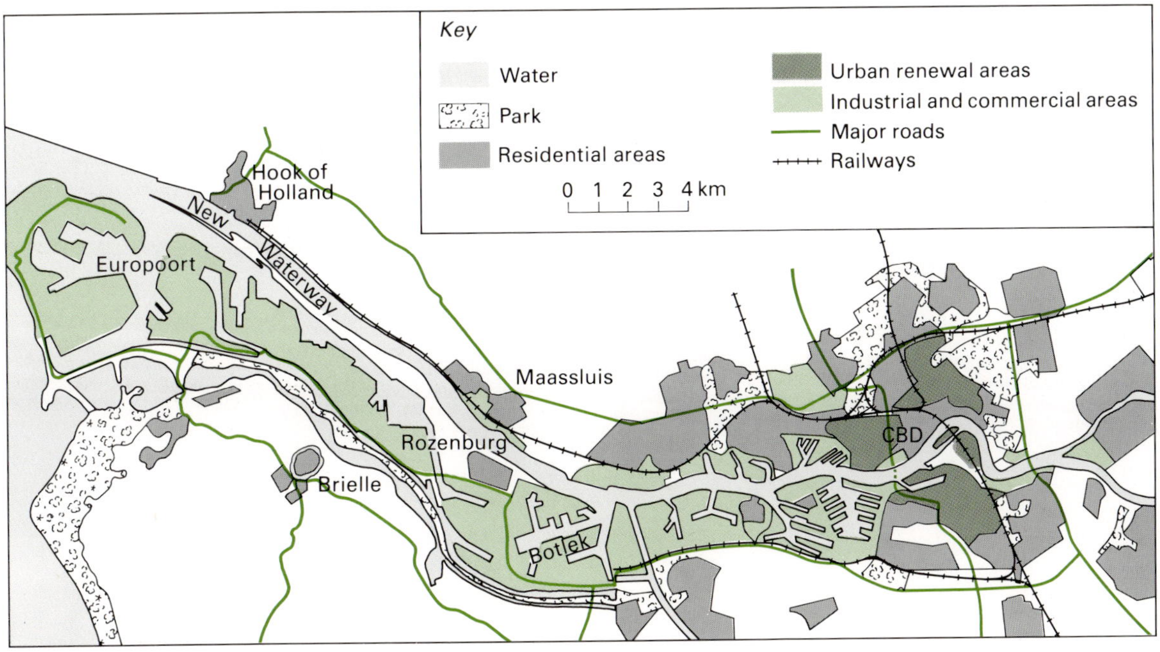

Fig. 6.8 *Land use in Rotterdam*

Fig. 6.9 *Rotterdam/Europoort*

Fig. 6.10 *Do industrial sites have to be unsightly? A new factory in Toronto, Canada*

Activities

1. Use the photograph of Rotterdam/Europoort in fig. 6.9. Identify as many different types of land use as possible. Which industries can be seen?
2. In what ways might the quality of life in the village of Rozenburg in fig. 6.8 be affected by its location?
3. Compare fig. 6.22(b) and (c) with fig. 6.10. What do you feel about the outward appearance of industrial buildings. Comment upon these examples.

Areas of space

Fig. 6.11 (*a*) *19th and* (*b*) *20th century playgrounds*

The school in fig. 6.11(a), was built at a different time from the school in fig. 6.11(b). The photographs show the different attitudes, in time, of the people responsible for education. The large area of space in (b) can be compared to the limited area in (a).

Similar comparisons can be made about the use of space in settlements in general, and the changes in attitudes which have occurred. Most towns, especially in developed countries, grew up in an unplanned way, land-users competing for land which best suited their needs. Few communities had the foresight, the authority or the money to control the scramble for land which took place. The needs of the people were often the last consideration when land was allocated or sold. It has already been described how lack of space, narrow streets and congestion are typical features in CBDs.

There are different purposes for the use of space in towns (see fig. 6.12). One concept about physical space in towns is that there should be space between what man has built, buildings, roads, railways, etc. In CBDs, there is very little of this.

Fig. 6.12 *Suggestions for classification of space in urban areas*

1 *Physical space*
2 *Personal/individual space*
3 *Planned space*
4 *Unplanned space*
5 *Used space*
6 *Unused space*
7 *Territorial space*
8 *Open-plan space*

Some space can be classified as personal space and this is often jealously guarded by individuals. Take for example, four people sitting round a table in an Inter-city train. Their sitting space is clearly defined but do they have equal shares of the table surface? The arm-rest defines the seat space, but the table is open. What do you feel if someone takes a very large share of the table space?

Activities

1 Measure the floor area of your classroom, in square metres. How many people are present? Find out the space allocated per person, on average. Do the same exercise in your home, the floor area and the people living there.
2 Why are space allocations in photographs (a) and (b) in fig. 6.11 so different? How far does this reflect peoples changing attitudes?

The individual's needs for space have been recognised in modern house-building. Houses are built at much lower densities than previously, especially in suburban areas. Each dwelling or pair of dwellings (semi-detached) has an area of space around it. Contrast this form of planning with that of a high-rise block of flats, dozens or even hundreds of homes inside one building. The individual controls the space inside the flat but nothing else. Corridors, lifts and stairways are communal. Many services in the building are communal.

Space may have a clearly defined purpose for it in a settlement. A feature of many towns that grew up in 19th century Britain was the public park. A piece of land was preserved from building, often by well-meaning citizens leaving money in their wills, to buy land. In these spaces, a bit of the English countryside was preserved by planting trees and flowers, creating an island of beauty in a sea of bricks and mortar. Some of these parks went further and provided recreational facilities for people. Children's play areas were popular and adventure parks, skate-board and roller-skating areas came later. Tennis-courts, bowling greens and band-stands catered for different generations of people. In Nathan Phillips Square in Toronto, Canada, a decorative lake in summer becomes a public ice-skating area in winter.

In many towns, especially newer ones, use of space has been planned carefully. For example, towns built on rivers often have had the grassy and wooded banks converted into parkland, for public recreation. Using pronounced physical features such as this is a common feature of towns. It may be extensive enough to form a separate sector on the urban growth model in fig. 6.20(c). Sometimes, one of the nucleii in fig. 6.20(d) is public space.

Fig. 6.14 *Examples of pressure upon personal space*

1 *'This lift can hold up to 6 people'*
2 *'Desks in the examination room must be at least 1 metre apart'*
3 *'There is a maximum of 30 students per class'*
4 *'57-seater bus. No standing room'*
5 *'Fire regulations – maximum seating capacity is 250'*
6 *'Keep to the right on the escalator'*

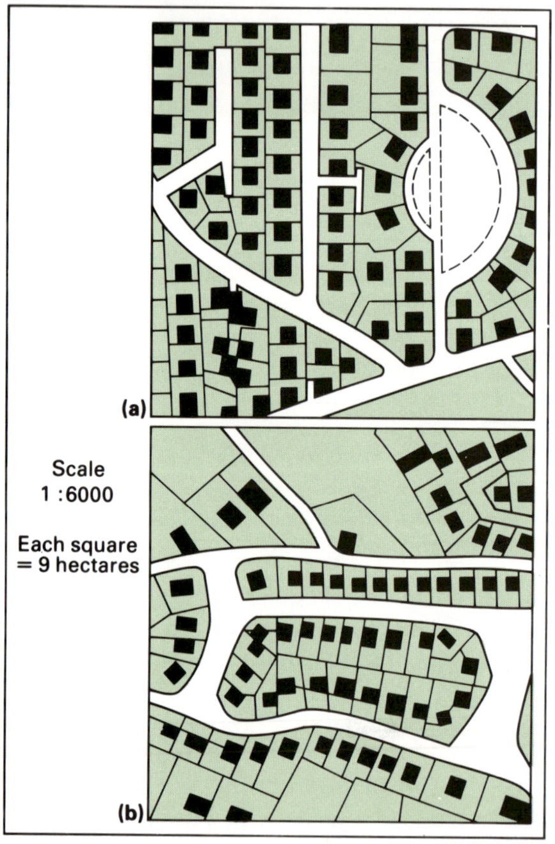

Fig. 6.13 *High density (**a**) and low density housing (**b**)*

Activities

1 Discuss the benefits and problems which can result from communal sharing of services such as refuse disposal. What is your attitude towards this? Which public services could be satisfactorily shared?
2 Use fig. 6.13. Calculate the average housing density in each map by counting the number of housing units in each square, which will give you the total per hectare. Allow an average of four people per house and this will give you the population density per hectare. Compare the two areas.
3 Use a large scale map of your own area to calculate housing densities in different parts of the town.

Fig. 6.15 *Unplanned space in a town – derelict land*

Where unplanned space exists in town, it is usually of a temporary nature. This is certainly true in developed countries. All land there is owned by someone, either privately or by the town authorities. This land will have long-term purposes which has not become apparent to the public. An example of such land is shown in fig. 6.15.

The land in fig. 6.16 was purchased by a builder for high-quality housing many years ago, but it has been 'held on to'. Over the years, the value of this land has increased greatly so that, when the builder eventually does build houses, they will be sold at a much higher price.

People's individual or family right to control their own personal space has been tested in recent years by open-plan housing policies. The traditional British desire for 'house and garden' has been deliberately ignored in many new towns. Figure 6.17 shows a row of terraced housing which share a space in front of them. Similar 'communal space' appears around the base of high-rise flats. These policies have been strongly criticised by many people.

In Britain, householders have traditionally been keen to identify their personal property, their 'territory'. Even on housing estates where large numbers of identical houses are put up, it does not take the new occupants very long to personalise or individualise the houses. Different paint colours, new styles of doors or garage doors, housing extensions and even highly individual garden lay-outs soon make identical houses look unique. Such alterations represent the idea of territorial space, an area where the individual has control and may wish to express his or her personality.

Fig. 6.16 *Space left unused in a commuter village. Can you suggest why?*

Fig. 6.17 *List arguments for and against communal space around housing*

Fig. 6.18 *Personalised housing*

Activities

Visit a housing estate and make a list of the different ways that people personalise their homes and property. What are your feelings about this?

Urban growth models

Figure 6.19 shows a model for urban growth in developing countries. Cities such as Lima in Peru, Quito in Ecuador and Lagos in Nigeria show many of these features.

Fig. 6.19 *Urban growth model in developing countries, Sao Paulo*

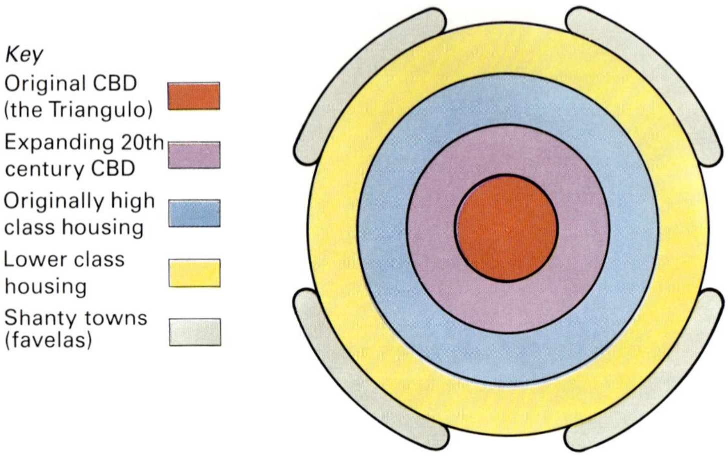

The growth of settlements in developed countries took a slightly different pattern from those in the developing world. In Europe and North America, demands for labour to work in factories in towns in the 19th century were the main stimulus to urban growth. Living standards in towns were so low at the time that high death rates kept natural population increases low. Most growth came from immigrants from rural areas. In developing countries, it was different. The very poor conditions and lack of opportunities in the rural areas attracted people to towns. Rapid natural population increase coupled with rural-urban migration and lower mortality rates caused the population 'explosions', seen in cities like Sao Paulo in the 20th century.

Figure 6.20 suggests models of urban growth for cities in the developed world. They do not state that all cities grew this way but these features are found in some way in most cities. The main features of Sao Paulo, a high class residential area around the CBD, poorer quality housing on cheaper land in the centre and around the edges of towns, are also found in developed countries.

Fig. 6.20 *Urban growth models*

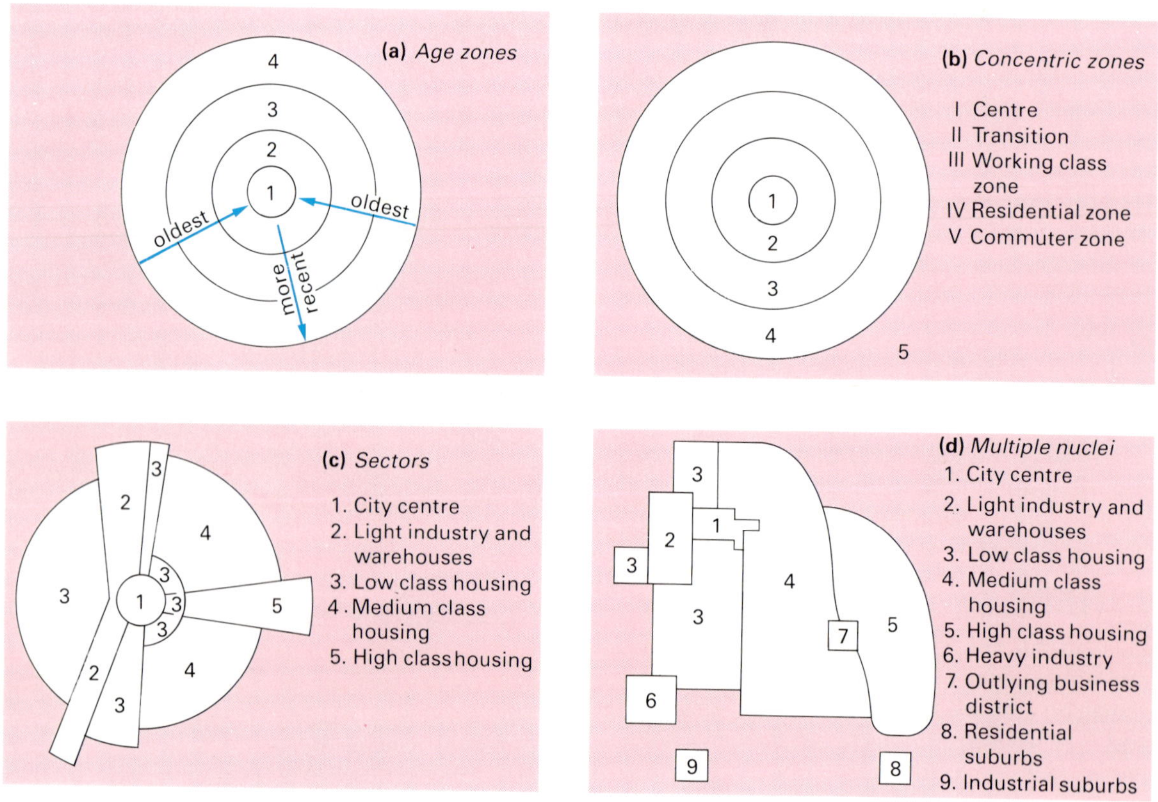

Many towns, especially in North America have grown up along the lines of one or more of these models. In Europe, the pattern is a little different. Because European towns are generally older, they tend to show a combination of the models.

The increased number of families owning a car after 1950 in Britain encouraged the growth of suburban housing estates. Town councils encouraged this by building new homes for people whose homes had been damaged in the war. Many people wanted to live on the edges of towns, near enough to get to work quickly but also to be able 'to live in the country'.

As towns developed many industries in CBDs found themselves on increasingly cramped sites. They looked for less congested sites with more space for expansion round them. The result was great changes in areas 2 and 3 on the model in fig. 6.21. Many premises became vacant, or changed their function (see fig. 6.22(a)). Houses became shops and offices and larger ones were converted into town flats. In some towns, the decline in quality of buildings and the quality of life in general in the transition zone outside the CBD, was so rapid that they became known as 'twilight zones'. This name described an area which had come to the end of its useful life, and was ready for some form of redevelopment.

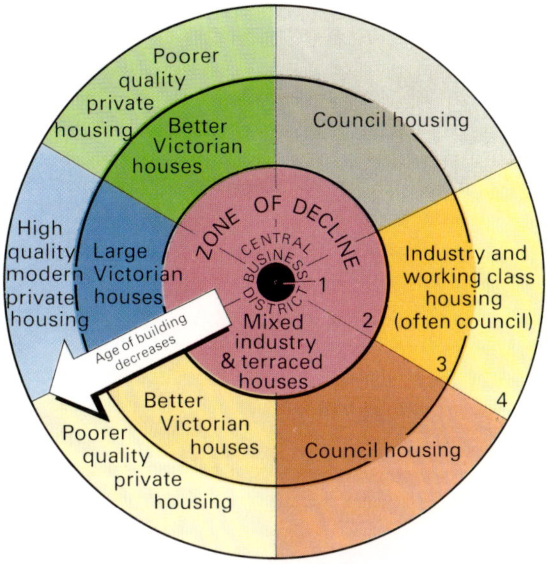

Fig. 6.21 *Urban growth model for European cities*

Fig. 6.22 *Changing functions*

(**a**) *19th century church used as a warehouse*

(**c**) *A new suburban factory*

(**b**) *Old factory in a CBD*

(**d**) *New suburban council housing*

(*e*) *Terraced houses, pre-1914*

(*f*) *Large town-house near a park, pre-1914*

(*g*) *New suburban private housing*

Activities

1 Draw a diagram similar to fig. 6.21 and locate on it where you think each of the photographs in fig. 6.22 might have been taken. Write down your reasons for each.

2 Read these statements:
'So many dull houses all the same. I wouldn't be surprised if people went into the wrong ones'.
'Why don't they paint houses in different colours to brighten them up?'
'It's nice here; just like being in the country'.
'Why do people buy a house then personalise it so much that you can hardly recognise it?'
Consider each of these attitudes in your discussion groups. Which parts of the model in fig. 6.21 do they refer to?

3 In fig. 6.21, where do you think a hypermarket would be located? Give your reasons.

4 In the street or area where you live, or a shopping area that you have studied, how many of the following have been sited in converted buildings, rather than new premises?
A bank. Solicitors. Insurance Company. An office. A warehouse. A small industry. Discuss reasons for this in your groups.

7 CHANGING SETTLEMENTS

Where people live

This section looks at new developments and redevelopment schemes in towns to see how society's attitude to and effect on the urban environment has changed over the years. Most towns in both developed and developing countries have grown up piecemeal, unplanned, and in response to market needs. Today, governments and town councils have much more knowledge and technology at their disposal. There are opportunities to develop settlements which provide for all the basic needs of people. By looking at a variety of schemes, at various scales, you will be able to judge for yourself whether planners are meeting these needs.

People have different perceptions about where they would like to live. Do you live in a nice place? Do you like where you live? Questions like these will usually be answered differently, even by people who live in the same place. Look at Activities on page 60 and fig. 7.2.

Fig. 7.1 *Main aspects of development schemes*

1. *Commercial buildings age, decay and need replacing.*
2. *Houses deteriorate and need refurbishment or replacement.*
3. *Householders expect higher standards of housing.*
4. *People expect a wider range of services in towns.*
5. *More space is required for recreational purposes.*
6. *Industries decline and need replacement.*
7. *Transport systems change, more vehicles, moving faster.*
8. *Interests of people, governments and private developers may not always be the same.*

Fig. 7.2 *Where would you like to live?*

Would you like to live beside a(n) . . .

Park	*Golf club*
Leisure centre	*Public house*
Bus station	*Woodland area*
Health clinic	*Youth club*
Airport	*Place where you work*
Your school	*Railway station*
Rubbish tip	*Shopping centre*
Coalmine	*Football stadium*

Fig. 7.3 *Different perceptions of where to live*

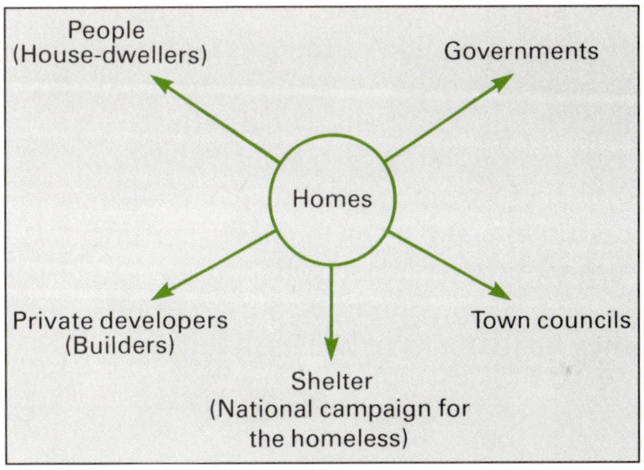

All the people and organisations in fig. 7.3 have reasons why they would like to see more houses built, or not as the case may be. Between 1945 and 1979 in Britain, political parties were in general agreement about the need for large-scale house-building programmes. Since then, greater emphasis has been placed upon the following:

1. Increasing the proportion of people owning their homes.
2. Selling council houses to their tenants.
3. Reducing the number of council houses being built.

While the number of new houses being built by private developers has remained fairly constant, the public sector (council housing) has been cut back strongly. See fig. 7.4.

Housing standards can affect people's quality of life. Houses in disrepair are a growing problem in developed countries like

Fig. 7.4 *House-building in Britain*

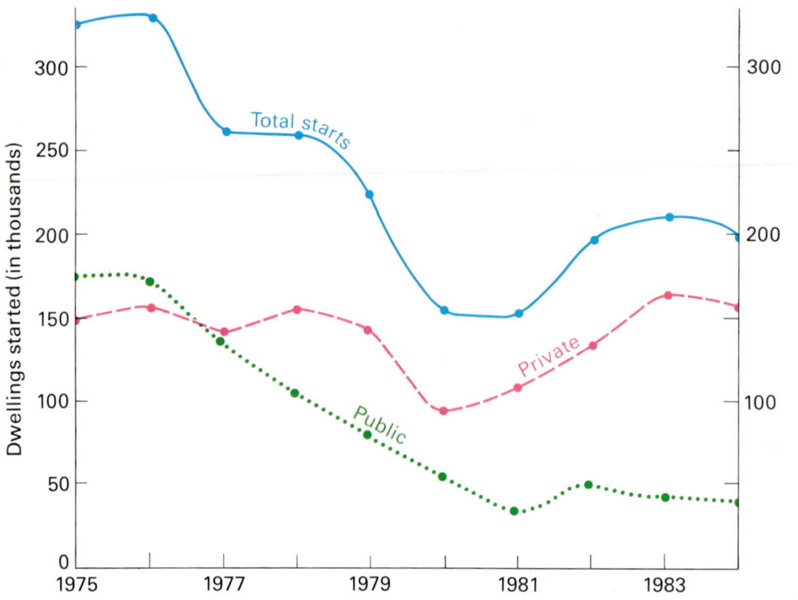

Britain. The National Campaign for the Homeless, 'Shelter', produces regular factsheets to draw attention to the decay of housing, as they see it. Some of this information can be seen in fig. 7.5.

Shelter's main argument is that not enough priority is being given to raising housing standards and replacing older houses. 'The English House Condition Survey in 1981 showed that 17% of homes in Britain needed at least £7000 worth of repairs done to them and another 24% needed at least £2500 spent on them.' (Shelter Fact Sheet No. 2 May 1986.)

Homelessness has become a serious problem in Britain. Shelter state that it is a direct effect of housing policies. The 1985 Housing Act makes it a duty for Local Authorities to house some categories of people, but not all. For example, families with

Fig. 7.5 *Information from Shelter factsheets*

A Types of disrepair (Housing Act 1985)

1 Fitness for habitation
2 Lack of basic amenities, eg hot and cold water, WC etc.
3 Cost of repair (at 1981 prices) estimated to be needed to bring a dwelling up to the improvement grant standard.

B 1981 Housing condition survey.

1 Of 18.1 million dwellings, 1.1 million were unfit for habitation.
2 0.9 million lacked basic amenities.
3 1 million required repairs of more than £7 000.
4.3 million required repairs of over £2 500.

C Who lives in houses of disrepair?

Household income as % of average wages		*Lacking amenities and some disrepair*
(a)	*Under 40*	*55*
(b)	*60–90*	*24*
(c)	*90–120*	*16*
(d)	*Over 120*	*5*

	Unfit for habitation and in serious disrepair	*Satisfactory*
(a)	*62*	*27*
(b)	*18*	*20*
(c)	*14*	*28*
(d)	*6*	*25*

D People complaining to Shelter of bad housing conditions.

Unemployed	*42%*	*Pensioners*	*11%*
Employed	*22%*	*Sick & disabled*	*4%*
Single parents	*20%*	*Others*	*1%*

Activities

Carry out a classroom survey. Find out about the sorts of places where you would like to live (the likes), and where you would not like to live (the dislikes). Use the list in fig. 7.2 for your survey. Each member of the class should list their 5 likes and dislikes in order of importance. Score five points for first, four for second and so on. Add up the totals for the class and display them for all to see. Discuss the results.

a) Do any items appear on both lists? Which ones and why?
b) Do boys and girls have different attitudes towards any of the items? Which ones and why?
c) In what ways would your lists differ from those of your parents? Ask them.

dependent children, people made homeless by an emergency such as flood or fire, and vulnerable people such as the elderly, must be housed. Any homeless person applying for a home must prove that they did not bring homelessness upon themselves. The gap between those who are housed and those who are not is growing. See fig. 7.8.

Fig. 7.6 *Homelessness in Britain*

Year	*Applications for housing*	*Acceptances under the Act*	*Gap*
1981	157 600	62 920	94 700
1982	157 500	70 010	87 490
1983	164 100	74 800	89 300
1984	170 190	78 240	91 950
1985	203 480	93 980	109 499

Fig. 7.7 *Categories of those accepted as homeless under the 1985 Act*

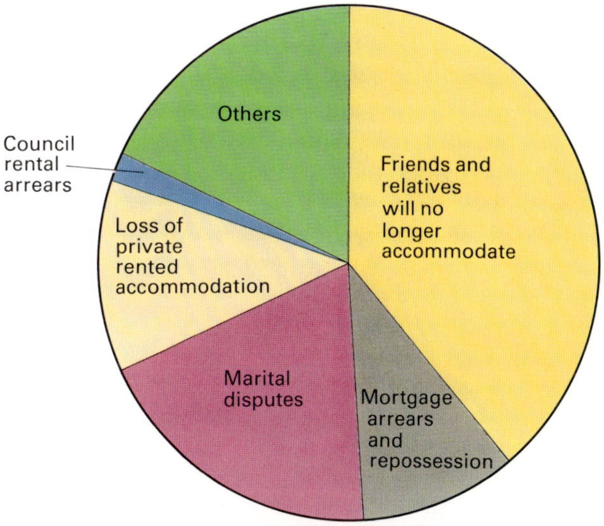

Fig. 7.8 *Homeless in Britain*

Activities

1 Study the Shelter Factsheet information in fig. 7.5. In your own words, state the main points that Shelter are making about housing problems.

2 Homelessness is a growing problem in many countries, including Britain. Summarise the information from Shelter in figs. 7.6 and 7.7. What is your attitude towards the policies for homeless people laid out in the 1985 Housing Act?

Since 1945 high rise development has occurred in many British cities. This was one response to the great shortage of housing after the World War II. After years of war damage and lack of repairs, many town councils were looking for a way to rehouse people quickly, and cheaply, and many turned to high rise building. The argument for them was strong as it provided modern housing at an affordable price. Figure 7.9 shows the sort of building which occurred. Large areas of slum housing were cleared away in twilight zones and tower blocks erected.

Hindsight has shown that high rise development has not been successful in providing people with good quality housing.

Activities

Study fig. 7.10.

1 Make a list of all the facts in the article which are related to people's quality of life.
2 Discuss in small groups the problems of living in tower blocks faced by i) Old people. ii) Disabled people. iii) Families with young children. Then write a paragraph to summarise the discussion.
3 What is your attitude towards the use of high rise buildings to house homeless people temporarily? How temporary should 'temporary' be?
4 What are the advantages of building high rise flats, like those in fig. 7.9?

Fig. 7.10 *Room at the top*

'A room at the top'

A few miles to the west of London's main shopping centre, the West End, in the twilight zone of the East End, live families whose attitudes towards tower blocks can be compared to being given the key for a jail cell. Outside is a vandalised world of wrecked, graffiti-covered corridors, staircases and lifts. Inside the tower block, they say it is even worse.

Jane is an unemployed, single parent with two young children. She relies upon social security and feels trapped in her 18th floor flat with little hope of rescue.

'This was supposed to be temporary', she said. 'It was OK at first, better than the bed and breakfast accommodation the council had provided before. This, at least, was my own home'.

Four years later, Jane suffers from stress. 'I've been refused a house on the ground so many times that I don't apply anymore. What can I do with two kids?'

'Don't open the doors to strangers', is another unwritten rule in the tower block. Milkmen and newspaper deliverers will not climb the stairs. The lifts rarely work. Jack, next door, is a pensioner and he rarely ever gets out. He hardly sees anyone now.

Fig. 7.9 *High rise building in Sheffield*

Uses of space

People make aesthetic judgements every day of their lives. What colour of seat covers for the car? What pattern for the living room curtains? These are highly personal decisions. In order to make towns more attractive places in which to live, who should make the decisions about how space should be used? Who should decide about decoration, landscaping and artistic creations in towns? Who should make decisions about many of the features of our 'townscapes', and the design of pedestrian precincts, the height and shapes of tower blocks, and so on?

One example of the different perceptions of people and planners about the use of public space occurred in Toronto, Canada. A committee of politicians and an airforce representative made the decision to place an airmen's memorial in a Toronto street. There was heated criticism about the artwork from the intended audience, the people of Toronto. For example local artists were joined by many angry citizens who picketed the memorial, charging that elitest decision making on the part of a closed committee had produced a work unsuitable for public places. As a result, in Toronto, all future artwork for public display will be reviewed by a committee representing the city's visual arts community as well as the politicians.

Fig. 7.11 *Rules for public art in Toronto, Canada*

1. *Must lend importance to the city's public places.*
2. *Must bring pleasure and enrichment to citizens and visitors.*
3. *Must support and encourage the city's own artists.*
4. *Must record the cultural development for future generations.*

This leads to the concept of 'a fit' between public art and its site, a successful relationship between art and its space. Such a success can become so powerful that it can provide landmarks in towns. Nelson's Column 'fits' into Trafalgar Square. Do some of the mosaic patterns on the walls of London's Underground 'fit'? Do bright coloured wall murals 'fit'? Are these appropriate in residential areas? These are personal decisions and can public areas be successfully decorated by millions of people, all making personal decisions?

Activities

Your school has been donated £300 in the will of a former student of the school, to provide a suitable memorial for him. Who should decide how the money is spent? Carry out a brainstorm to find possible ideas for such a memorial. Decide where it should be located. Then, analyse the process by which decisions were reached.

Separating people and traffic

Daily movements of people can cause problems in towns. Figure 7.13 shows daily movements to work of eight teachers in a town centre school. The figures show two of the ways in which distance can be measured.

1. Linear distance – the length of a journey in kilometres along a particular route from home to school.
2. Time distance – the length of time such a journey takes.

These movements of people in towns can lead to problems of traffic congestion and accidents. For many years, town planners struggled with the problems of separating people and traffic. Some of the methods they used are shown in fig. 7.15.

Fig. 7.12 *Daily movements of people in Toronto*

Activities

Use the statistics in fig. 7.13. Draw a graph outline similar to that in fig. 7.14. The x axis shows distance linear, and the y axis shows distance time. Plot the statistics. What does the graph show?

Fig. 7.13 *Distance to work for 8 teachers*

Teacher	*Linear distance in km*	*Time distance in minutes*	*Mode of travel*
1	1.5	12	Foot
2	2.6	4	Car
3	16	45	Bus and on foot
4	1.6	6	Cycle
5	15	30	Train and on foot
6	4.3	15	Bus
7	23	18	Car
8	15	54	Bus (twice)

Fig. 7.14 *Graph outline*

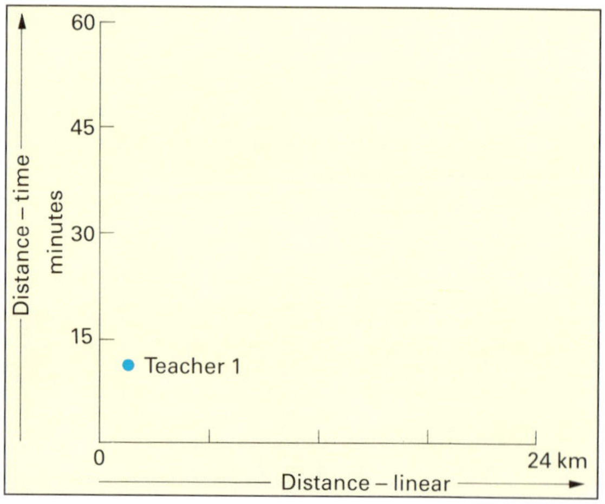

Fig. 7.15 *(**a**) A pavement (**b**) railings (**c**) zebra crossing (**d**) car-parking. How do these traditional methods separate people and traffic?*

Many towns have introduced pedestrianisation schemes. In these, roads and streets are converted into traffic free 'precincts'. It is admitted that both people and traffic need access to the CBD but in the past, traffic access has been more or less unlimited. Increasingly people are being attracted to hypermarkets outside the CBD because of the danger, congestion and pollution of town centres. The towns have fought back by introducing traffic-free areas. These are not easy to create and contain several elements:

1. Provision of off-street parking.
2. Providing access for public transport.
3. Replacing roads with pedestrian areas.
4. Building ring-roads and by-passes around the CBD.
5. Removing some buildings and facilities and replacing them with others.

The photographs in fig. 7.16 show some of these features in a pedestrianised CBD.

Fig. 7.16 *Newgate shopping centre, Bishop Auckland. Traffic-free market place, Darlington. Pedestrianisation, Newgate St, Bishop Auckland*

Activities

1 Study fig. 7.15 (a) to (d).
Can you think of any other ways that people and traffic have been separated in towns?

2 What is your attitude towards pedestrianisation? In what ways does it help to revive social life in town centres? Which groups of people are most likely to object to it?

Fig. 7.17 *Underground walkways in Toronto.*

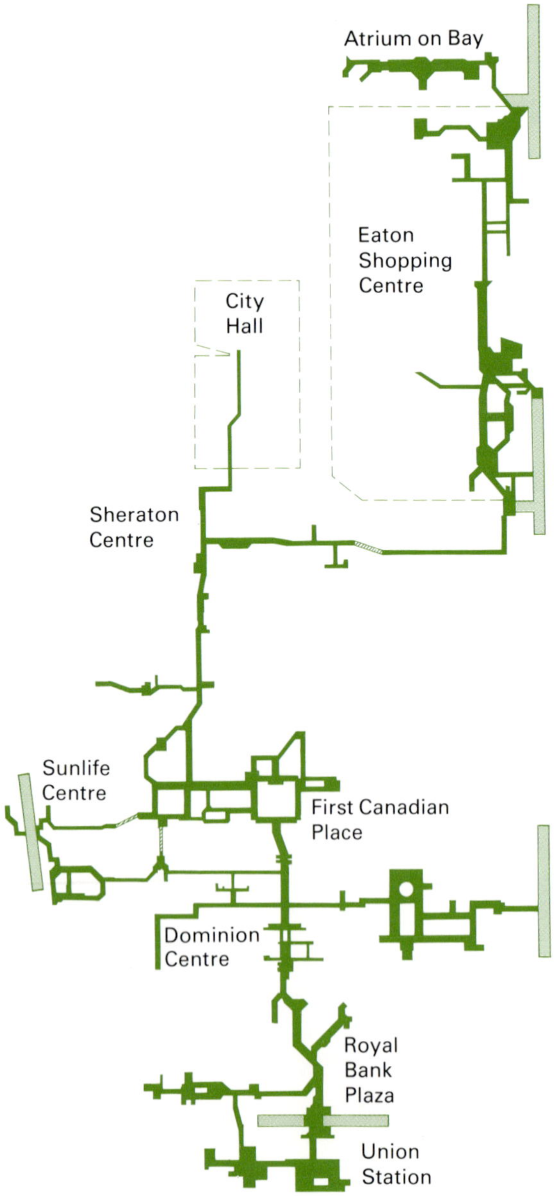

A very different approach was taken in Toronto, Canada. Today it is possible in this large city to walk underground the 1½ km from Union Station to City Hall. This is part of an underground network of walkways which extends about 3.5 km.

The scheme was started in 1961 and now 70 000 square metres of shops, restaurants and banks line the walkways. How did it all come about?

The sidewalks of downtown Toronto were becoming increasingly crowded throughout the 1950s. Traffic was increasing and public open space was almost non-existent. On top of these problems, the severe Canadian winter weather with heavy snow and deep slush made pedestrian life in the CBD very unpleasant. An experiment in underground shopping began in 1964 with the introduction of shops under the Dominion centre and the Richmond/Adelaide Centre.

Fig. 7.18 *Pedestrianised area, Toronto, Canada*

Subsequent developments have encouraged underground links and have led to today's elaborate network. Planning has made it possible for disabled people in wheelchairs to use the system. Most entry/exit points have especially designed escalators which will take wheelchairs. The benefits of walking to work underground in winter are obvious. Even in summer, the attractive clean, air-conditioned walkways are more attractive than the noisy, air-polluted streets (see fig. 7.17).

Suburban changes

There have been changes in attitude towards suburban planning. Much of the planning in large towns during the last forty years was based on assumptions which have now become dated. Some of today's realities are shown in fig. 7.19. Suburban areas need a larger number of small housing units, not just large family houses. Community facilities such as health care, shopping centres and schools need to be provided in the suburbs. Increasingly, jobs are being provided there.

Until about 1970, the number of office jobs continued to grow within CBDs and it was industries which moved to 'greenfield sites' in the suburbs. However, increasing congestion and higher land prices in CBDs have led to many town councils developing policies of *decentralisation*. Many town councils deliberately tried to reduce the number of office jobs in the city centres and encouraged their growth in the suburbs. At the same time, offices and shops voluntarily resited in suburbs where land prices were cheaper. Hypermarkets, needing large areas of land for storage and parking, have also developed on the outskirts of towns.

It was a natural step for planners to develop new 'business districts' or, as they are called in France, commercial nodes, outside the CBD. In the developed countries, these 'downtowns' have grown rapidly in recent years. Figure 7.21 shows that they have several common features.

In Toronto, Canada, several of these commercial nodes have appeared in recent years. They are linked together by the city's rapid transit system as well as the major roads such as the McDonald-Cartier Freeway.

Fig. 7.19 *Planning assumptions and realities*

1950s assumptions	1980s realities
Married couples move to suburbs	*High numbers of senior citizens in suburbs*
Families had an average of 2.8 children	*Birth rate has been halved*
Mothers stay at home to look after children	*In many families, both parents work*
Fathers commuted to town centres, often by car	*High unemployment*
Social and recreational life was based upon the suburban neighbourhood	*Many single parent families*

Fig. 7.20 *Suburban shopping centres, Toronto*

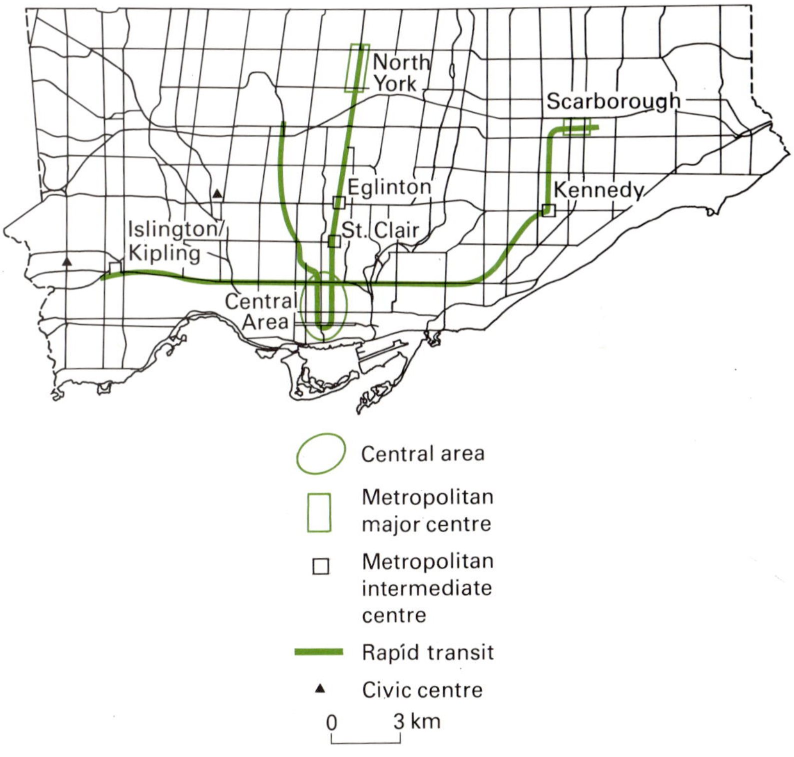

Activities

From the realities of the 1980s in fig. 7.19, how would you plan suburban housing areas for the year 2000AD?
Discuss each item in the chart in your groups then write a planning report.

1. *A variety of human activities in a small place*
2. *Located centrally for their markets*
3. *Pedestrian orientated*
4. *Active beyond the eight-hour day*
5. *Focus of suburban transport systems*

Fig. 7.21 *Features of suburban business districts*

Large redevelopments

Usually inner city redevelopment is small scale, for example a shopping centre. Occasionally, a new ring-road or a pedestrianisation scheme allows quite large scale planning. It is only rarely that a whole region of a city is cleared and finance found for development such as has occurred in the London Docklands.

The London docklands

In London a great opportunity for redevelopment has occurred in the former docklands of the East End. The area is shown in fig. 7.22. Along the Thames downstream from Tower Bridge there was a large area of warehouses, docks and offices which had grown up in the nineteenth and early twentieth centuries and which by the 1970s had fallen into disuse. During the 1960s and 1970s, the container revolution in the shipping industry combined with the decline of British shipping to close down all the docks. In 1981 the Government stated that 'the area displays more acutely and extensively than any other area in England the physical decline of the Inner City and the need for urban regeneration.' The London Docklands Development Corporation (LDDC) was established to deal with the redevelopment.

Fig. 7.22 *London's Dockland*

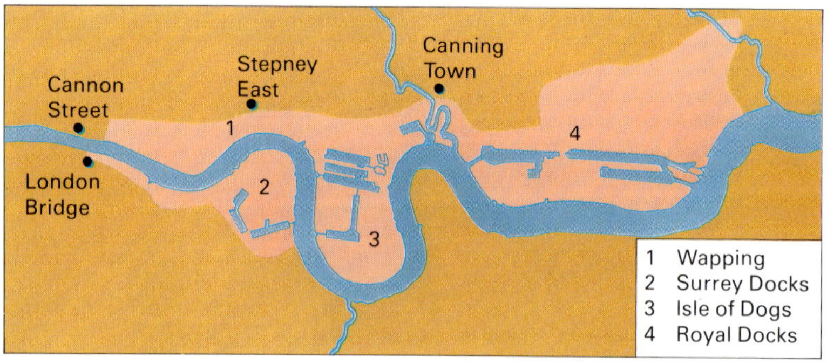

Fig. 7.23 *Isle of Dogs, London*

The Docklands area stretches from Tower Bridge to the Royal Docks and has been divided into four areas for development. One of these, the Isle of Dogs, shown in fig. 7.23, shows all the problems of the area and most of the proposed developments.

The LDDC plans for this area of Docklands have several objectives.

1 *Improvement of infrastructure.* The overall improvement of roads throughout Docklands including the east-west link, the A13, includes much of the upgrading of roads in the Isle of Dogs. A perimeter road as well as access to central sites will be built. Probably more important, the Docklands Light Railway will connect the area to London's Underground.

Fig. 7.24 *Docklands Light Railway, London*

2 *Creation of an enterprise zone.* This has been set up by the LDDC to attract new industries to the Isle of Dogs. Eight national newspapers have already opened premises there (see fig.

Fig. 7.25 *Guardian building, London Dockland*

7.25). 'Skylines' is a professional village of forty separate housing units. Each one is designed for owner-occupation by small professional or service organisations. The wide choice of internal lay-out was so attractive to buyers that they were sold immediately. These small buildings contrast with the very large Canary Wharf development, a financial centre with over a million square metres of floor space.

3 *Housing provision.* Plans for housing include the refurbishment of existing housing and the building of new ones, mainly along the riverside. In 1981, 83% of housing in Docklands was Local Authority housing. One objective of the LDDC was to increase home-ownership in partnership with local authorities. Forty percent of the sales of new houses by the end of 1986 was to local people. A wide variety of homes at different price levels are being built to cater for many types of buyer.

4 *Environmental improvements.* Docklands has a relatively flat landscape. The removal of derelict buildings on such a large scale has given opportunities to introduce tree-planting, moundings and embankments which will add variety to this otherwise level area. The 88 km of waterfront of Docklands will allow development of many water-related leisure activities. Conservation of riverside landmarks is built into the plan. For example St Matthias Church in Poplar, built in 1654, will be conserved and restored, as far as is possible, to its original condition.

The responsibility for planning Docklands is in the hands of the independent LDDC. Some of the developments have been constructed in response to the needs of commerce and industry for cheap, rapidly built premises. Should such an important opportunity be left to market forces? Or should the best architects and planners in the country have been involved to ensure that what was built fitted in with an overall plan for the area that was aesthetically pleasing?

Fig. 7.26 *Skylines professional village, London Dockland*

Fig. 7.27 *Enterprise zone sign, London Dockland*

Fig. 7.28 *Main objectives of the London DDC*

1 New housing at an affordable price
2 New industrial development and job retraining
3 New recreational facilities
4 New commercial developments
5 Environmental improvements and conservation
6 New transport systems
7 To end the LDDC as soon as Docklands' prosperity becomes self-generating.

Fig. 7.29 *Traditional dockland before redevelopment*

Fig. 7.30 *Modern industry in the Isle of Dogs, London*

Activities

1 Study the four main objectives for the development of London's Dockland on pages 68–69. Do you agree with any of them? Discuss them in your groups.
2 Send for copies of the LDDC Development plans for the whole of Docklands. Try and work out who will be the main beneficiaries of these plans. Do you think that such a major redevelopment as this is being properly organised?
3 Look at the planning in Toronto on pages 66 and 67 and that for Brasilia on pages 78 and 79. Compare the attitudes of people and governments in these examples with the development of Docklands in London. Which do you prefer and why?

Whole-town redevelopment

Many settlements which grew up very quickly over the last 100 years have suffered very rapid decline recently. This is especially true of industrial towns in developed countries. During the Industrial Revolution, factories sprang up in favoured locations near ports and railways. People were drawn to jobs there and large areas of cheap housing were built to house them. Much of this was built in a very unplanned way.

The Dundee Project

One such settlement was Dundee in the Tayside Region of Scotland. It grew, in the 19th century, into Scotland's second largest industrial city, from a small market town to the largest manufacturer of jute and linen in the world (see fig. 7.31). Its population grew sixfold in 70 years and at the peak of jute manufacturing about half the total workforce (40 000 people) was employed in the industry.

Today (1989) the figure is less than 1000.

Fig. 7.31 *Position of Dundee*

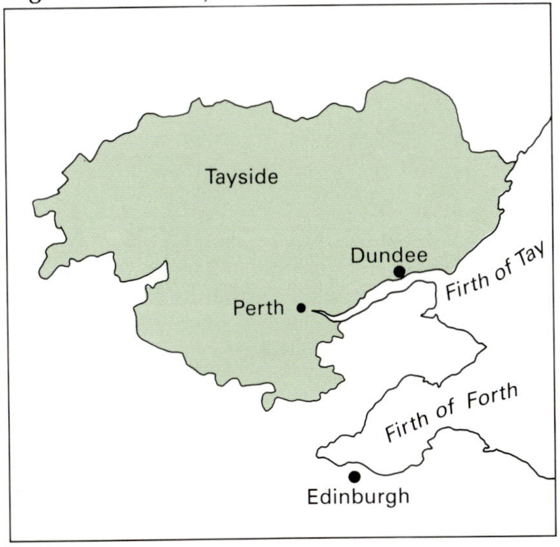

What happened to Dundee was typical of many industrial towns in Britain. The jute industry which had brought so much employment and wealth to the city, collapsed. The dramatic nature of this collapse is shown in figs 7.32 and 7.33 and its effects upon Dundee were large scale dereliction of land and the emergence of much run-down housing in the centre of the city.

Fig. 7.32 *Decline of Dundee's workforce in jute making*

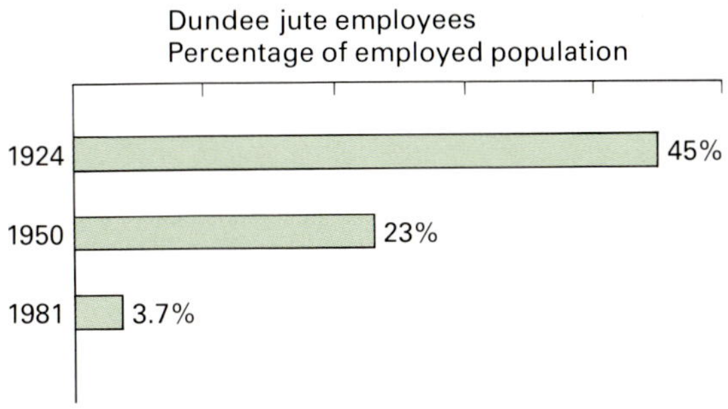

Fig. 7.33 *Occupational structure for Dundee, 1911 to 1981*

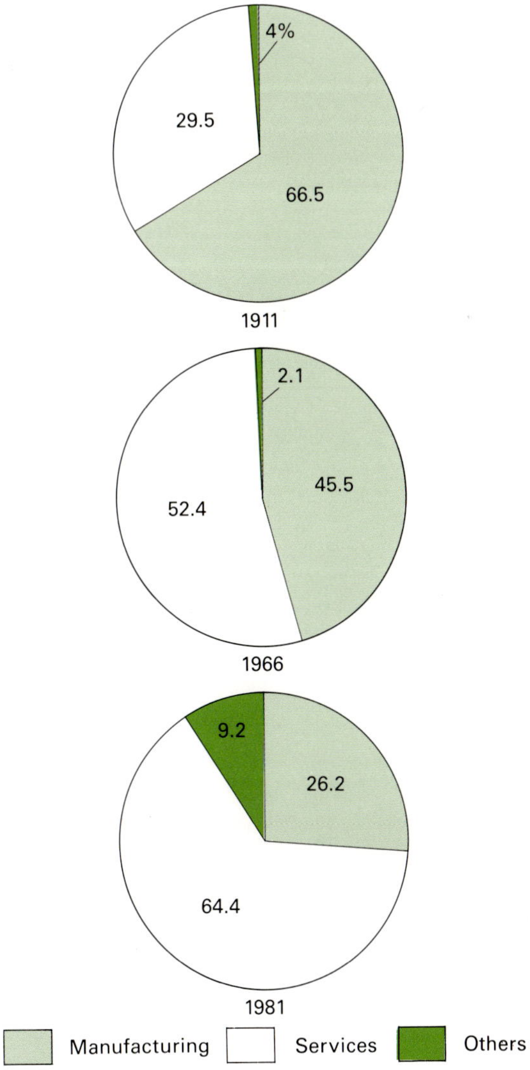

Fig. 7.34 *Blackness area of Dundee*

The once thriving Blackness area of the centre of Dundee, shown in fig. 7.34, was left with narrow, winding streets between declining tenement housing and empty jute mills. Such an environment was very unattractive to any new industries which were attracted to Dundee during the decline of jute making. Most of them opened up on suburban sites outside Blackness. The scene shown in fig. 7.37 was very common in the centre of the town. The decline of the inner city was rapid.

It was against this background that a £40 million scheme known as the 'Dundee Project' was born. Its stated aims were to increase investment and employment opportunities in Dundee by focusing upon development of high technology industries and upon specific sites across the city. In doing so, it brought together national, regional and local planners in an integrated city-wide project. Dundee was already a special development area and six parts of the city had been designated as Enterprise Zones. It was the job of the project team to integrate all these bodies, the Scottish Development Agency, Tayside Regional Council and Dundee City Council, to use the grants and other financial benefits of development areas and Enterprise Zones, so that Dundee could recover from industrial decline.

Fig. 7.37 *Derelict land, Blackness area, Dundee*

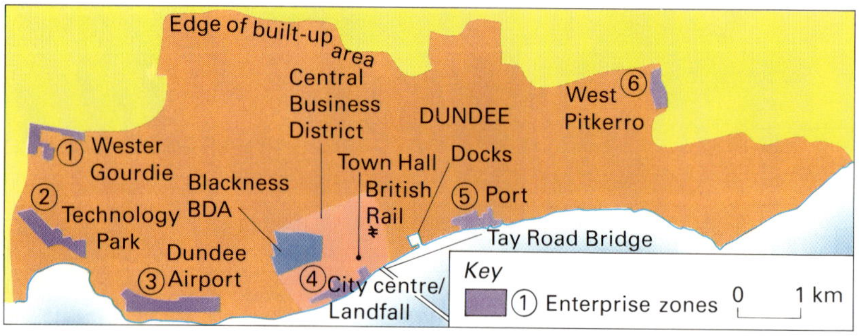

Fig. 7.35 *Enterprise zones in Dundee*

Fig. 7.36 *The Enterprise zones of Dundee*

Name of zone	*Area in hectares*	*Ownership of land*	*Details*
1 Wester Gourdie	12	Mainly Scottish Development Agency	Modern industrial estate. Offshore engineering, printing and computer companies already established.
2 Technology Park	48	Scottish Development Agency	Greenfield site. Designed for high-tech industries.
3 Dundee Airport	12	Dundee District Council	New industrial estate near airport. Airport related industries, eg air cargo handling centre.
4 City centre Landfall	12	SDA, British Rail Tayside Regional Council and Dundee City Council	City centre office developments, commercial and industrial uses and residential.
5 Port area	12	Dundee Port Authority	Beside a Ro-Ro ferry terminal. Contains an oil terminal and off-shore supply bases.
6 West Pitkerro	12½	SDA and Dundee City Council	Part of a 35½ hectare industrial estate. Variety of new processing and manufacturing industries.

Fig. 7.38 *Technology Park, Dundee*

Urban renewal in Dundee has taken several different forms. In suburban areas, land in and near Enterprise Zones has been allocated for residential as well as industrial uses. A most ambitious scheme for industrial development has been planned in the form of a Technology Park. See fig. 7.35 and fig. 7.36. High-tech industries are being encouraged to open on this site. The already attractive 'green-field' site overlooking the Tay estuary is being enhanced by careful landscaping and tree planting. A high standard of amenities will be provided to attract industries whose highly skilled workers would expect such standards.

In the older parts of Dundee, environmental improvements also have a high priority. In some areas, 'face-lifts' have greatly improved the environment, as fig. 7.39 shows. In the port area of Dundee, a more elaborate policy, of land clearance, has had to be introduced. Old factories and railway yards were cleared on a 12 hectare site known as the Central Waterfront. The land use plan, with mixed ownership of the development agencies and British Rail, shown in fig. 7.40, combines new housing areas with office development, commercial and industrial uses.

Fig. 7.39 *A 'face-lift' in Westport, Dundee*

Fig. 7.40 *Planned land-use in the Central Waterfront Enterprise Zone of Dundee*

Activities

1 Read the section about the Dundee project. Make a list of all the different types of development schemes which make up the urban policy of Dundee.
2 What are the different organisations involved in the urban renewal of Dundee?
3 Find out about 'development areas' and 'enterprise zones'. Discuss them in your groups.
4 Discuss in your groups the ways that the Dundee Project has tried to satisfy the needs of the people in Dundee. Make a list of these ways.

The largest and perhaps the most difficult scheme in the Dundee Project concerns the 'twilight zone' of Blackness in the centre of the city. Many local companies had drawn attention to the fact that the poor appearance of the area was a drawback to business confidence. It gave such a poor impression to visitors and potential newcomers that something exceptional would be needed to revive the area for business.

The concept of a Business Development Area (BDA) was created by the project team. It was accepted that there was a need to inspire confidence in the people of the area in order to stimulate revival.

Clearing away dereliction (see fig. 7.37) and making environmental improvements were an obvious starting point. But the project aimed higher. Several different schemes were introduced. Tayside Regional Council's Business Adviser started advice sessions for small firms in the area in October 1981. By 1984, there were over 50 new firms operating in Blackness. The number of people working in the BDA reached a low of 2 700 in 1983 but has since picked up, to over 3 000. Making grants and loans services available, encouraging local educational centres to run 'be your own boss' courses and improving the local infrastructure has led to a transformation in business confidence.

Environmental improvements have been a major part of the scheme. Two new roads, including the University By-pass, have improved access to Blackness. The legacy of narrow streets designed for horse and cart traffic was difficult to overcome. A traffic management scheme has helped. This was particularly important because of the increasing number of commuters to the city centre using Blackness streets for car parking. New off-street car parks are part of the scheme. Street lighting has been improved to enhance traffic safety and to eliminate dark corners and cul-de-sacs which attracted vandalism.

A third element in the Blackness scheme involved improvements to existing buildings. A new image was needed for the area and small scale, often quite simple, face-lifts were vital. Stone cleaning and repointing, repainting and often embellishing with wall murals had a striking impact. The Scottish Arts Council and the Scottish Development Agency gave grants for a variety of schemes. Even new street name-plates had an impact.

Westport, shown in fig. 7.39 is a good example of what has been done. The Blackness Project, the Cleghorn Housing Association and a private developer have combined to save the area not only from dereliction, but probably from demolition. Craft shops, cafes, restaurants and bars have made this area into a thriving community again.

Activities

Extended writing – 'For one large town that you have studied, describe and explain the development of functional zones. Explain how recent developments in the town have affected these zones'.

New towns

Figure 3.22 shows how one British city, Leicester, has grown during the last century. It has spread well beyond its original boundaries into the surrounding countryside. This is called urban sprawl. It has happened in many West European cities at various scales and has long been recognised as a serious problem.

The Green Belt was one attempt to arrest the growth of urban sprawl in London and was copied in other cities later. It was a zone of countryside around the edges of the urban area, in which further building was very restricted. As well as limiting the sprawl, it also provided much needed recreational areas for urban dwellers.

London's Green Belt was quite effective in

slowing down urban sprawl, during the 1920 to 1945 period. However, after World War II, urban renewal was called for on a large scale and a massive rehousing programme was planned to deal with the war damaged inner city and areas of derelict land. Government policy encouraged the new housing to be built at a lower density than in previous decades. As a result, large numbers of people had to be rehoused elsewhere. This led to the concept of 'overspill populations', the name given to populations rehoused elsewhere. London's answer was to the problem was to 'leapfrog' beyond the Green Belt and to build several New Towns around its perimeter, such as Hemel Hempstead, Harlow, Stevenage and Crawley.

The problem of housing the overspill populations put severe pressure upon the Green Belt idea and planners looked for other ways to control urban sprawl. Green Wedges were tried in some towns. These were wedge-shaped areas of space between 'growth zones'. Copenhagen has used a variation of this wedge idea in its 'finger plan' (see fig. 7.41). New building has been limited to five growth zones, fingers, to the west of the city.

Fig. 7.41 *Methods used to control urban sprawl*

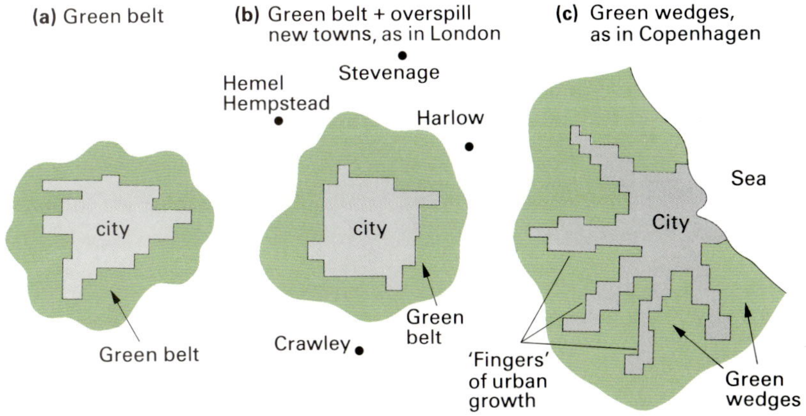

Fig. 7.42 *Green buffers and green heart, Randstad*

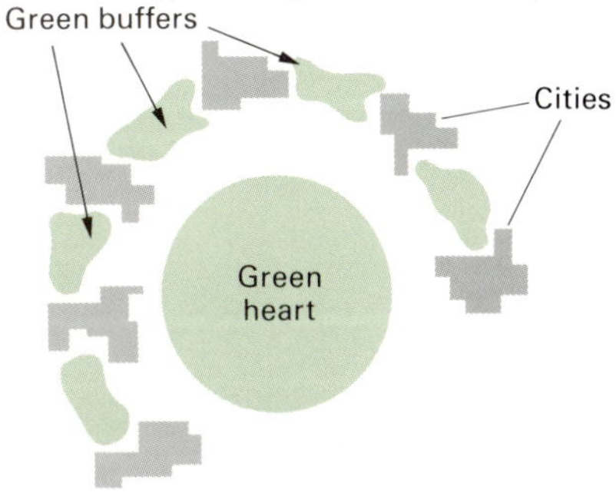

The Netherlands

In the Netherlands, another approach was tried in the very congested conurbation of Randstad ('Ring city'). One attempt to prevent urban sprawl in a crescent shaped urban area stretching from Dordrecht to Utrecht was made by the Dutch by introducing Green Buffers. These were areas of space between settlements acting as buffers to new development. The buffers were accompanied by a Green Heart, a large area of countryside in the centre of the circle formed by the Randstad cities. But the changing population of the Netherlands and the needs of urban renewal combined to make this an insufficient response. The Dutch had to plan further. They did this by adapting a national plan for new polder development in the Lake Ijssel area of the country.

The New Polders of the Netherlands were planned originally to extend the country's farmland. Indeed the early polders such as Wieringermeer were used for this purpose. Since then, the overspill population problems of Randstad have led them to develop the North East Polder differently. This 50 000 hectares of new land already has a population of 40 000 people, about half of it in a new town of Emmeloord, and the rest in the rural area and ten large farming villages. This area is shown in figs. 7.44 and 7.45.

Fig. 7.43 *Randstad, Netherlands*

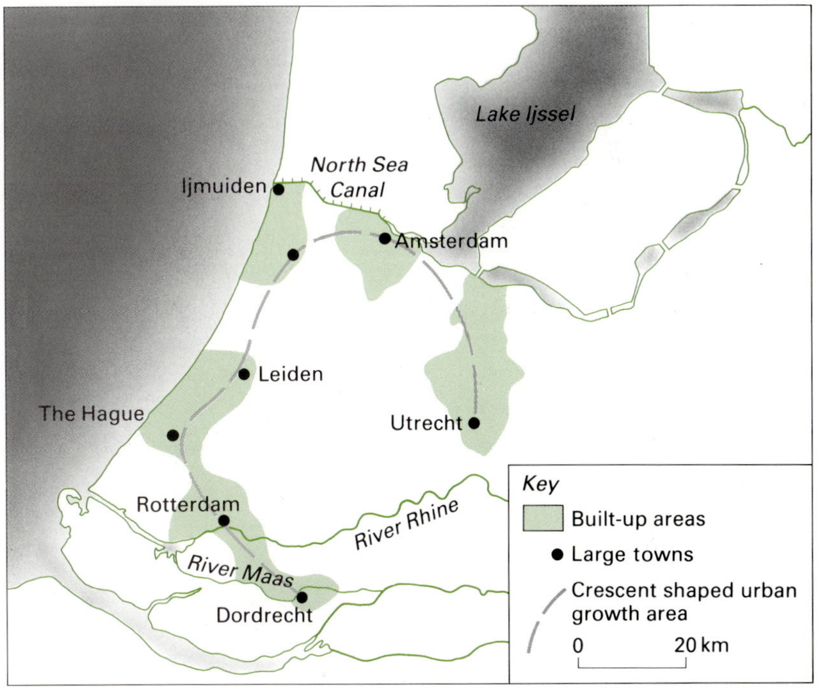

Fig. 7.44 *Farming settlements in NE Polder, Netherlands*

Fig. 7.45 *Emmeloord new town, Netherlands*

Activities

1 Find out about growth zones and New Towns in Paris. Compare them to those in British cities.
2 Which people are likely to favour or oppose Green Belts, or the preservation of 'green areas'? What are the advantages and disadvantages that you can identify?
3 What problems can arise from moving overspill populations out of declining urban areas?

Telford

Telford New Town in Shropshire was developed to accommodate the overspill population of the West Midlands (see fig. 7.47). The original plan was to develop Dawley as a new town but the scale of overspill was so large that two other settlements, Oakengates and Wellington were included and the town was named Telford. As in most new towns, careful planning separated residential from industrial areas and transport networks were extended to provide good access both to the town and within it.

Look at fig. 7.46 which is a pictorial map illustrating the attractions of Telford. Make a list of these attractions. The reality of living in a new town may not be quite the same. 'New Town blues' is a phrase used to describe 'strangeness', 'newness', 'lack of community spirit' and a 'sense of not belonging' which residents of new towns have described. These are difficult problems to overcome. In the early days some of the amenities and common features of established towns may not have been developed.

Fig. 7.46 *Attractions of Telford*

Fig. 7.47 *Telford New Town*

Fig. 7.48 *Attractions of New Towns*

Attractions	*New Towns*						
	Telford						
Good housing							
Variety of housing							
Schools							
Shopping							
Entertainment							
Environment							
Government grants							
Other financial benefits							
Good labour force							
Available sites							
Good communications							
Central location							
Modern (& high tech) industry							

Activities

Use figs. 7.46 and 7.48.

1. Tick all the attractions claimed for Telford in fig. 7.46 in the first column of fig. 7.48.
2. Either collect press cuttings for New Towns or send to the New Towns for their advertising information. Then complete other columns in fig. 7.48.
3. If you live in or near a New Town, complete one column from your own knowledge and experience. Find out if New Town attractions live up to their advertising claims.
4. Suggest some of the possible causes for the problems people have experienced in adapting to living in new towns.

Fig. 7.49 *Brasilia*

Brasilia

Capital cities were often once new towns. Many countries at different times in history have built brand new capitals. Louis XIV in France in the 17th century removed his capital from Paris to Versailles, a 'splendid palace' to reflect his view of his own importance. The new independent American government in the 18th century built Washington in a district (Columbia) outside the influence of any of the states. In Australia, Canberra was built roughly equidistant from the two most influential cities of Sydney and Melbourne. Nigeria is planning a federal capital in the centre of the country hoping that it will be a unifying influence (see fig. 1.23).

The idea of building Brasilia, a capital city in the centre of the country, had been in the minds of Brazilians for over 200 years. The concept features in the constitution of 1891. In 1955 the site in the Goias Uplands of Central Brazil was chosen. It was equidistant from the two dominant cities of Sao Paulo and Rio de Janeiro. It was also very near the territorial centre of the country. Probably more important was its position in relation to 'the march to the west', the opening up of central Brazil.

In 1955 the government then announced a competition for the right to plan the city. Professor Costa, an urban designer, won and from the outset, careful planning was vital. He divided the future city into three zones, residential, industrial and administrative. A Brazilian architect, Oscar Niemeyer, designed a grandiose, futuristic CBD.

The site was near the junction of three rivers: Sao Francisco, Tocantius and Paraná, where three regional boundaries met. It was a symbolic meeting place 'of the Brazils'. The R. Paraná was dammed to form a lake. Its

Fig. 7.50 *Location of Brasilia*

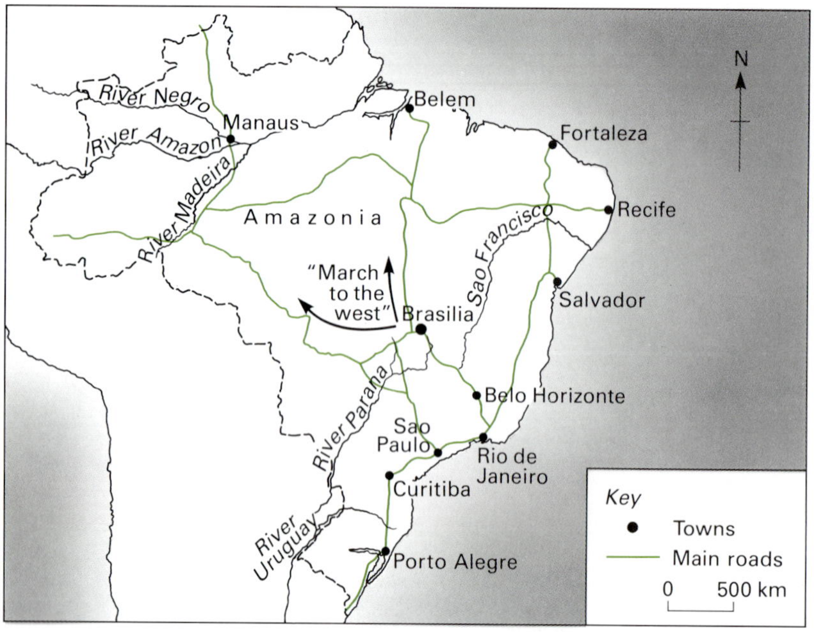

situation was very significant. Within three years, major roads were completed, making Brasilia the focus of a national network. In 1968, a rail link was built to South-east Brazil. The city plan was very dramatic. The city was laid out in the shape of an aeroplane, the main public buildings forming the cockpit, the business, and commercial areas the fuselage, and residential areas the wings. Industries developed around 'the tail'. The residential area, where homes were offered free at first, consists of over a hundred neighbourhood 'superblocks', each one self-contained with over 10 six-storey apartment buildings, a school and a shopping centre.

Where planning was less successful was in the developments which have occurred since completion of the city. It was not foreseen that many construction workers would stay on. Satellite towns have sprung up outside Brasilia, taking overspill populations. Here, medical, educational and other amenities are not as good. These are dormitory settlements. However, the favelas, common in other Brazilian cities have not developed to the same extent. The population of Brasilia and its satellites is already 1.2 millions and job possibilities are strong 'pull factors'.

The effects of the massive capital investment in Brasilia upon the country's finances will never be known. The drain on resources undoubtedly helped to cause the decline in the Brazilian economy in the 1950s and the collapse of the government in 1964. One Brazilian minister is reported to have called the cost of Brasilia a crime against the country's economy.

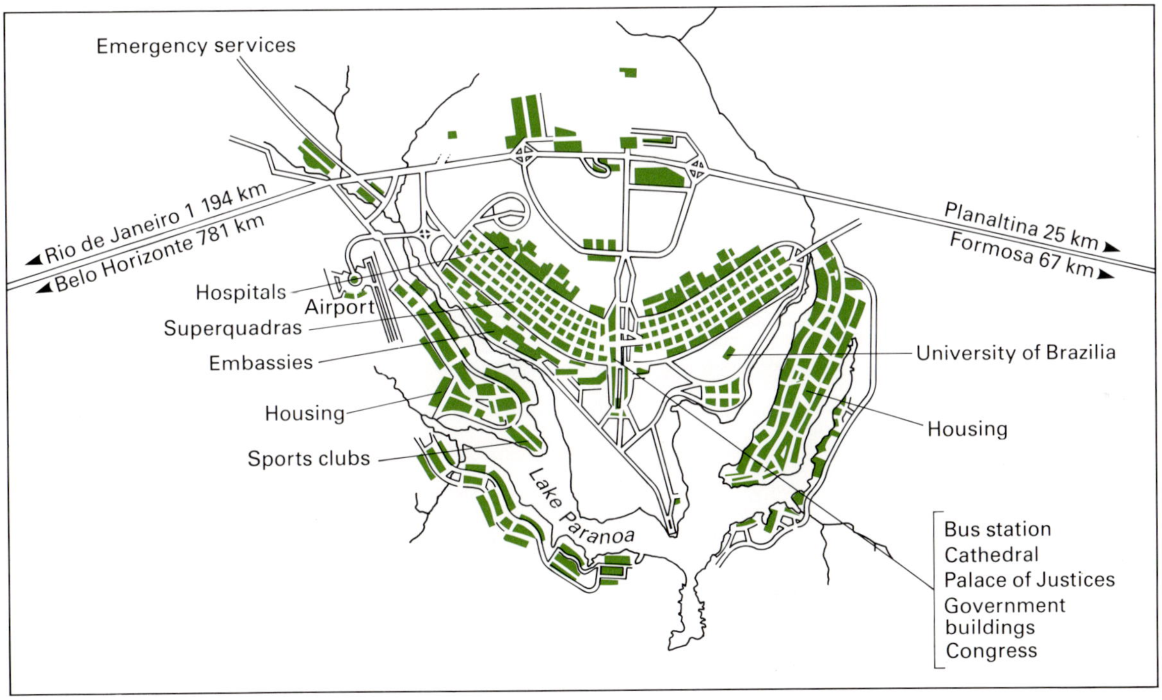

Fig. 7.51 *Brasilia*

Activities

1 Make a list of the different reasons for building new national capitals, including Brasilia.
2 Find out about 'the march to the west', the opening up of Amazonia in Brazil.
3 What is your attitude towards the policy of investing heavily in one scheme at the possible expense of the rest of the country? Does it happen in Britain?
4 Compare the location of capital cities in Italy, Chile and Norway with those in France, Mexico and New Zealand. Comment upon the shapes of these countries. How has this affected the locations? What problems could occur in countries like Chile and Norway?
5 Is there a need for a new national capital in Britain? Where would you locate it? Discuss in your groups the advantages and disadvantages of such an idea.

PART THREE PRODUCTION

8 INDUSTRY

Industry and Welfare

Fig. 8.1 *'Smokestack industry' A glassworks in Chesterfield*

Fig. 8.2 *The 'North-South' division of the world (from the Brandt Commission, 1980)*

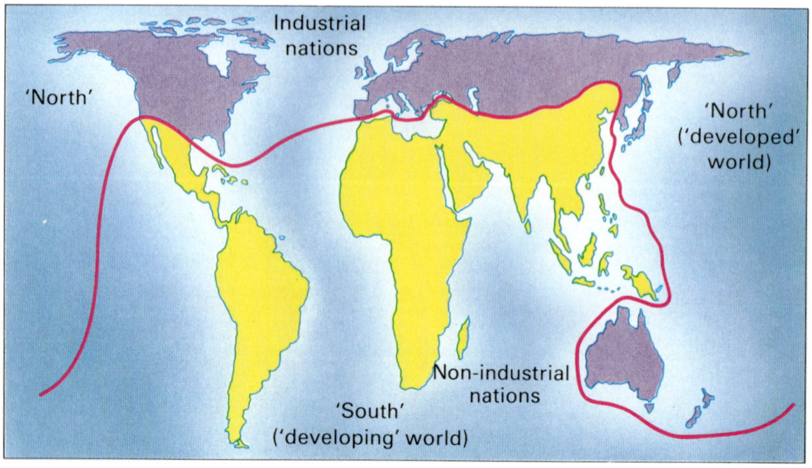

People have very different images of industry. Many associate it with dirty factories, grime and pollution. Figure 8.1 fits this popular, narrow image. However there is much more to industry than factories and coal mines. Industry has a broader meaning and includes paid work of all kinds, teaching, office work and factory jobs, that lead to the production of goods and services. Compare the industry shown in fig. 8.1 with that shown in fig. 6.10, which shows the popular image is not always true.

Industry is important because it has an effect upon human welfare. It is a wealth-creating activity. The more goods and services produced by industry, the greater will be the wealth (economic welfare) of the community and perhaps the quality of life of people.

Developed countries are usually highly industrialised. They are found in three main areas of the world – North America, Western Europe and Japan. Developing countries, on the other hand, have reached various stages of industrialisation. Some have very few productive industries; some are newly industrialised and some are industrialising very quickly. Figure 8.2 shows how the world was divided by the Brandt Commission in 1980, according to industry and wealth, into 'North' and 'South'.

One way to compare levels of economic welfare between countries is to use an indicator such as the Gross National Product per person. Turn back to fig. 4.11 which shows GNP per head for several countries, and suggest which of these countries are in the 'North' and which in the 'South'. There are two important problems associated with this method of measuring human welfare:

1. GNP per person does not measure human happiness and people's total well-being. There is more to life than money, and a satisfying way of life may not be associated directly with high economic welfare. People on low incomes in a developing country may be as happy as those with higher incomes in a developed country.
2. GNP per person is only an average and does not show how wealth is distributed across the population of a country. There are pockets of poverty in developed countries and small numbers of people with high wealth in developing countries. Figure 8.3 shows the variations in human welfare within Italy. Look back at figs. 4.8 and 4.9 to see that some people in Brazil are wealthy.

Another indicator is the Physical Quality of Life Index (PQLI). This tries to put a value upon the quality of people's lives. Figure 8.4 shows the Index for five countries in 1986. It is calculated using three indicators:

1. the infant mortality rate
2. life expectancy
3. the literacy rate

A high figure shows a high quality of life.

Fig. 8.3 *Some factors affecting levels of welfare in Italy*

Factors	*Regions of Northern Italy*	*Regions of Southern Italy*
Rate of unemployment (%)	9.7	13.3
Population living below official Government poverty line (%)	3.8	27.2
No. of motor vehicles (per '000 inhabitants)	306	93
Meat consumption (kgs per head p.a.)	40	19
Domestic & Electricity consumption (kws per head p.a.)	148	74
% employed in agriculture	11.1	29.9
% employed in service industries	34.8	26.0

The Index can be used to give a clearer picture of how people's basic needs are being met. It shows whether developments in industry benefit ordinary people's lives. The figures in fig 8.4 show a wide difference in the quality of life between developing countries, but a narrower gap between some of these countries and developed countries. It must be remembered that many quality of life indicators are closely related to GNP per person. A country (eg Nigeria) can have a higher GNP per person than another (eg India) but a lower PQLI. What does this tell you about the two countries?

Fig. 8.4 *The PQL Index and GNP per head for five countries*

Country	Physical quality of life index (0–100)	GNP per head 1986–US$
UK	96	8570
Sri Lanka	83	360
India	43	260
Nigeria	25	730
Ethiopia	16	110

Activities

Before you start to study industry, find out about your own and your class' perceptions of industry. Carry out a brainstorm (see Activity 2.2) to answer the question: 'In a word or phrase, what sorts of things do you associate with industry?'

Sectors of industry

Classifying occupations

The jobs and industries in which people work can be classified into groups. One classification used worldwide has nine groups. Each of these groups falls into one of three broad categories of industry. These categories are known as sectors. Figure 8.5 shows that the sectors are linked. Explain how they are linked.

When jobs and industries are classified into groups and sectors, the employment structure of a country is shown. Work in each of the three sectors produces economic welfare.

Fig. 8.5 *Some relationships between the sectors of industry*

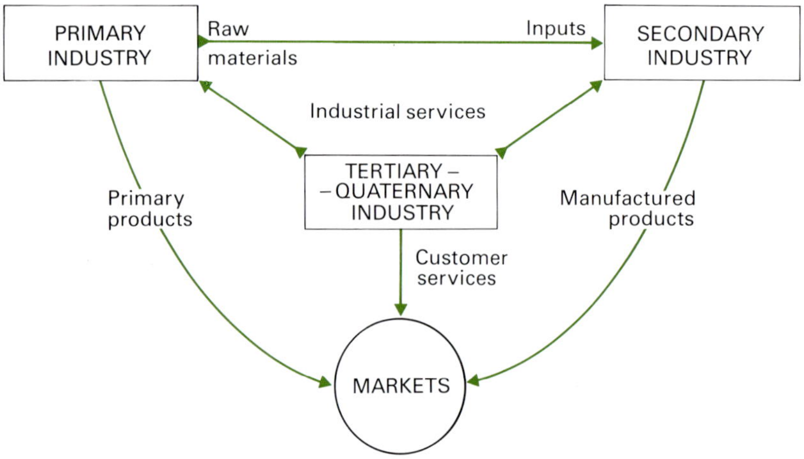

Fig. 8.6 *Employment structure of selected countries*

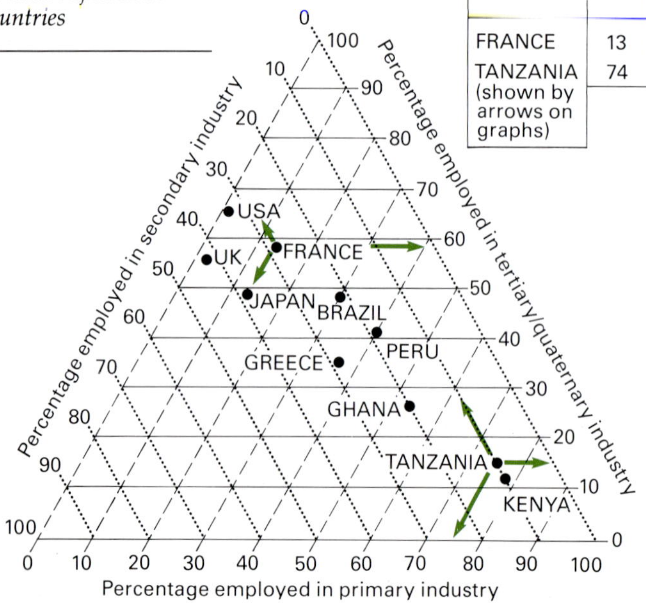

	Prim.	Sec.	Ter/ /Quat
FRANCE	13	29	58
TANZANIA (shown by arrows on graphs)	74	10	16

Fig. 8.7 *Employment structures of France and Tanzania*

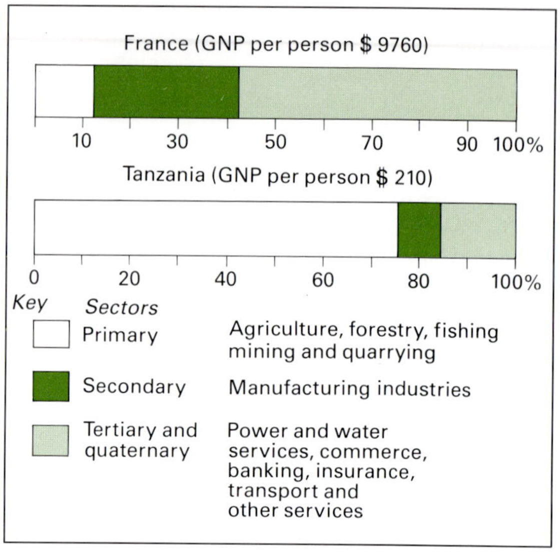

Figures 8.6 and 8.7 show that 59% of France's economic welfare is produced by tertiary and quaternary industry, 29% by secondary industry and 12% by primary industry. This contrasts greatly with the origin of Tanzania's wealth. Developed countries depend heavily on tertiary and quaternary industry whereas much of the wealth of developing countries is created by primary industry. The size of the various sectors is a good general indicator of a country's level of economic development. Figure 8.8 shows that as a country develops economically, the proportion of its labour force employed in the primary sector declines. At first this produces a rise in the secondary sector and later, a rise in the tertiary and quaternary sector. Britain's changing employment structure has seen a swing from manufacturing to services since the 1950s.

The structure of employment also varies within a country. For example, fig. 8.10 shows the differences in the size of sectors between northern and south-east England. The tertiary/quaternary sector in France, for example, in fig. 8.7 shows that 52% of the working population is included. However, there is a much higher percentage of such workers in the Greater Paris area, which does not show up on the bar-graph for France. Government offices, headquarters of major companies and service occupations in the national capital provide much tertiary/quaternary employment. On the other hand the primary sector for Great Paris is much smaller than that for the whole of France.

Fig. 8.8 *Stages in economic development and employment structure*

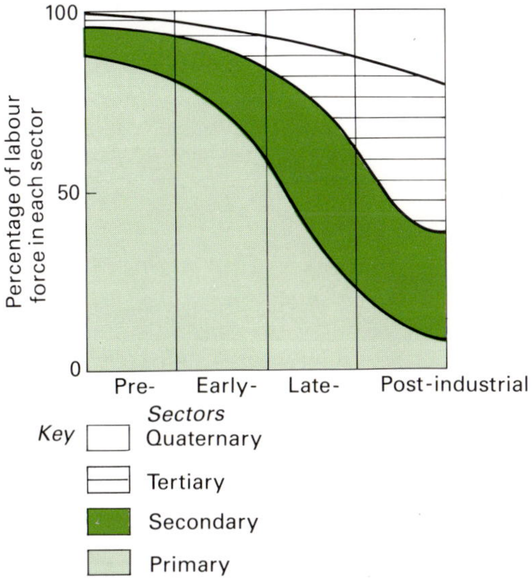

Fig. 8.9 (**a**) *Nairobi, modern CBD.* (**b**) *The informal sector in Nairobi, Kenya, converting cans and aerosols into oil lamps*

Some people work outside these formal sectors of industry. In all countries there is an informal sector of people who do not work regularly, and when they do, do work which does not fall into the primary-secondary-tertiary and quaternary classifications. Street traders, shoe cleaners, window cleaners and carters are common in many developing world cities. In South America it is thought that about 40 per cent of the population of working age are involved with the informal sector. A 'black economy' and 'moonlighting' occur in developed countries such as Britain.

Fig. 8.10 *The employment structure of two regions of England*

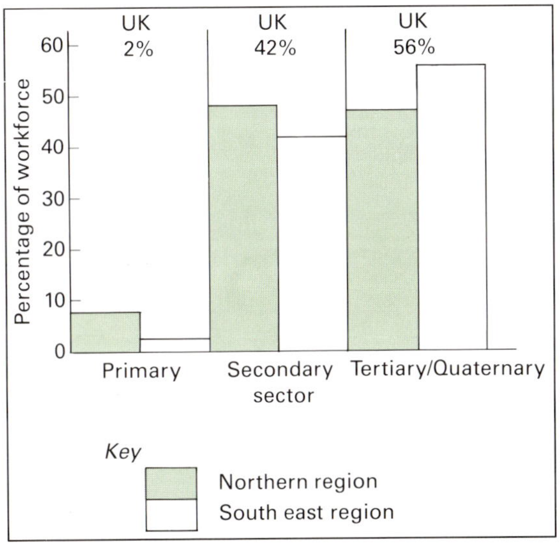

Activities

1 Name three primary jobs, six secondary jobs and six tertiary/quaternary jobs.

2 Use information from fig. 8.6 to complete the table below.

Country	Percentage employed in sector		
	Primary	Secondary	Tertiary/Quaternary
USA			
UK			
Japan			
Brazil			
Ghana			
Kenya			

3 Choose one developed and one developing country from this chart and draw bar-charts to show employment structures, similar to those in fig. 8.5.

9 FARMING

Farming and food production

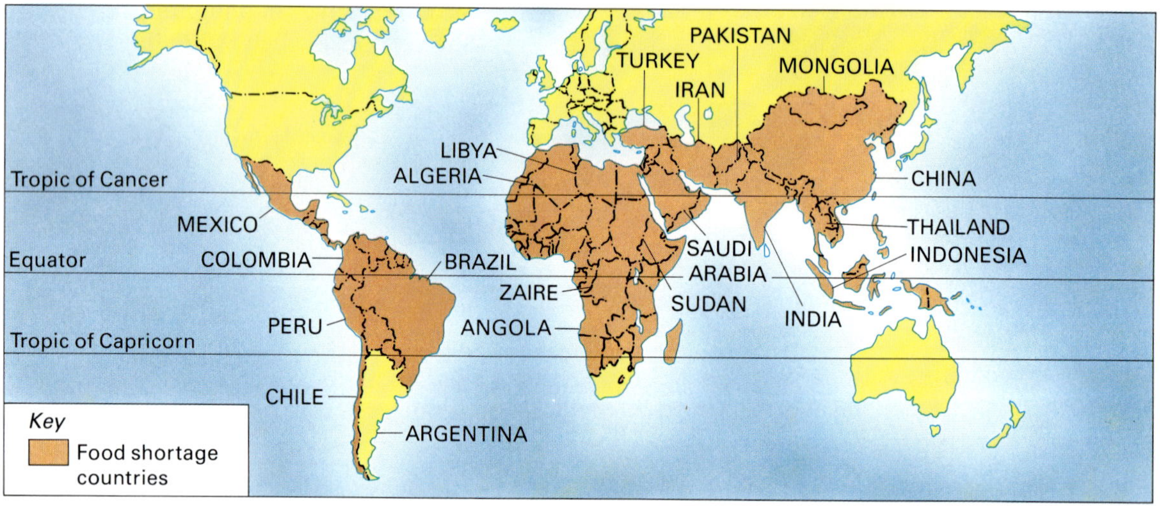

Fig. 9.1 *Countries with food shortages*

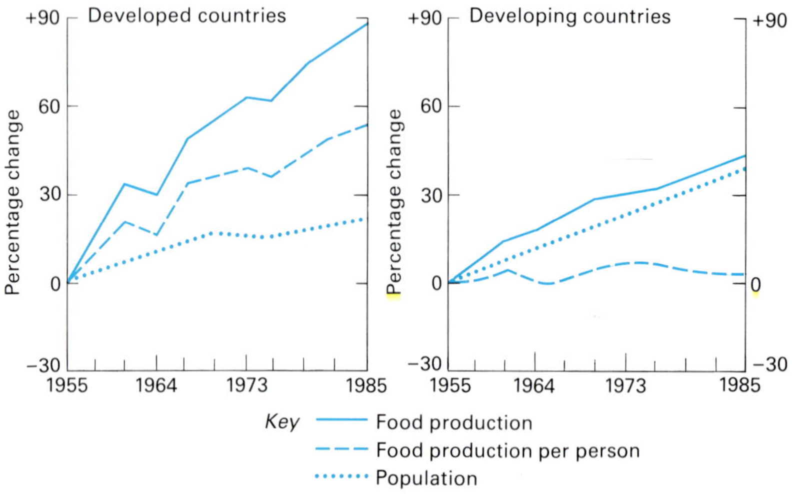

Fig. 9.2 *Changes in food production and population*

Farming is the name given to people's use of their environment to produce food. Farms are our main source of food supply. They are also a source of raw materials for industry such as wool. Food is produced either for farmers and their families, which is called *subsistence* farming, or for sale to other people, which is called *commercial* farming. In some countries the major farming system is subsistence.

Food shortages occur in many parts of the world. Figure 9.1 shows that these happen mainly in Africa, Asia and South America.

World food production has grown faster than world population. About half of the food produced is eaten in the developed countries, but these countries have only about one quarter of the world's population. Changes in food production, population and food production per head in both developed and developing countries are shown in fig. 9.2.

The demand for food

World demands for food match changes in population and wealth. Farm production has to be increased to meet the ever increasing demand for food. There are two basic ways of increasing production:

1. Use more land for farming.
2. Use farmland more productively so that output from a certain area of land, the *yield*, rises.

In 1984 the United Nations recommended five ways of increasing world food supply. These are listed in fig. 9.3.

In North America and Western Europe more food is produced than is needed, a surplus exists. Here, farming is often called agri-business. Farmers work as business people trying to get as much income as possible by

Fig. 9.3 *United Nations' recommendations for increasing world food supply in 1984*

1. *Increase the present low level of human inputs into farming in developing countries eg modern management methods, fertilisers, pesticides, technical equipment . . .*
2. *Grow crops more suited to local soils and climates in developing countries*
3. *Grow crops in developing countries with higher calorie contents*
4. *Use all the possible farmland for farming*
5. *Encourage freer movement of food from areas of surplus to areas of shortage*

adapting their farming to the environmental and economic conditions, by using fertilisers for example.

In parts of Africa on the other hand, there are severe food shortages, especially in the seven Sahel countries shown in fig. 9.5. The causes of these food problems include:

- Rapid population growth – more and more mouths to feed.
- The 'great drought' since 1968. Lower rainfall and the spread of the desert has made soil conditions worse and has led to smaller harvests.
- Civil wars and political instability have made farming more difficult and have caused many people to leave the countryside.
- Government farming policies:

a) There has not been enough financial investment in farming and agricultural training.

b) The storage, marketing and distribution of food is poor and leads to much wastage.

c) Rural-to-urban migration of people has been allowed to reduce the size of the farming population.

Fig. 9.4 *Agri-business*

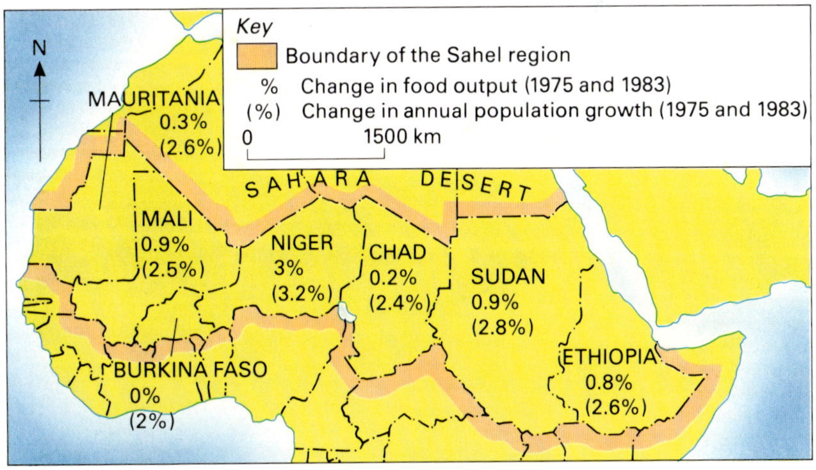

Fig. 9.5 *The African 'famine belt'*

Activities

1 Carry out a whole-class brainstorm (see Activity 2.2). What is your image of farmers and country people? Analyse the results by making a negative list and a positive list.

2 Divide your class into five groups. Each group should discuss one of the statements below about farming:

a) Farming ruins the natural environment.

b) Urban areas should not be allowed to spread into the countryside.

c) Former industrial land in urban areas should be re-used for farming.

d) The countryside is there for city-dwellers to drive through and picnic in.

e) Farmers are more interested in quick profits than animals.

After your discussions, one member of each group should report to the whole class about the group's findings.

3 Individual work (at home). Write a paragraph or make a list about each of the five topics to summarise your class' attitude towards farming.

Farming as a system

Fig. 9.6 *Farming as a system*

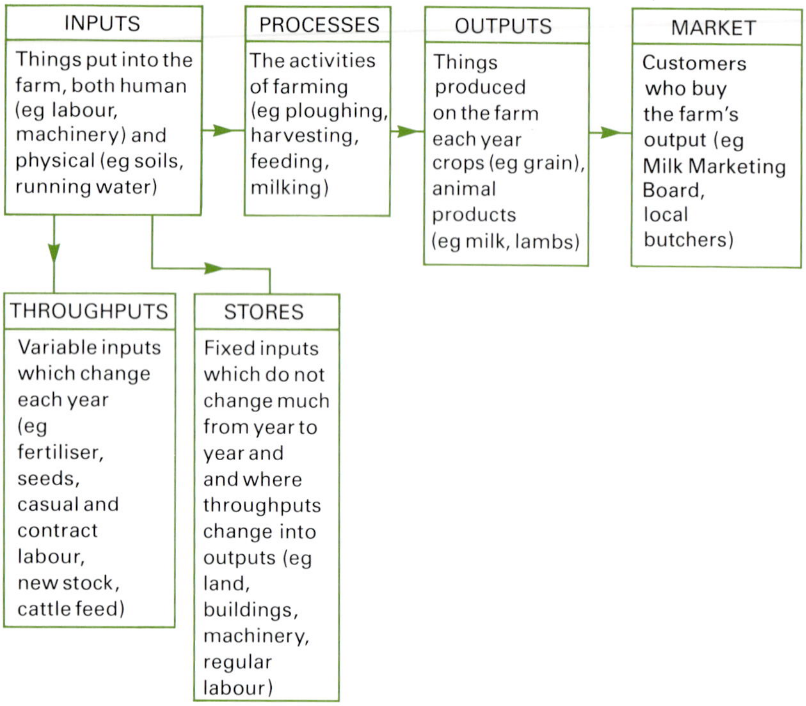

Farms can be studied as food producing systems. Food is an output from the farming system, produced when inputs to the system such as seed and labour combine with processes of farming such as ploughing and feeding. Figure 9.6 shows farm inputs, processes and outputs, as a system. Each farm works as an input–process–output system. A change in one of these parts affects other parts. For example, output should rise if the farmer increases inputs. Farmers trying to increase output have to increase the inputs into their system such as more land, more fertilisers. In a system, inputs influence outputs. You only get out in food what you put in as inputs. The parts of a system are dependent upon each other. These relationships or links are shown by means of arrows on the systems diagram.

Fig. 9.7 *A systems diagram for a Pennine sheep farm and dairy farm*

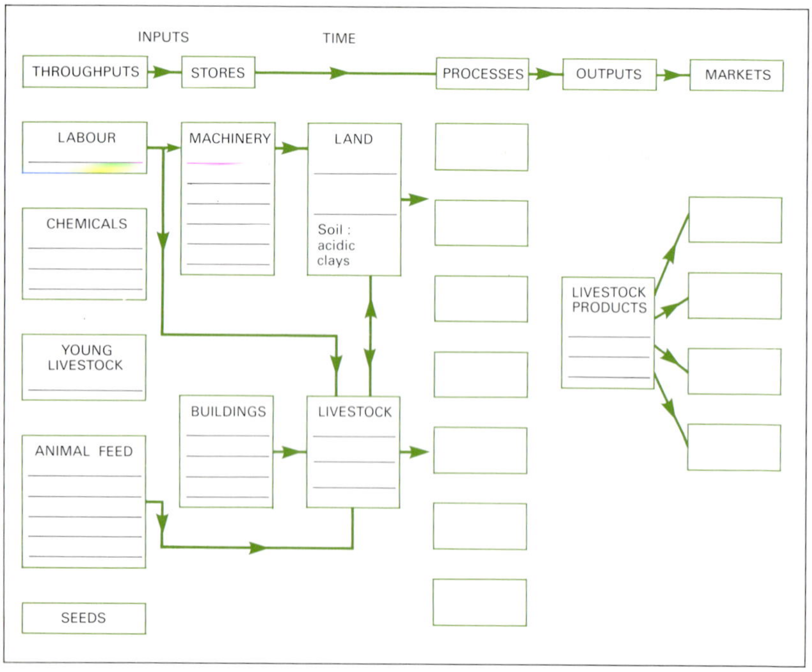

Activities

1 Use the systems diagram, fig. 9.7, which shows a sheep farm and a dairy farm in the Pennines and the list of throughputs, stores, processes, outputs and markets which relate to this farm. Make your own copy of the system and complete it using the information provided.

Local butchers
3 tractors
Harrow
60 Freisian cows
150 hectares of moorland
Shearing
Milk
55 Guernsey cows
Sheep dip
Silage clamp
Wool Marketing Board
Lambing
Muck spreading
Milking parlour
Wool
Muck spreader
Calves
Milking machines
Sheep dipping
250 sheep
Milking
Barns
Silage maker
Trailers
210 hectares of pasture
Milk Marketing Board
Sheep
Fertilising
Machinery, maintenance and repair
Fertiliser spreader
Local cattle market

2 Add six further arrows to the diagram (or write six statements) to show relationships or links within the system which are not shown at present.

Differences in farming systems

Farming systems differ from place to place and from time to time. Figure 9.8 compares a mixed commercial farm in Britain to a subsistence farm in Nepal.

Fig. 9.8 *Contrasting farming systems – a British farm (**a**) and a Nepali farm (**b**)*

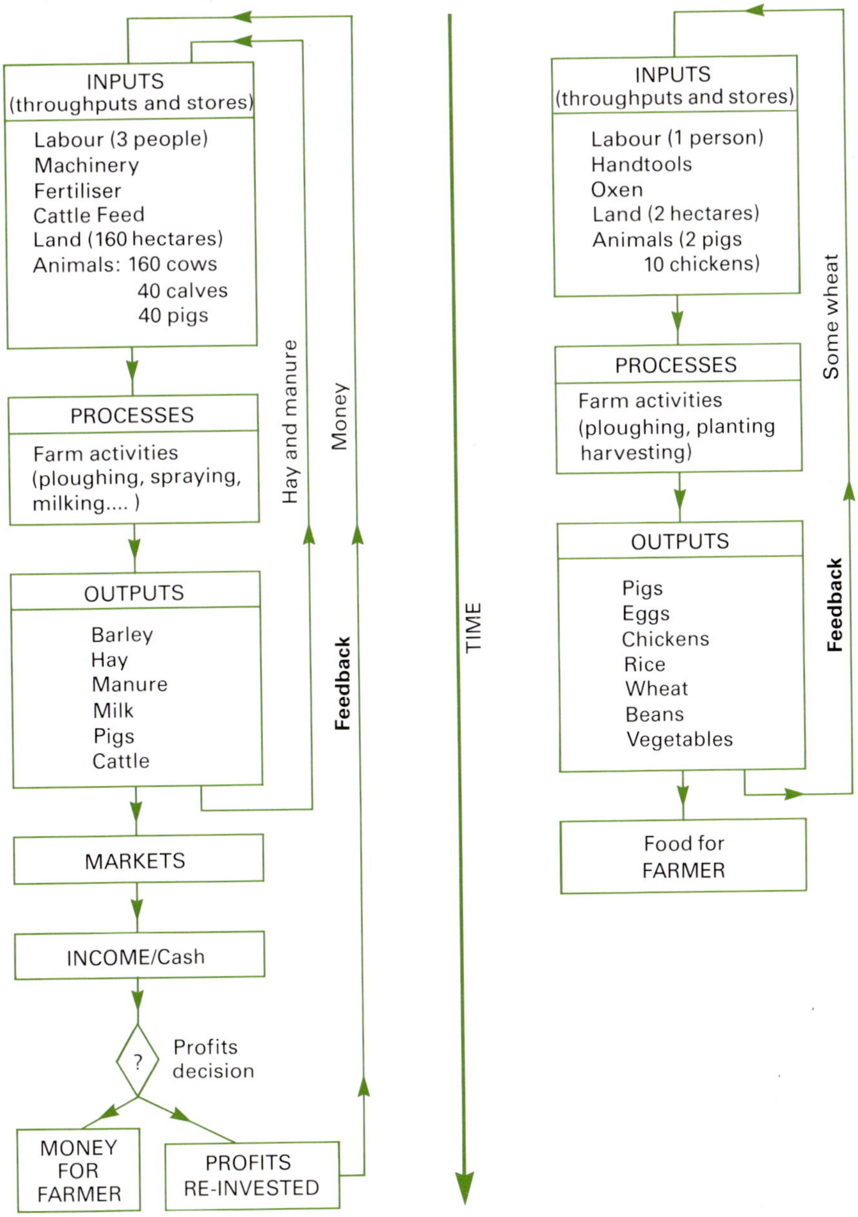

Classifying farms

Fig. 9.9 *The main types of farming in the world*

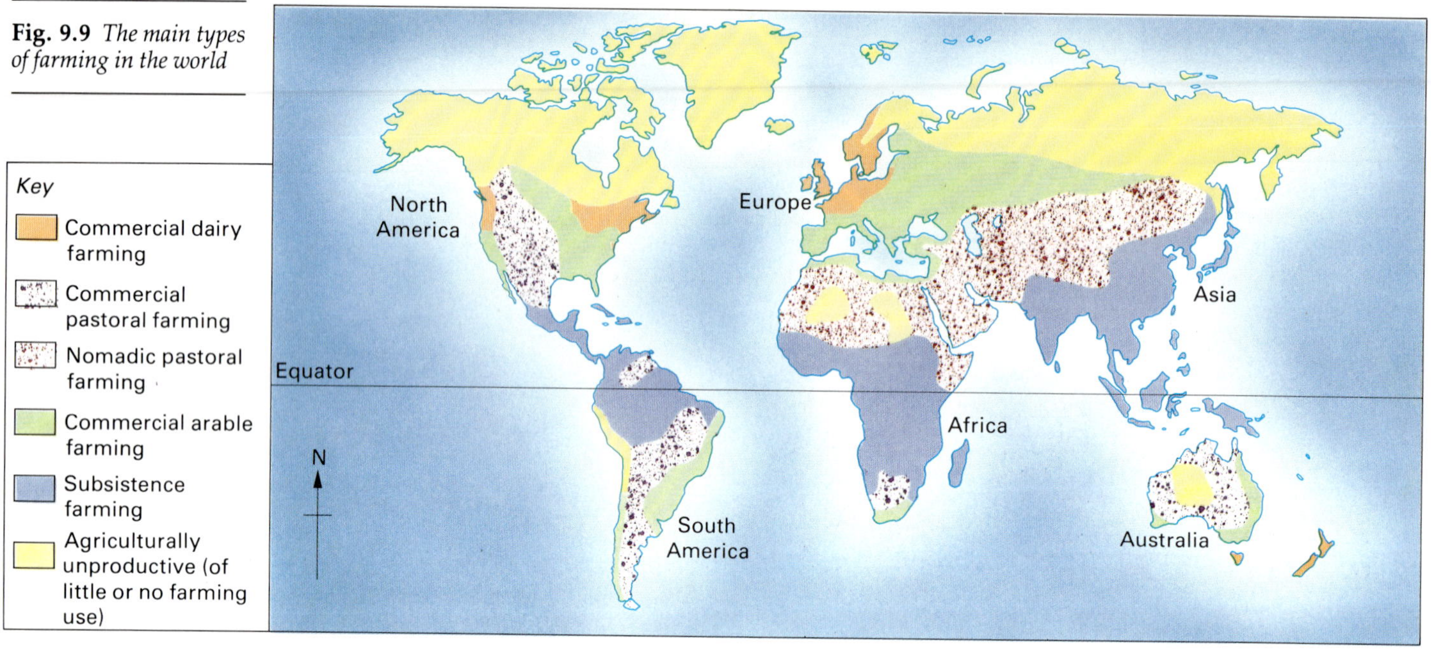

1 *Type*. There are many different types of farming and the main ones are shown in fig. 9.9. This classification into main types is based upon the processes and outputs from farms.

Farming type	Process and output
Arable farms	– land is ploughed to grow crops like grain.
Pastoral farms	– animals are reared for either milk (dairy cows), meat (beef cattle) or other products such as wool.
Mixed farms	– farmers grow crops and keep animals in roughly similar proportions.

The output from farms is either for family needs (subsistence) or for sale to a wider market (commercial farming). Another output factor which helps to classify farms is whether they are monocultural or polycultural. Some farms such as large plantations specialise on one crop or product only. The coffee farms of Brazil and rubber plantations of Malaysia are examples of monoculture. Farms with more than one output are called polycultural.

2 *Inputs*. Each type of farming is a different system. Figure 9.11 shows the different combination of inputs of land, labour and capital (money invested in buildings and equipment) in three different types of farming. These combinations can lead to another method of classification. Where a high proportion of land is used in relation to labour and capital, a farm is called *extensive*. *Intensive* farms have a high proportion of labour and capital in relation to the land. (Look at fig. 9.10).

Fig. 9.10 *Intensive and extensive farming systems*

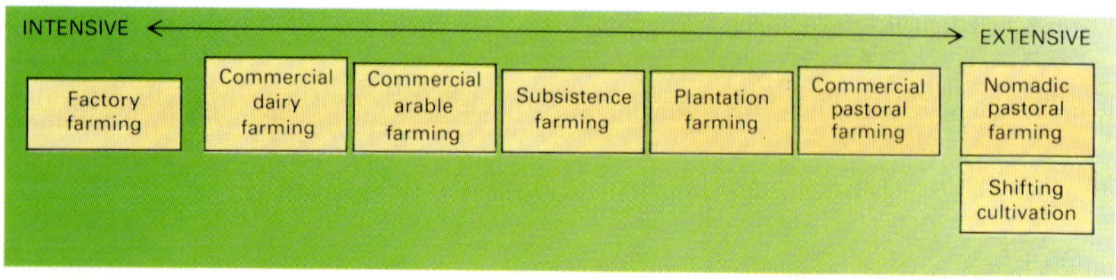

Fig. 9.11 *Inputs of land, labour and capital to three types of farming*

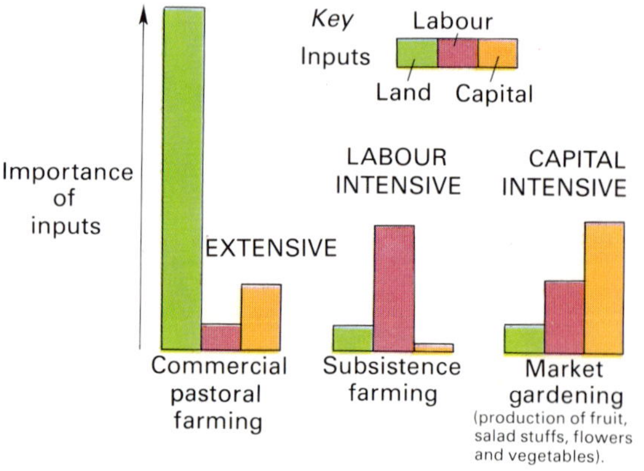

3 *Size of farm*. Extensive farms such as Australian sheep farms are usually large in area. They often make use of marginal land as well (land which is only just agriculturally productive). Intensive farms like the vegetable growers on the edges of British urban areas are usually quite small. A great deal of money is invested in inputs such as fertilisers, machinery and labour to produce as much from each hectare of land as possible. For example, greenhouse crops such as tomatoes need a great amount of expensive hand labour (look at fig. 9.12).

4 *Land tenure* (who owns the farmland). In Brazil, there are five million farms. These range from *latifundia*, over 1000 hectares in size, to *minifundia*, under 10 hectares. Latifundia are usually cattle ranches or cocoa, coffee or sugar plantations. They are often owned by absentee landlords who often live in cities and appoint managers to run the farms. Workers may be paid a wage in cash or given a plot of land for their own use as part or all of their wages. Most minifundia are owner-occupied, owned by working farmers. Another type of land tenure is the tenant farmer who rents the land and buildings from a landlord. Rents are paid from any profits the tenant can make. Many small and medium size farms in Western Europe are this type. Farms may even be communally owned, rather than privately. Many villages in India have this type of land tenure. In China and the USSR this is known as *collective* farming. China has over 50 000 collective farms or communes, each run by local people through workers' committees.

In many countries, people and governments are dissatisfied with systems of tenure. Many land reform schemes have been introduced. In parts of Southern Italy, latifundia have been broken up into smaller farm units. In Southern France, on the other hand, government policies encourage the combining of several scattered plots of land into one medium sized farm (*remembrement*). This is similar to what happened in Britain during the enclosure movement before the 18th century.

Fig. 9.12 *'A green house farm'*

Activities

1 Find out about the types of farming listed below:
plantation farming shifting cultivation subsistence farming nomadic pastoral herding.
Match each type with one of the statements below:
a) People grow enough food to live on but have little left to sell.
b) People wander from place to place living on milk and meat from cattle, sheep or goats.
c) A single cash crop is grown on a very large, tropical farm. It is usually grown for export.
d) Crops are grown on newly cleared land for a short period of time. Then the farmer moves on to another clearing.

2 Carry out a group enquiry into communal farming. Find an example of a village farm, a collective farm or a commune and make notes about it. Produce a wall display for the rest of the class which includes:
a) A sketch map to show location, size and lay-out of the farm.
b) How the land is used.
c) The part played by private enterprise (private land, private markets etc.)
d) How decisions are made.

Farming decisions

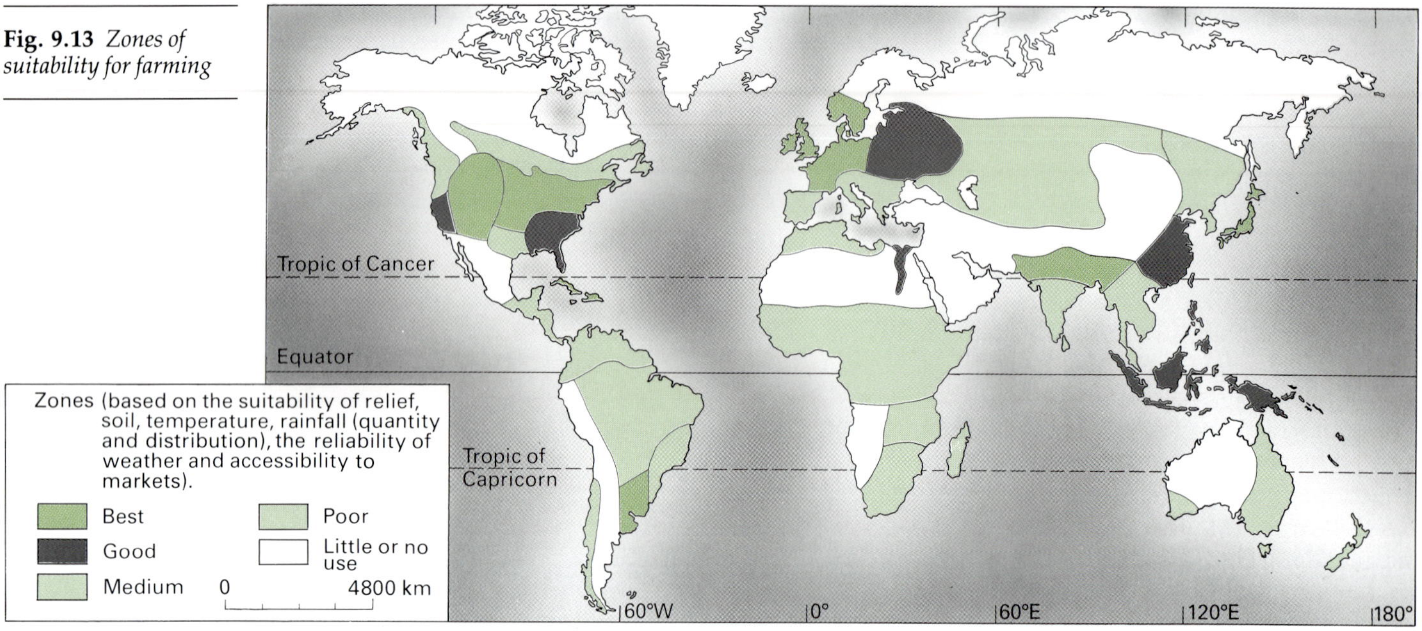

Fig. 9.13 *Zones of suitability for farming*

Some farming areas are more suitable for growing crops than others. Figure 9.13 shows the world divided into zones of suitability.

Western Europe is shown as one of the best areas, for example, and farmers have a wide choice of land use.

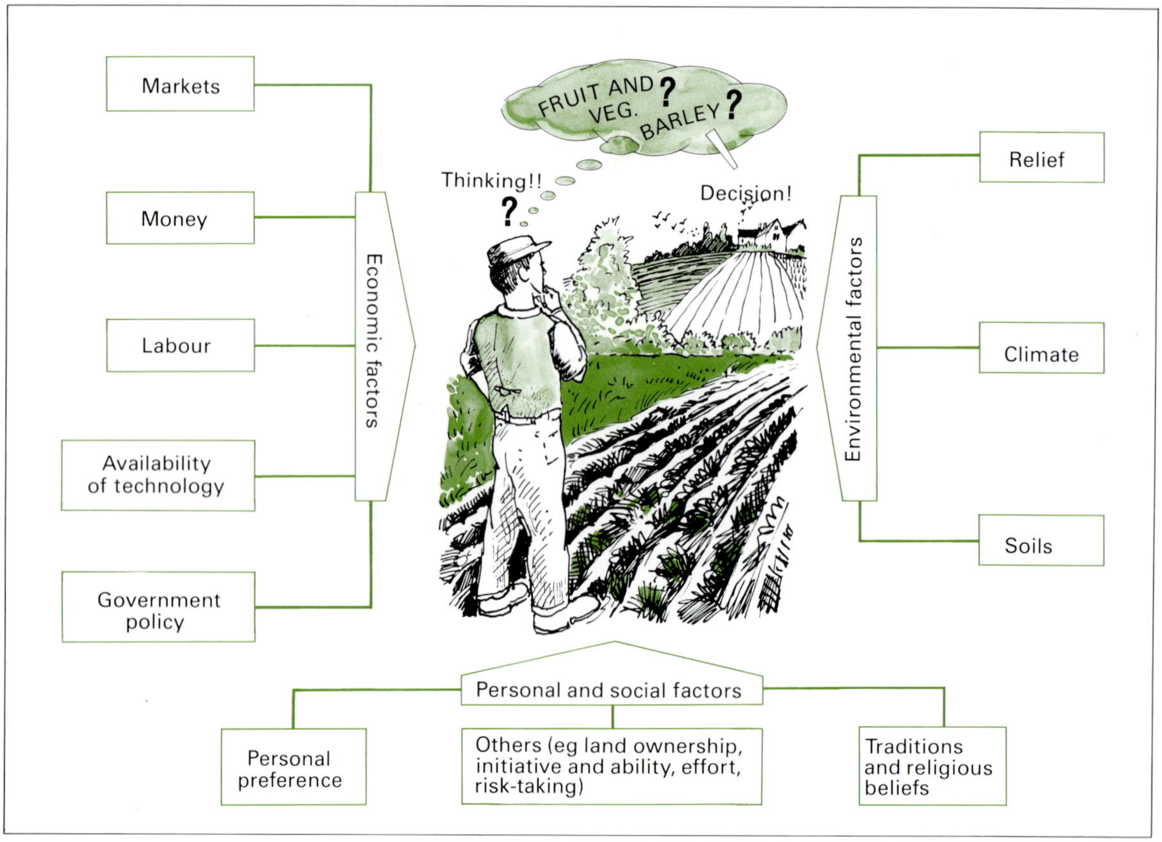

Fig. 9.14 *The farmer's choice – what to grow*

Imagine that you have been left a plot of land, in someone's will. It is in one of the best zones on fig. 9.13, and you decide to farm it. You would have to make some important decisions – what crops to grow, which animals to keep, in which fields? All farmers have to make similar decisions. Many factors influence the choices they make. Figure 9.14 shows the main factors that influence what farmland is actually used for. It shows the factors which farmers might think about when deciding how to use land. The world's farmers rarely have a free choice. Sometimes, only one type of farming is possible because of physical factors over which the farmer has little or no control. The climate and the steepness of slopes around a farm cannot be influenced much by a farmer. Factors which cannot be influenced or controlled are known as constraints. They are much more likely to be environmental (physical) factors than economic, personal and social (human) factors. It is possible to change access to markets for example and to improve labour supply. It is less easy to alter the climate or relief of the area where a farm is located. However as can be seen in fig. 9.16 it is possible to overcome climatic constraints.

Activities

1 Make a list of the decisions a farmer must take before starting production.
2 Using an atlas locate one country or area in each of the five zones shown in fig. 9.13. For each, suggest reasons for its level of suitability for farming.
3 Study fig. 9.15 in small groups. For each farm, rank the four factors in order of their importance in influencing the 'what-do-I-do' decision. Then, compare the rank orders of your groups.
4 Look at fig. 9.16. What inputs are being used in this example?

Fig. 9.15 *Factors affecting farming type*

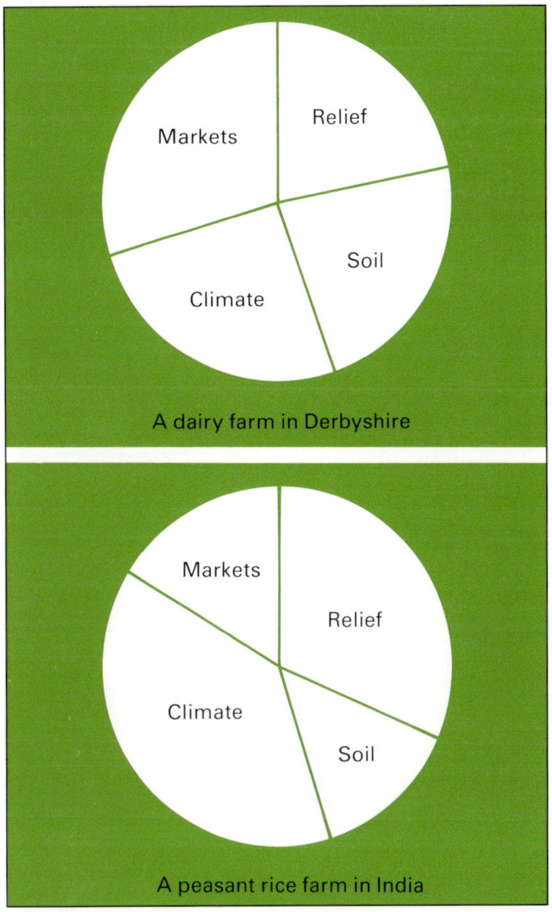

Fig. 9.16 *Greening the desert in Saudi Arabia. Circular crop rings irrigated by centre-pivot sprinklers*

Farming and the environment

Farming is strongly influenced by the environment. In Britain, the Ministry of Agriculture, Fisheries and Food uses five grades for farmland. The differences between Grade 1 land (high yields) and Grade 5 land (of little agricultural value) come mainly from variations in relief, soil and climate.

Fig. 9.17 *Suitable weather conditions for five farm products*

	Conditions	
Product	*Temperature*	*Rainfall*
Wheat	over 15°C in summer	less than 750 mm a year; more than 30 mm a month in late-autumn and early winter for winter-sown wheat
Oats	maximum of 15°C in summer	over 1000 mm a year
Sugar beet	over 15°C in summer	less than 650 mm a year; less than 40 mm in harvesting month
Dairy cows	below 15°C in summer; over 6°C in winter	more than 800 mm a year
Sheep	can put up with below freezing temperatures	can put up with over 1500 mm a year

Climate and weather

All plants need warmth and moisture to grow. The requirements of five types of farming in Britain are shown in fig. 9.17. Study fig. 9.19 carefully. Maps B to F show the climatic variations in Britain that farmers have to consider. They help to explain the pattern of farming shown in Map A.

Variations in weather from year to year are also important to farmers. Heavy rains, high winds, late frosts and droughts can all have damaging effects. Changes from 'normal' weather affect farmers' incomes. Hence, they have to cope with a degree of risk. Figure 9.18 shows the damage done to cereal yields in Britain by the unreliable rainfall of the 1976 growing season.

In Nigeria unreliable weather is also a regular problem for farmers. In Northern Nigeria only 1 to 3 months in the year have over 100 mm of rainfall. In the south, there are 7 to 9 months. Not only does the total amount decrease northwards, but it also becomes more unreliable. In seven of the years between 1970 and 1985 rainfall in the north was well below average and in two of the years almost none. Figure 9.20 shows the farming changes from south to north in Nigeria which are affected by these climatic changes.

Fig. 9.18 *Cereal yields per hectare in Britain 1969 to 1979*

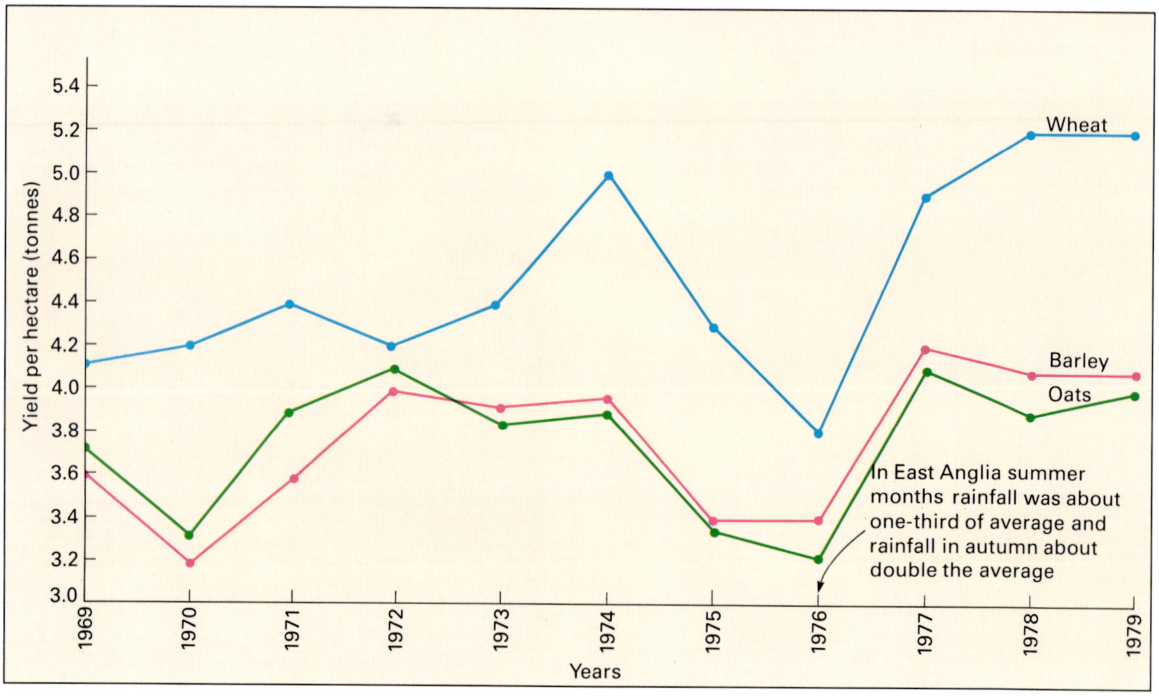

Fig. 9.19 *Farming and physical influences in England and Wales*

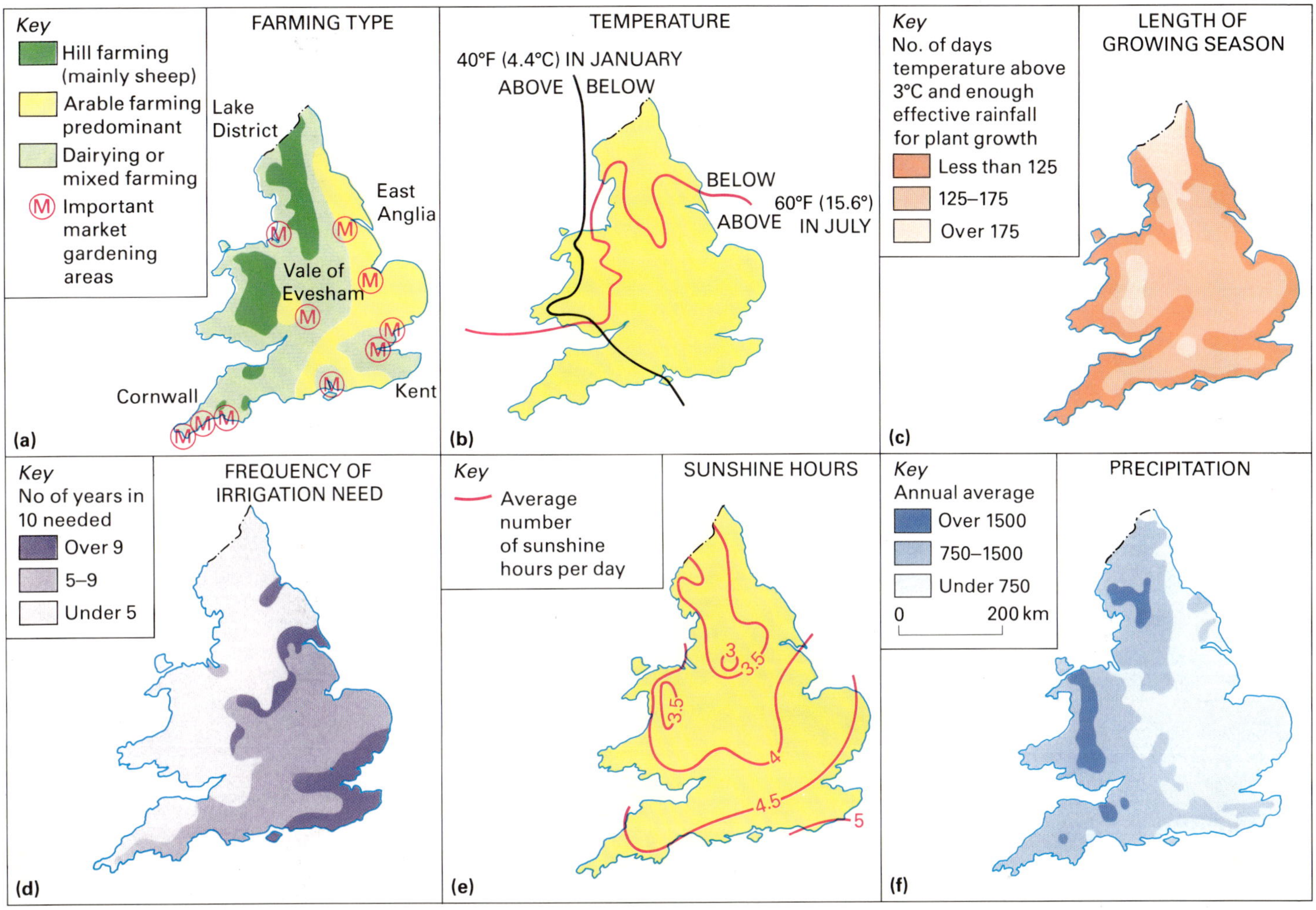

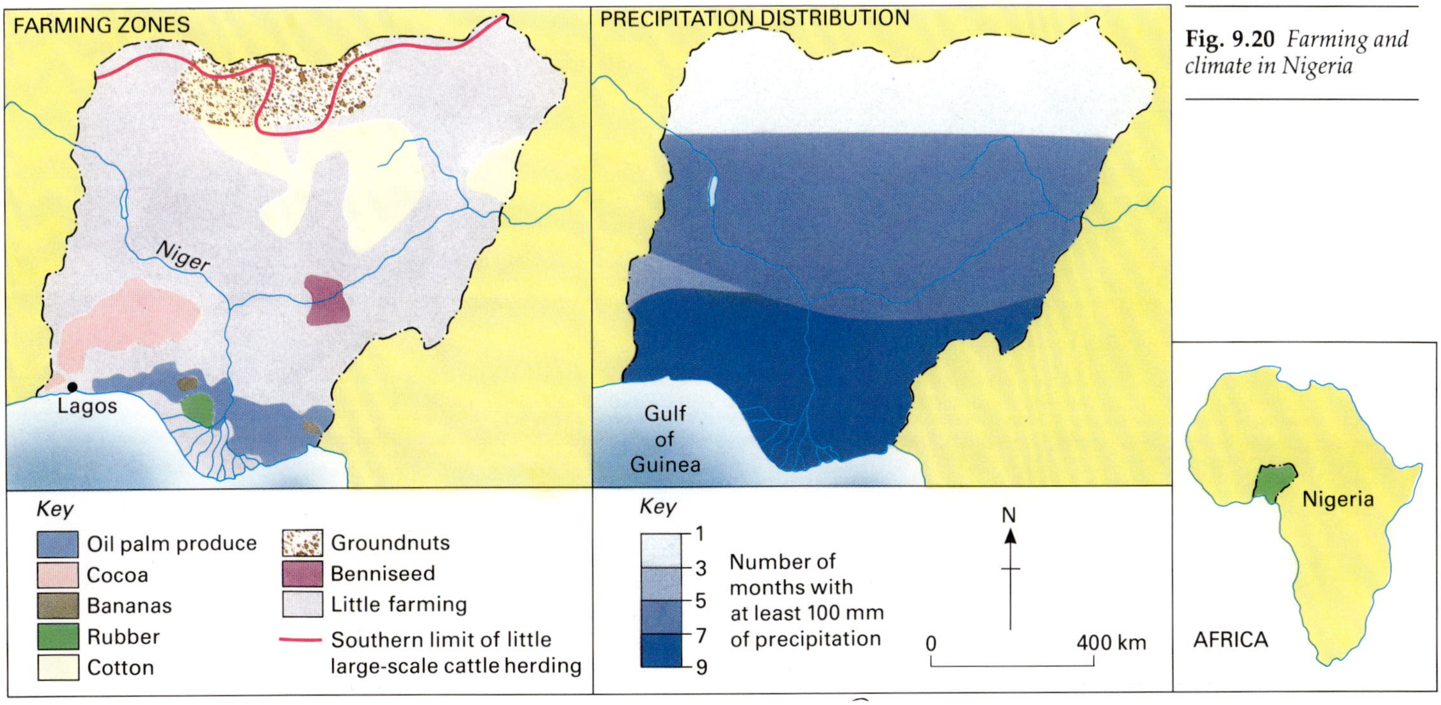

Fig. 9.20 *Farming and climate in Nigeria*

Relief and soils

The fertility of the soil, its depth, how well drained it is, how easily worked it is and how quickly it warms up are all important questions for farmers. The part played by soils in farming is so important that farmers are continually trying to improve them. They do this by ploughing, and adding fertilisers and manure.

Figure 9.21 shows a Derbyshire dairy farm. The decisions about what to produce have been strongly influenced by soils and relief. Study the map carefully to find out about the relationships between relief and soils and the types of farming.

Fig. 9.21 *Plan of Eastwood Farm, Derbyshire*

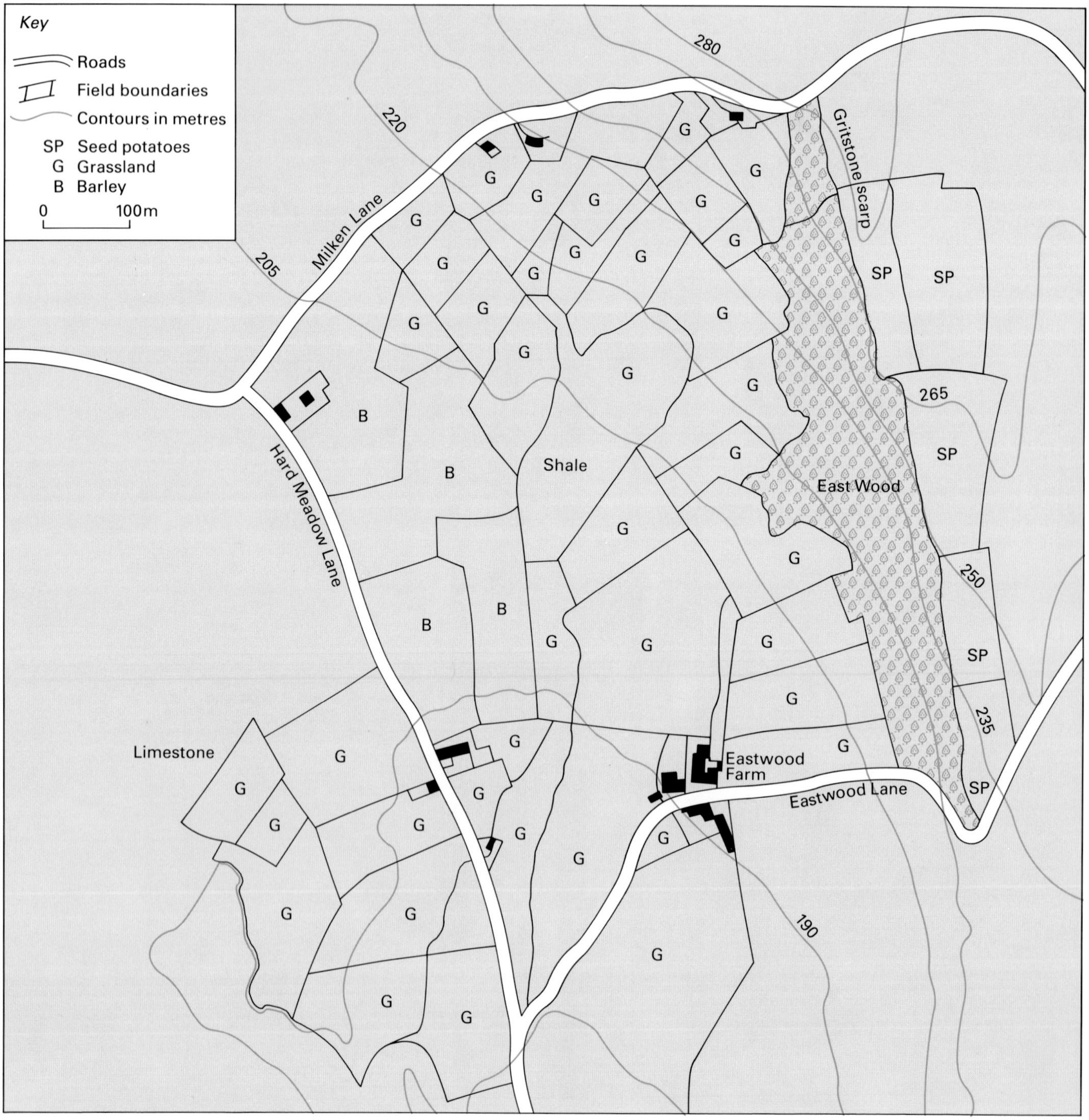

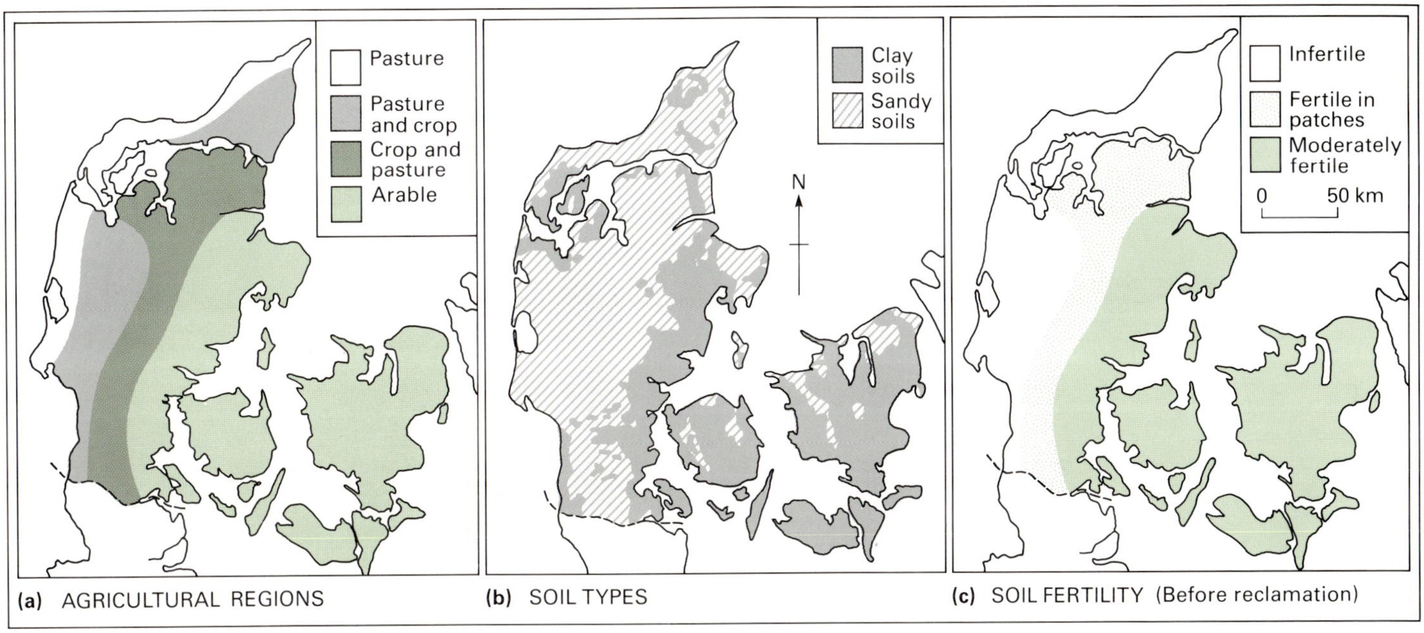

Fig. 9.22 *Soils and farming in Denmark*

Relief not only affects soils and land drainage but also directly affects farming. Steeply sloping land makes the use of machinery difficult. In the Lake District for example, this is one strong reason why sheep farming continues. Flat or gently sloping land is generally most suitable for farming as long as the land does not flood.

Farming in Denmark also shows the influence of these factors. Figure 9.22a shows the changes from pasture and dairying in Western Denmark to arable farming in the east. Does the information in maps b and c explain this? Also, does the change from wetter, milder maritime climate in the west to the more continental climate of Eastern Denmark help to explain these changes?

Fig. 9.23 *Central Valley water control and irrigation project in California*

Key

Upland over 200 m

▲ Pumping station

A Delta Cross Channel
B Delta–Mendota Canal
C San Luis Canal
D California Aqueduct
E Madera Canal
F Friant–Kern Canal

Station	Annual rainfall (mm)	April–September rainfall (mm)
Fresno	149	20
Sacramento	471	58
Redding	663	92
Tahoe	2429	1010

Activities

This activity will involve you in some individual or group research work. Figure 9.23 shows the Central Valley Irrigation and Water Control Project of California. You will need to find out about these three topics:

a) irrigation, and what it is.
b) The climate of the Central Valley, especially its rainfall.
c) The amount and types of farming in the Central Valley.

1 Using fig. 9.23, find out how the problems of bringing water from the Sierra Nevada Mountains to the Central Valley have been solved. The main features of the scheme are shown on the map but you will need to find out how it operates.

2 From your research test this hypothesis:
The very productive farming of the Central Valley would not be possible without irrigation.

Farming and economic factors

Decisions about farming systems depend upon economic factors as well as physical factors. These include the size and nearness of the market, the customers who buy the farmers' output, and government agricultural policies.

Markets

The distance from a farm to its market has a strong influence on what the farmer decides to produce. It leads to the kind of land use pattern around urban areas in Western Europe shown by fig. 9.25. Near the urban areas, market gardens produce fruit and vegetables, and dairy farms producing fresh milk are often found. Further away from the market, farmers often specialise in arable farming and livestock rearing. Why should this be so? Look at fig. 9.24.

Fig. 9.24 *The profits obtained from 4 types of farming at various distances from the centre of a city*

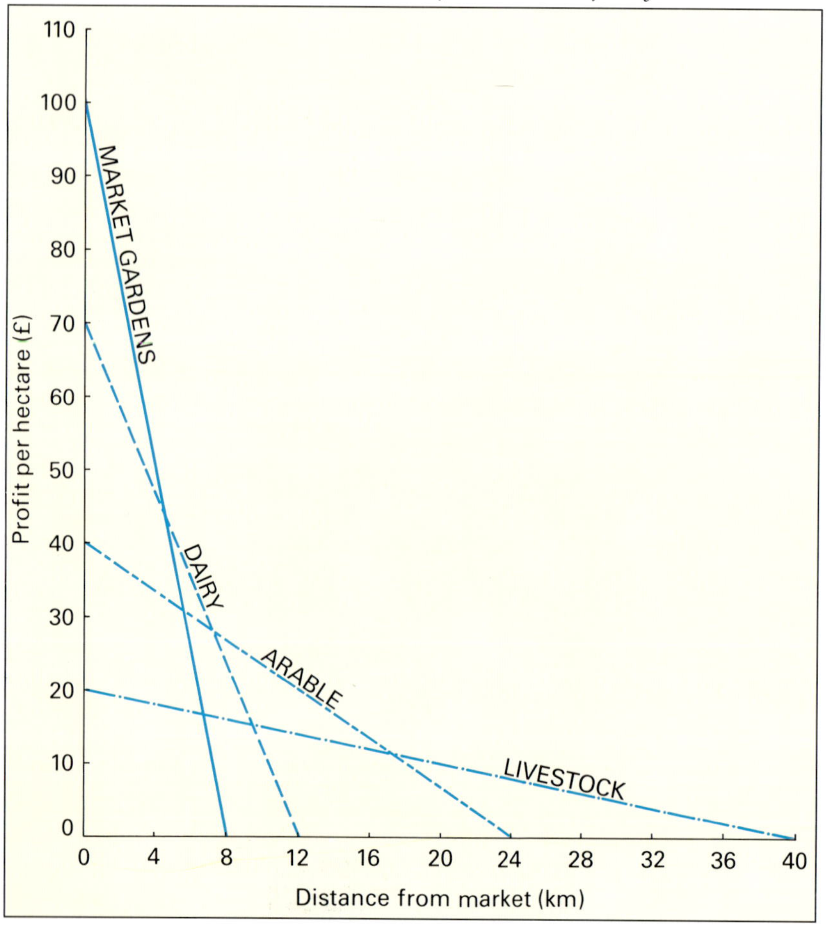

Fig. 9.25 *Pattern of farmland use round a city*

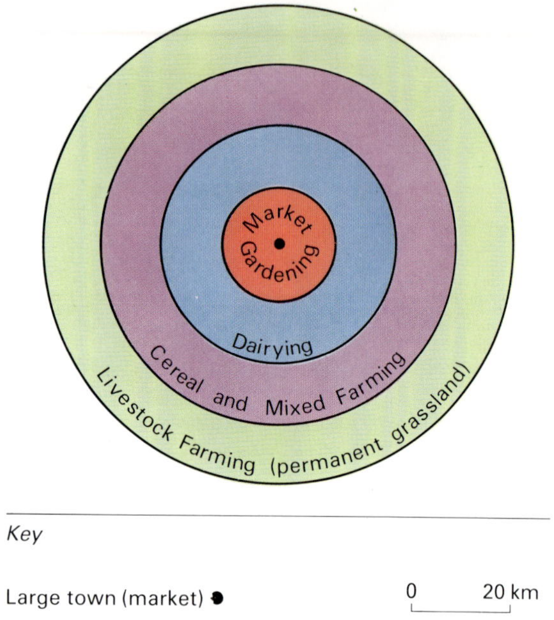

Market gardening and dairy farming are examples of intensive farming. They use land with a high value near and in urban areas (up to 8 km from the centre on fig. 9.25). Vegetables and milk are bulky perishable goods and rapid, low cost transport is required. Market gardens and dairy farms are usually very accessible using major roads and railways to the large towns and cities. At about 8 km from the city centre, on fig. 9.25, there is a change from dairy farms to wheat fields. This is because arable and livestock farming become more profitable away from urban areas. The lower land values enable more extensive farms to compete. Wheat and beef are less perishable products, so speed of transport to market is less important. The high transport costs to market faced by beef farmers can be covered by the higher prices that meat fetches.

Land use, transport and distance to market are closely linked. They help to explain how patterns of land use change with scale. Figure 9.26 shows how it can work at the local scale. In West African villages the intensity of land use decreases with distance from the village. A similar pattern can be seen at the national scale in Uruguay, fig. 9.27. The map shows market gardening around Montevideo where approximately 39 per cent of Uruguay's

Fig. 9.26 *Farmland around a village in Nigeria*

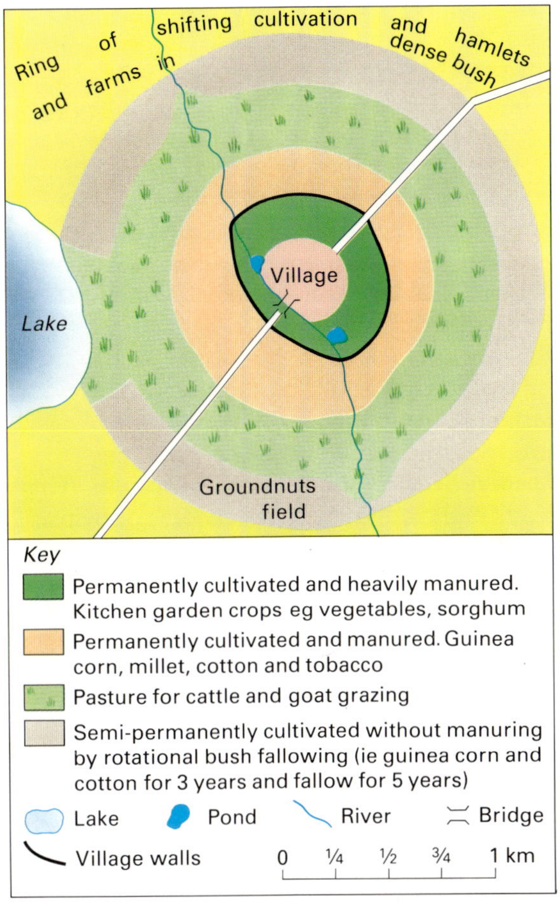

population live. Dairying followed by cereals or stock raising appear at greater distances from the city.

Because there are many factors influencing the farmer's decision, patterns vary in time and space. Transport improvements change patterns. One effect of modern transport, for example, is to move the boundaries of the various zones further away from the market. Figure 9.28 shows that the market may be a great distance from the farmland.

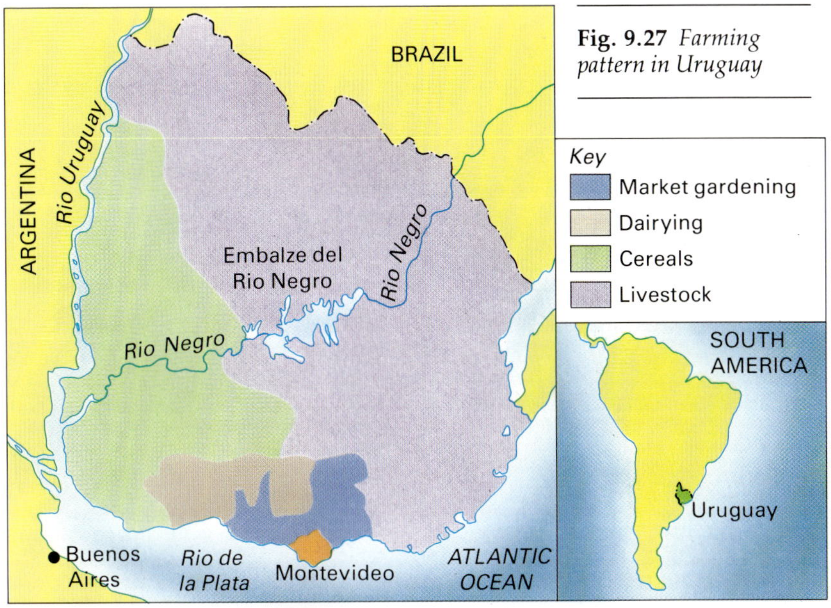

Fig. 9.27 *Farming pattern in Uruguay*

Fig. 9.28 *A selection of exotic fruits, imported from Africa and other countries, worldwide*

Government policies

Governments of many countries give help and support to farming. This can influence farmers' decisions. Without government intervention farmers are never sure of how much money they will make. If, for example, a farmer produces more milk than shops need, the price would probably drop. If not enough milk was produced, there would be a shortage in the shops and the price would rise. As a result, prices can go up and down from time to time.

Fig. 9.29 *Food mountains in the European Community*

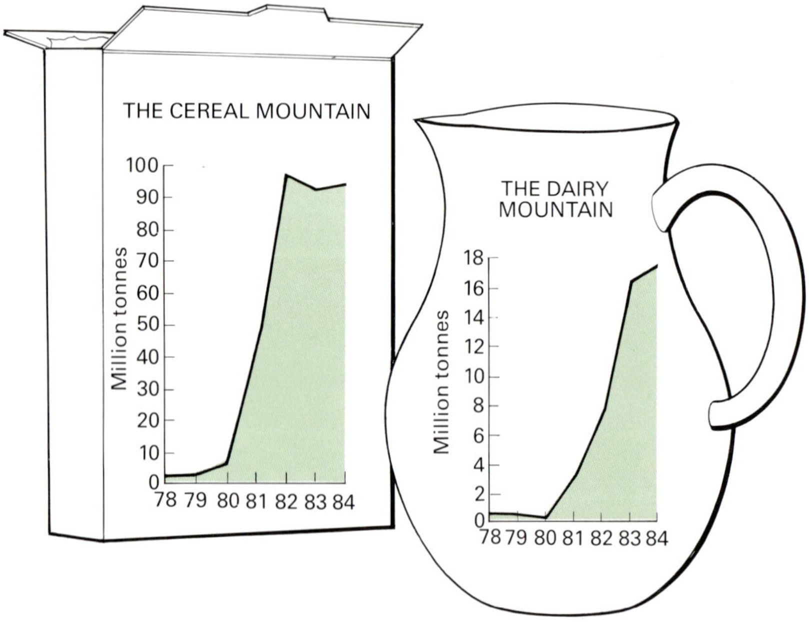

European Economic Community

The EEC countries, including Britain, have a Common Agricultural Policy, developed to help their farming industries. This policy fixed the price of farm produce regardless of whether there was too much or too little. It aimed to guarantee farmers a good price, a stable amount of money each year, and to keep prices for shoppers stable. Problems have appeared because European farms using modern technology are very efficient. They have been able to increase production too much. All the over-production or surpluses that are not needed in the shops, are bought up by the European Community so that farmers can get their money. Buying up produce that cannot be sold encourages farmers to carry on producing surpluses. This leads to the build up of huge stores of crops,

Fig. 9.30 *The European Community had enough grain in store to feed Britain for a year (1987)*

Activities

1 Many farmers who have land near urban areas carry out market gardening but there is no guarantee that the land will be physically suitable for this use. Discuss in your groups what each of the following mean for farmers:
a) Infertile soil b) Waterlogged soil. c) Aridity (lack of precipitation)
d) Frost. e) Wind.

2 Each class group should use a separate farm plan to test the following hypothesis: The intensity of farming drops with distance from the farmhouse. Write a report about your findings.

3 Carry out a brainstorm (see Activity 2.2) to identify the main features of the Common Agricultural Policy of the EEC. In three separate groups, discuss the following:
a) The need for large food stocks.
b) The policy of being generous to farmers.
c) Can food mountains be removed?
Each group should report its findings to the whole class and then, write individually, a paragraph or make a list to summarise the class' attitudes.

meat and milk ('butter mountains, grain mountains, beef mountains and wine lakes') which the Community cannot sell (see figs. 9.29 and 9.30).

Food gluts which are still produced today are very expensive to store. In the case of milk, storage was costing so much that dairy farmers were given a top limit which they could produce (known as a *quota*). Anyone going over the quota would be fined. Milk production did fall but not by as much as was hoped. Keeping to the limits can make some marginal farms bankrupt. This political decision, in 1984, caused some farms in Britain to close down and others to change what they produced.

The Common Agricultural Policy also provides for loans and grants of money to be given to some farmers to enable them to buy new equipment, to encourage them to improve their land or to grow certain crops. The many fields of yellow oil-seed rape seen in Britain today are largely the result of the financial subsidies which that crop has attracted.

Farming in Nigeria

As well as changing over time, government agricultural policies vary from country to country. The Nigerian Government has agricultural policies which are aimed at increasing food production and making the country self-sufficient. The government:

- sets guaranteed minimum prices for certain products hoping that this will get farmers to produce more
- gives subsidies to farmers to pay for human inputs such as fertiliser, pesticide, machinery and improved seeds
- offers financial help to farmers of certain crops eg rice.

Extending the area of farmland and reducing the number of subsistence farmers are the main aims of these policies. It is often the case that economic factors such as these have most influence in the farmer's decision about a farming system.

Fig. 9.31 *Modern farming in Nigeria*

Two farms in developed countries

Decision-making by farmers produces patterns on a land-use map, since farmers in the same area usually come to similar decisions about what it is best to produce. Patterns occur at different scales. National patterns for Britain and Nigeria are shown in figs 9.19 (map A) and 9.20. A smaller scale for Nottinghamshire is shown in fig. 9.32.

Fig. 9.32 *Farming pattern of Nottinghamshire*

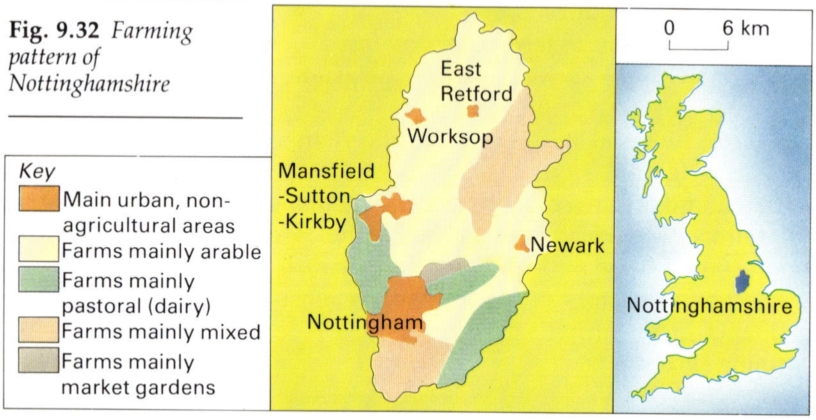

Fig. 9.33 *Barrow farm, Nottinghamshire*

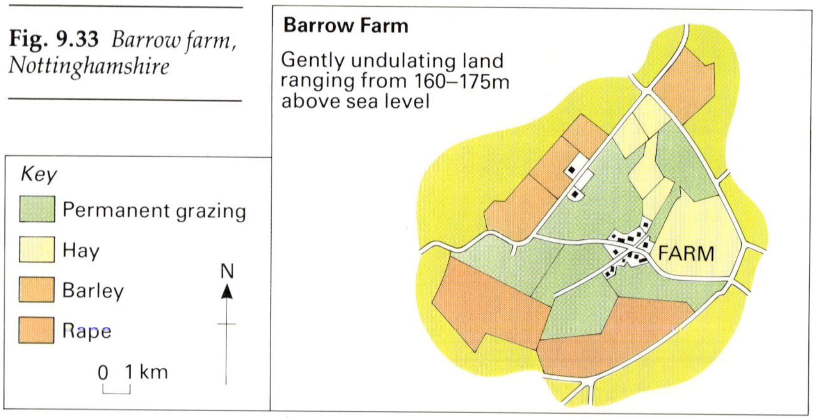

Barrow Farm, Teversal, Nottinghamshire

David Wentworth and his father rent and own a total of 59.3 hectares of land. This is shown in fig. 9.33. Their farm is mixed but there is a strong emphasis on dairying which provides 80 per cent of their income. The milking herd contains 90 Freisian cows, all of them bred on the farm. They are milked twice a day and give high yields. Eight cows can be milked at a time in the milking parlour. The milk is taken by pipe from the cow into bulk storage tanks. It is collected by a Derby Milk Marketing Board tanker each day. A cow produces milk for over a year after the birth of a calf. In order to

Fig. 9.34 *Barrow Farm, Nottinghamshire*

maintain continuous milk production, each cow is artificially inseminated at the AI centre each year with semen from a Freisian or Limousin bull. During the seven or eight years that the cow remains in the herd, it will produce a calf once per year on average. Each year, around one hundred calves are born. About twelve heifers (female calves) join the milking herd when they are about fifteen months old as replacements for older cows. Calves unwanted by the farm eg bull calves, are sold at market in Matlock at about the same age. The herd grazes the pastures from April to October and is kept inside in winter.

The winter feed is silage (hay) made from grass and barley mixed with concentrates (often dried cattle feed bought by the farmer). A large quantity of straw is needed for bedding the animals indoor. Most comes from the barley harvest of a nearby farm. The main purpose of having their own arable land is to provide winter fodder although the rape crop is sold at market in Liverpool. Each year some of the grassland is ploughed up and re-seeded. This enables manure to be added to the soil and weeds to be controlled without much chemical spraying. A four-year crop rotation of three years barley and one of rape, is used on fields. Barley takes a lot of nutrients out of the soil while rape helps to restore its fertility.

The farm is well-equipped with four tractors, a combine, a forager and a mower for cutting and collecting grass. There is also a baler, a 'muck' spreader and various attachments for the tractors for ploughing, lifting and carting. The farm employs two full-time workers.

Bealby farm, near Regina, Canada

Jack Bealby and his two sons farm 194 hectares of land which they own, outside Regina. This is shown in fig. 9.35. This is below the average size for a farm in the Prairie Provinces. It is basically a cereal farm, but like many other Prairie farmers they have diversified their farming recently. They have moved away from monoculture (farming one product). The Canadian Department of Agriculture has been encouraging farmers to grow crops other than wheat because production has continued to grow faster than demand. Jack Bealby has reduced the total dependence his father once had on wheat. Now oats and barley are also grown as winter feed grains. This is partly for their own small herd of 30 Friesian cows, but mainly for sale to cattle ranches in southern Alberta. The Friesians graze on the pasture and cereal stubble after the harvest, between April and October. They are stall-fed during the winter. Flax is grown for its oilseed and sold in Edmonton.

Hard red wheat remains the chief cereal crop and is grown on two extensive hedgeless 'prairies' to the south of the farm buildings (fig. 9.36). It is called spring wheat because it is sown in spring, following the April/May thaw of the frozen winter ground. Growth is rapid in the rising temperatures and moist soil of early summer. The hot, dry summers ripen the crop which is harvested from late-August to mid-September. Two extra workers are taken on for harvesting and ploughing. Five combines are used. The grain is of high quality and exported. Ploughing and fertilising takes place after the harvest at a time when the first winter frosts appear.

The other great farming change since his father's days is mechanisation. The farm now uses very advanced technology and the very latest in scientific farming such as computer analysis of soil fertility and crop spraying by helicopter.

Fig. 9.35 *Bealby Farm, near Regina, Saskatchewan*

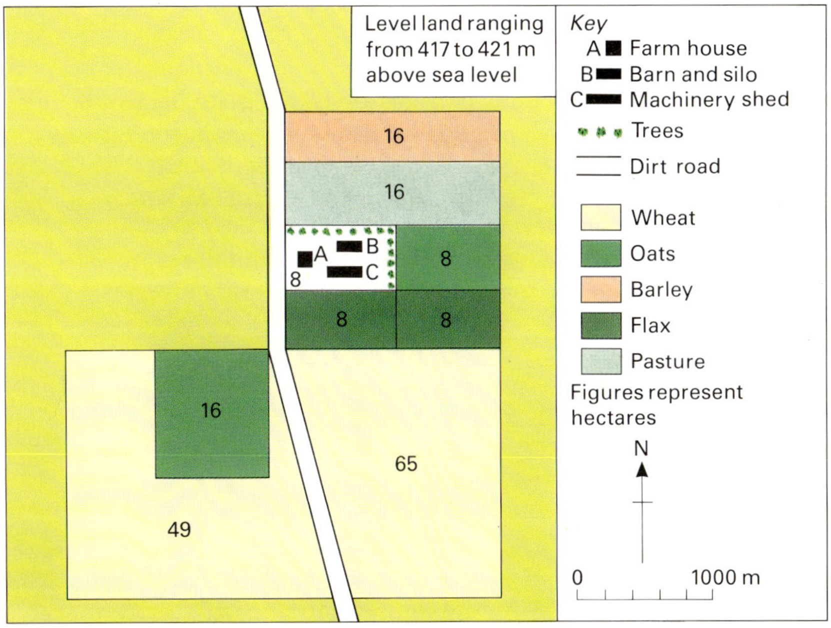

Fig. 9.36 *Harvesting on the Canadian Prairies*

Activities

1 Copy and complete the following table. One difference has been entered for you

Similarities between the two farms	Differences between the two farms
	Dairy farm – labour intensive Cereal farm not

2 Another way to compare these two farms is to draw a calendar of farming activities for the year for them.

Farming issues in developed countries

Many changes are taking place in farming in developed countries. The main changes are:
- a drop in the area of farmland
- a drop in the number of workers in agriculture
- a rise in the area of land per worker
- an increase in the output of food from farms as a result of rising yields per hectare and per person
- the increased use of farm mechanisation
- the increased use of fertilisers and pesticides
- an increase in the size (area) of farms
- increased specialisation on farms
- new methods such as factory farming and 'pick-your-own' farms (figs 9.37 and 9.38).
- more contract farming between farmers and food processors
- fewer strict crop rotations with the exception of 'break' crops such as peas being grown
- a switch in land use from rough grazing to permanent pasture and from grassland generally towards arable.

Fig. 9.37 *Viner's Pick-your-own farm, Kent*

Fig. 9.38 *Brockbanks Pick-your-own farm, Essex*

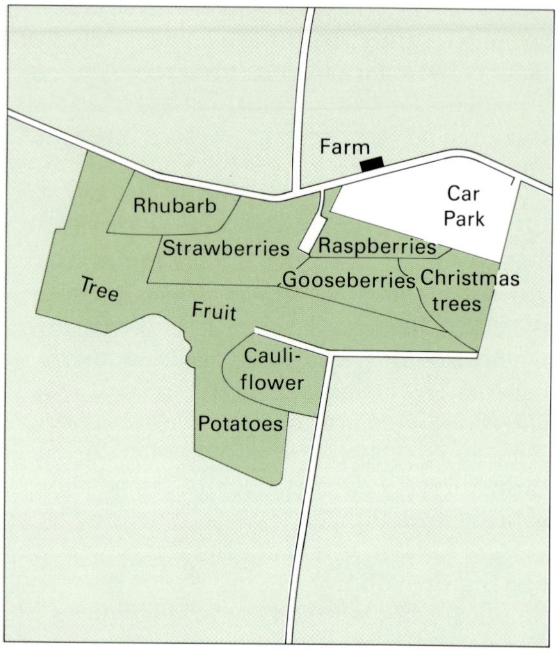

These changes cause conflict between farmers and people. Study fig. 9.39 carefully. The development of factory farming and the increased use of chemical fertilisers and pesticides can cause arguments between people other than farmers themselves.

New farming activities and some of the modern changes in farming strongly affect environmental conditions. For thousands of years farming has shaped our landscape. Today there is a growing concern over the effects which modern farming is having on the rural landscape, people's environment generally and wildlife. Some of the main areas of concern are:

1. Hundreds of millions of pound's worth of chemical fertilisers and pesticides are spread over Britain's farmland each year (look at figs 9.41 to 9.43). This is believed by many to harm the health of farm workers and the general public, and to damage wildlife. But a return to more traditional farming using manure, may lead to lower output and higher food prices.

2. The removal by farmers of the hedges which enclose their fields is sometimes known as *prairification*. It may be to the advantage of the farmer to have slightly more farmland and bigger fields so that machinery can be used

We can manage with just the family and get a new YTS trainee each year.

I need high yields – everybody uses fertilisers and pesticides now.

I'm not in debt to the bank. While the farm pays its way, I have no worries.

I need bigger machinery to increase my yields. I need large fields for my big new combines.

I like a mixed farm – there's always a good income coming in and I can keep my work force busy all year.

Muck spreading is my answer. I don't like all these chemicals on the land.

With these high profits, Dad, paying off the half million bank loan is no real problem. EEC subsidies make this type of land use our only real future. You grow whatever brings the biggest profit.

You have to make changes. You can't be sentimental and worry about the cows and such like.

I like to see a nice hedgerow. They shelter the fields and animals. Those cows in the fields are just like family friends.

Fig. 9.39 *Farmers' changing attitudes to farming in Britain today*

more easily. However there is a greater risk of soil erosion. Wire fences appear in the place of hedges and more wildlife is destroyed.

3. Farming and leisure interests can cause conflict in National Parks. Some hill sheep farmers are ploughing and fencing moorland to grow root crops and more productive grass for extra animals. In National Parks such as Exmoor, there is a conflict between farmers who live and work on the hills all the year round and people who visit for leisure purposes. Traditional sheep farming may give visitors access to the moors, but it does not allow the farmer to increase output.

4. Smoke from stubble burning can be a hazard for road users. Some rivers have become heavily polluted with farmyard slurry and silage run-off from sheep and cattle farms.

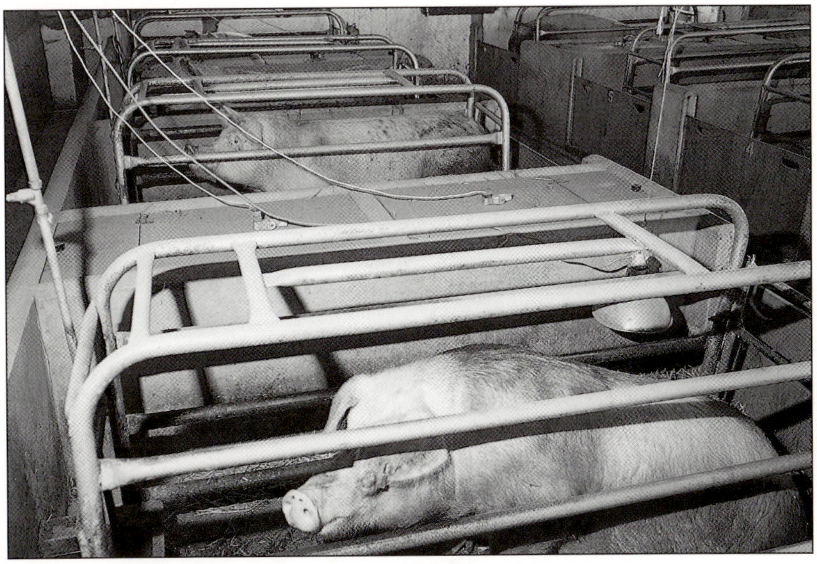

Fig. 9.40 *Factory farming of pigs*

Activities

SHOULD WE FACTORY FARM ANIMALS?

YES

A factory farmer might see nothing wrong and say:

- it is the best way to achieve a reliable supply of eggs, poultry and pig meat at reasonable prices.
- animals are kept in generally humane conditions which are subject to a strict code of conduct.

NO

An animal rights campaigner might believe that:

- keeping and breeding animals in cages is against their natural behaviour.
- animals have a right to be 'happy' and their welfare considered.

Can you add any more points to either side of the argument? What other organised groups might wish to take part in this argument?

There has been a steady loss of farmland to urban, industrial and recreational uses in recent years. There is competition for land and farming has to compete with other uses. The 'food mountains' in Europe and the poorer prospects for some farmers, have encouraged the use of some farmland for housing, forestry, recreational facilities and food processing plants during the 1980s. A recent government plan in Britain to free unneeded farmland for these sorts of developments has led to conflict between farmers and 'country-lovers'.

Fig. 9.41 *Pesticide spraying. Discuss the advantages and disadvantages of using pesticides?*

Fig. 9.42 *Pollution from fertilisers*

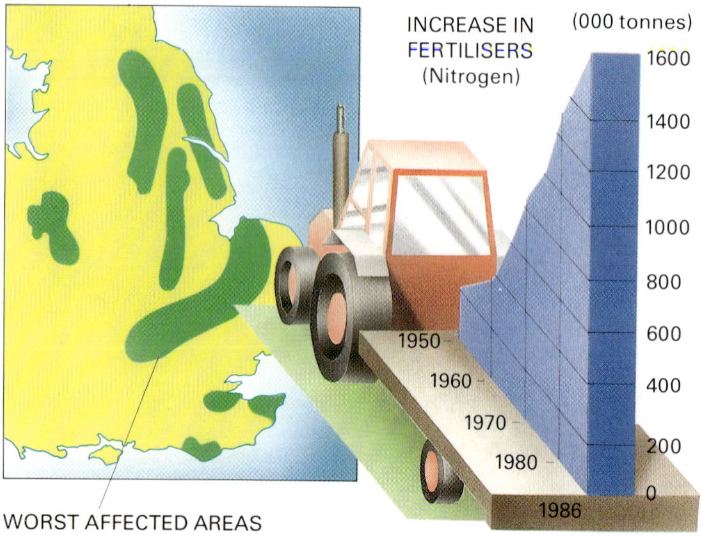

Fig. 9.43 *Extract from Ripon Gazette 20/2/87*

£440,000 plan after water alert

A £440,000 scheme to tackle high nitrate levels from fertilisers in water supplies in the Baldersby area, west of Thirsk has been approved by Yorkshire Water after it was found chemical levels failed to meet EEC standards.

High nitrate levels in water endanger babies by lowering the amount of oxygen in their blood (the 'blue baby syndrome').

As a precautionary measure, Yorkshire Water already provides a special household delivery service of low nitrate water to home where there is a nursing mother with babies under six months old.

Fig. 9.44 *Countryside at risk*

COUNTRYSIDE AT RISK

More farmland in Walton looks set to be scrapped to make way for housing.

Two fields between Somersby Avenue and Somersall Park are next in line for residential development if council planners give the go-ahead.

An application to build on the land has been made by William Davis – based at Forest Field, Forest Road, Loughborough, Leicestershire.

The plans are on view at the Town Hall, Chesterfield.

Activities

Group role play. Two members of the group should be young farmers trying to convince others of the need to change to new farming practices. Two others should be older farmers trying to defend traditional farming practices. Two more members should represent the rest of the family who are not on either side at first but are prepared to listen to both sides.

After discussion, the whole group should vote whether to change or not. Everyone should write a summary of the main points argued and how a conclusion was reached.

Wet rice farming in the Ganges Delta

Villages in the Ganges Delta of India depend upon subsistence rice farming. Rice is the staple food of most of South east Asia. The rice is grown in small plots in widely scattered fields, covered by water during the growing season. It is a type of farming very well adapted to local conditions and closely related to climate and population:

- the growing season is timed to benefit from the high rainfall of the monsoon (fig. 9.46). Level relief, perhaps achieved by cutting terraces into sloping land is important for flooding the fields.
- the farming is very labour-intensive in this area of high population densities. The land is intensively farmed using a large labour force. Productivity levels per worker are low and largely subsistent. Capital inputs are generally small.

The system, though subsistent, does generally meet the large demand for food.

Fig. 9.45 *Rice growing in the Ganges Delta, India*

More progressive farmers by using fertilisers, higher-yielding varieties or buying the land they farm have been able to raise their output and become commercial farmers. Where IR8 rice has been grown, higher yields and two crops a year (multiple cropping) have been achieved.

Fig. 9.46 *Climate of the Ganges Delta, NE India*

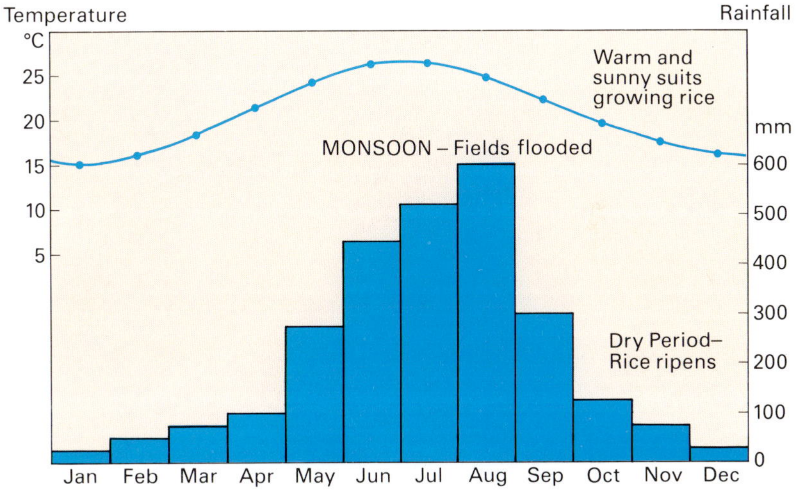

Jan to April	May	June–July	Aug–Nov	Dec
Quiet period. Weeding, ploughing and manuring. May be some vegetables grown (intercropping)	Sowing in nursery seed beds	Seedlings trans-planted to paddy fields	Growing season 160 days. Hand weeding continues	Harvested by hand. Bundling, drying and threshing

Activities

Your group has been given the task of advising the leaders of a village in the Ganges Delta of India about how to improve its wet rice output. You are aiming at an increase in commercial production. You should consider these points:

a) Forming farmers' cooperative, sharing costs and work.
b) Introducing new high-yield varieties of seed.
c) Using more fertilisers and pesticides to increase yields.
d) Using more mechanised forms of farming to make better use of land.
e) Nationalising the land and working it as a collective farm or commune.

After your discussions, write a report for the village leaders.

Farming issues in developing countries

For a large proportion of the population of many developing countries, farming is the main form of livelihood. This is true despite recent drifts of people to the towns. Low production occurs on many farms and there are low yields per hectare. Food shortage is a big issue in many developing countries. Subsistence farmers with low living standards make up much of the large rural population.

Fig. 9.47 *Low output farms*

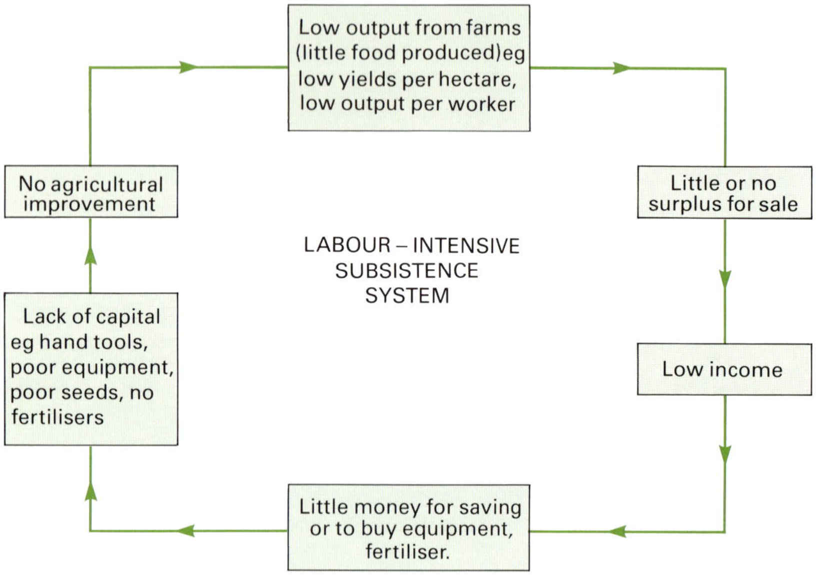

There is great variety of farming systems throughout Africa. Most of them face these problems:

1. Recent population increases have increased the demand for food and put extra pressure on farming. 1986 was the first year in Africa since 1970 that food production rose faster than population.
2. Land ownership is often a barrier to improving food production. Many farmers are tenants working small plots of land which they do not own.
3. Farming tends to be extensive and labour-intensive, and not capital-intensive. Investment in machinery, fertilisers and pesticides is generally low.
4. The natural environment is a constraint for farmers in some areas. Drought, soil erosion, floods and the threat of locusts and other insects create difficulties for farmers in much of Africa.

The low production and poverty amongst farmers is the result of a vicious circle. Figure 9.47 helps to explain some of the difficulties farmers face. Breaking this circle of poverty has proved difficult. Figure 9.48 shows how farming improvements can increase output and provide the farmer with more money. This money can then be used to finance the farm improvements.

Fig. 9.48 *Model of agricultural development in developing countries*

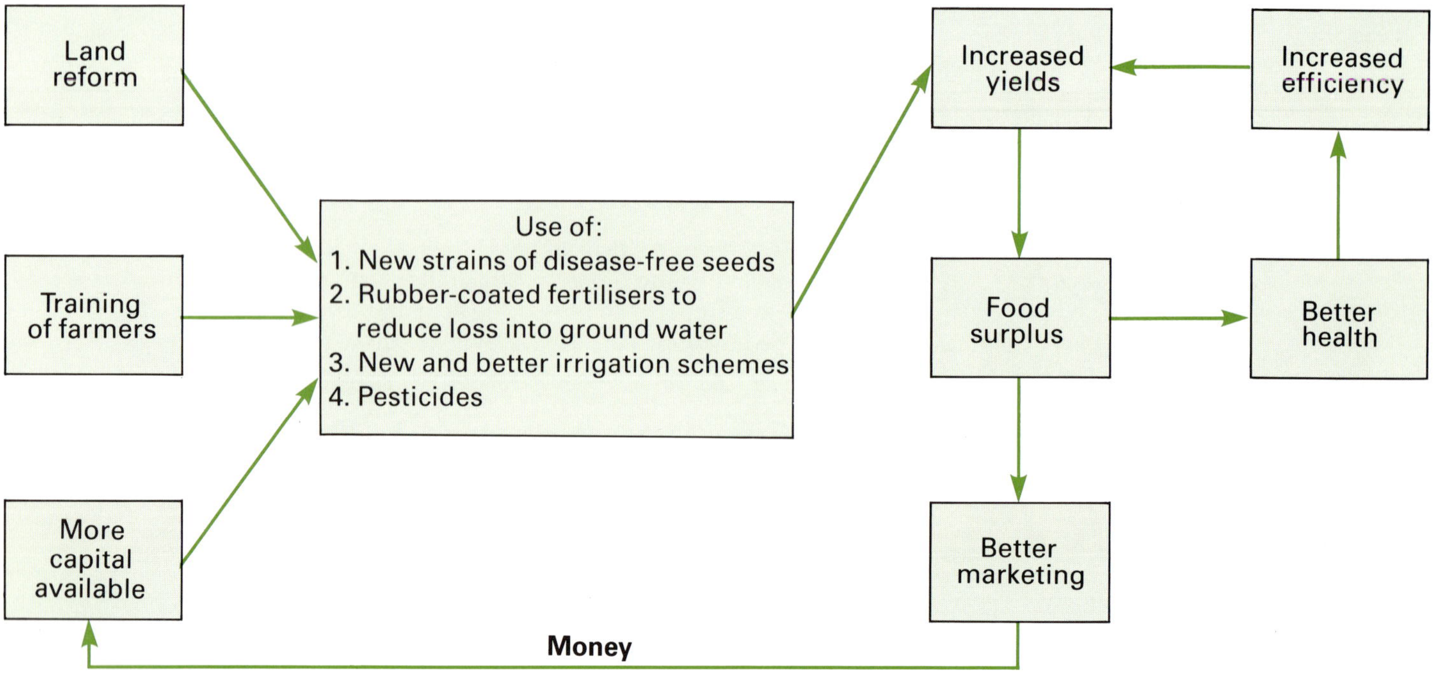

The 'Green Revolution'

This term has been used since the 1960s to describe the attempts to improve farming and to help to solve the food problems of developing countries. New, fast-growing and high-yielding crops, such as IR8 rice, have been developed. India, especially the state of Punjab, is a good example of the success of the 'green revolution'. Over the past twenty years crop yields per hectare and grain production have grown faster than population. The use of fertilisers and irrigation has greatly increased. Common problems in the Punjab are:

- farmers need to be shown new methods
- high-yielding varieties need the correct dose of expensive chemical fertilisers and weedkiller
- technical equipment such as irrigation pumps and cultivators has high maintenance and running costs.

Many areas could produce more food if there was greater investment in fertilisers, pesticides, technical equipment and modern management methods. Crops such as coffee and strawberries grow well in places, with the aid of these inputs, and they are exported. More financial aid for farming and food markets which give better prices to farmers would help to increase the supply of food for the local population.

Some of the traditional farming methods are well adapted to local conditions. They help to increase output. Others are less helpful. More careful management of an area's resources is required in places. For example, the Polnoroeste project in the state of Rondonia in north west Brazil was an unsuccessful land reform scheme. Farmers in the overcrowded south of Brazil were offered the chance of owning their own land at no charge.

New farmland was to be brought into use by clearing the rainforest, where traditionally the 'slash and burn' method of shifting cultivation was used. It was hoped that the deforested land would be used for cash cropping but the soil was found to be low in fertility and unsuitable. The environment has been damaged by forest clearance. Some erosion has occurred and species have been threatened with extinction. Despite a large input of money, time and effort , little has been achieved except a small increase in output, mainly by cattle farming. Animals overgrazing grasslands is an environmental danger which occurs in many countries. In Botswana, in southern Africa, Livestock III was a plan to increase beef production for export by 50 per cent. However overgrazing has had disastrous effects on the grasslands by causing soil erosion.

10 MANUFACTURING

Classifying manufacturing industries

Manufacturing industries, which make up the secondary employment sector, can be classified. This is done by using the International Standard Industrial Classification (ISIC). It recognises the fifteen main types of manufacturing industry which are shown in fig. 10.1. In each of these industries raw materials are processed into finished goods to increase their value.

A simplified type of classification is shown in fig. 10.2. This gives the percentages of people employed in the various groups of industries in 1970 and 1985. The classification is based on the nature of the product or output. It provides an easy way to compare

Fig. 10.1 *International Standard Industrial Classification*

1 Food, drink and tobacco.
2 Coal and petroleum products.
3 Chemicals and allied industries.
4 Metal manufacture.
5 Mechanical engineering.
6 Instrument engineering.
7 Electrical engineering.
8 Shipbuilding and marine engineering.
9 Vehicles.
10 Textiles.
11 Leather.
12 Clothing and footwear.
13 Bricks, pottery, glass and cement.
14 Timber and furniture.
15 Paper, printing and publishing.

Fig. 10.2 *Percentage of total labour force in various manufacturing industries in the UK 1970–85*

Manufacturing classification	*1970*	*1985*
Food, Drink and Tobacco	3.9%	2.8%
Coal, Petrol and Chemicals	2.4%	1.9%
Metal Manufacture	2.5%	1.3%
Engineering	16.9%	12.2%
Textiles, Leather and Clothing	5.3%	2.8%

Fig. 10.3 *Some industrial differences between Nigeria and the UK*

Group	*Nigeria*		*United Kingdom*	
	No of employees ('000s)	*Percentage of employees in manufacturing*	*No of employees ('000s)*	*Percentage of employees in manufacturing*
1 Food, drink and tobacco	60	28	761	10.5
2 Wood, furniture, paper, printing	32	15	801	11
3 Textiles, clothing and shoes	54	25	933	13
4 Chemicals	19	9	588	8
5 Rubber products	11	5	116	1.6
6 Iron and steel	0.3	0.1	386	5.3
7 Metal products	16	7.5	692	9.5
8 Machinery	0.2	0.1	873	12
9 Motor vehicles	2	1	472	6.5
10 Other transport equipment	1.5	0.7	441	6
11 Electrical goods	4	2	680	9
12 Other manufacturing industries	14	6.6	562	7.6
Total manufacturing workforce	214	100	7305	100

manufacturing industries of different countries. In fig. 10.3, the manufacturing industries of the United Kingdom have been compared to those in Nigeria. It is valuable to do this because manufacturing industry is a major contributor to economic development. Both the quantity and the kind of manufacturing tend to vary between developed and developing countries.

Manufacturing is often classified as heavy or light industry. Some industries such as iron and steel make large or bulky products. These are referred to as heavy industries. Others, because they involve the manufacture of smaller products such as household goods are called light industries.

Fig. 10.4 *Industries classified according to location*

Group	*Characteristic*
Raw Material-orientated	Located near the source of the raw materials they process
Market-orientated	Located near their consumers
Footloose	Free from the restriction of materials and markets and not tied to any location

Activities

1 Study fig. 10.1 in your discussion groups. For each of the 15 main types of manufacturing in the International Standard Industrial Classification decide whether it is heavy or light industry.
2 Use fig. 10.2. Discuss the changes in manufacturing employment in the UK between 1970 and 1985.
3 Discuss the meaning of a) raw material orientated industry; b) market orientated industry and c) footloose industry. Which one(s) best fit each industry in fig. 10.1?
4 Use fig. 10.3. What are the main differences between the industries of Nigeria and the UK?

All manufacturing industry, whether heavy or light, shows the following organisational structure;

TYPE OF MANUFACTURING INDUSTRY – (the large-scale of manufacturing)
↓
Firm – (the company is the basic organising unit)
↓
Plant (or factory) – (the small-scale of manufacturing)

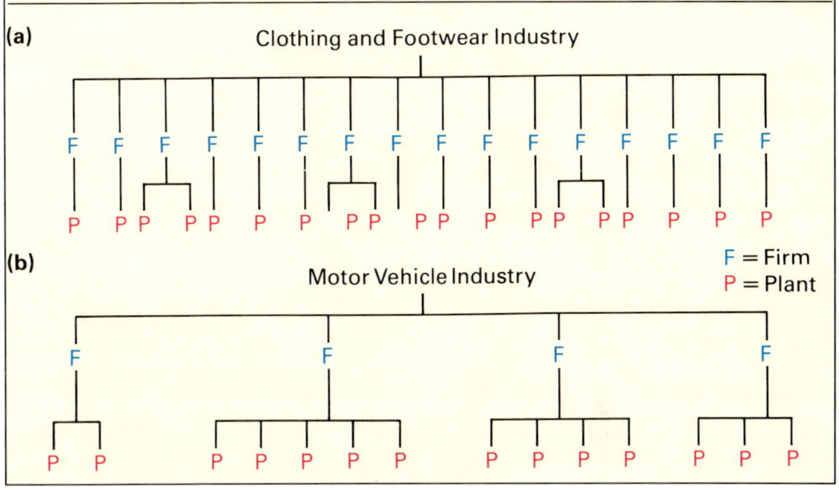

Fig. 10.5 *Simplified model of the clothing and footwear and vehicle industries*

Some industries are dominated by a few large firms while others have many small firms. Figure 10.5 compares clothing and footwear industries to the vehicle industry. Figure 10.5(a) shows that many small, single-plant firms are common in the clothing and footwear industry. The factories are themselves often small. However, fig. 10.5(b) shows that large multi-plant firms with large factories exist in the vehicle industry. Mass production is used to make a large number of products. This is achieved through labour specialisation and the use of machinery. Today, manufacturing industry is increasingly dependent upon high capital investment. These are highly technological firms employing fewer and fewer workers.

There has been a growth of multi-industry firms. This is where a firm makes many products and has plants in more than one industry. For example, Unilever consists of over 8000 firms around the world making products such as food and drink, chemical products, paper, plastics and detergents. There are many other differences between industries which could be used to classify them. These include the size of factories, the scale of production, the number of workers employed, the methods of production and the choice of location (look at fig. 10.4).

Manufacturing systems

Manufacturing industry can be studied as a system

Each firm or plant/factory depends upon three elements in a system.
1. Inputs are things which are put into production such as raw materials.
2. Processes are the way in which articles are produced.
3. Outputs are things which are produced, including by-products and waste. The idea of a system is that all these elements involved in the production of goods are linked together. It is these interrelationships or links which make it a system, so that a change in one part of the system will have effects on another. For example, if the demand for a product rises, it will be necessary to increase inputs. This will allow output to rise to meet the increased demand. Equally, if the supply of inputs falls, the output is also likely to fall in terms of finished goods or financial gain to the factory owner. You only get out what you put in! As one plant may be linked with other plants by the transfer of materials and products, a change in one system may influence other systems.

Figure 10.6 shows the manufacturing system as a flow diagram with the inputs, processes and outputs arranged in sequence, that is, in the order in which they occur. All production requires the input of resources, called factors of production of which there are four groups:

1. *Land*. This includes all the free gifts of nature, the land and soil itself, the minerals in the earth's crust, and all the other natural resources around.
2. *Labour*. All the physical and mental characteristics of working people, ranging from enterprise and initiative to manual work, are referred to as labour.
3. *Capital*. Tools, machinery and all other human aids used to produce goods and services for consumers are called capital.
4. *Knowledge*. This fourth type of resource is a special type of capital, human capital. It includes all the information and understanding that people have accumulated over the years which is stored in books, people's heads, etc. and is available to producers.

Manufacturing uses various combinations of these factors to produce goods. Many modern industries have increased output by increasing the input of capital and knowledge.

Some systems' diagrams are quite complicated. Look at fig. 10.7 which shows a systems flow diagram with throughputs, stores, decision-making and feedback. The diagram also gives examples of the kinds of decisions that have to be made at various points. Inputs can be split into throughputs and stores. Throughputs are those inputs whose supply can be varied, such as the amounts and quality of raw materials like coal, iron ore and fuel. Stores, on the other hand, are the fixed inputs like land, buildings and machinery whose supply does not generally change much. Figure 10.7 also shows the

Fig. 10.6 *Manufacturing system*

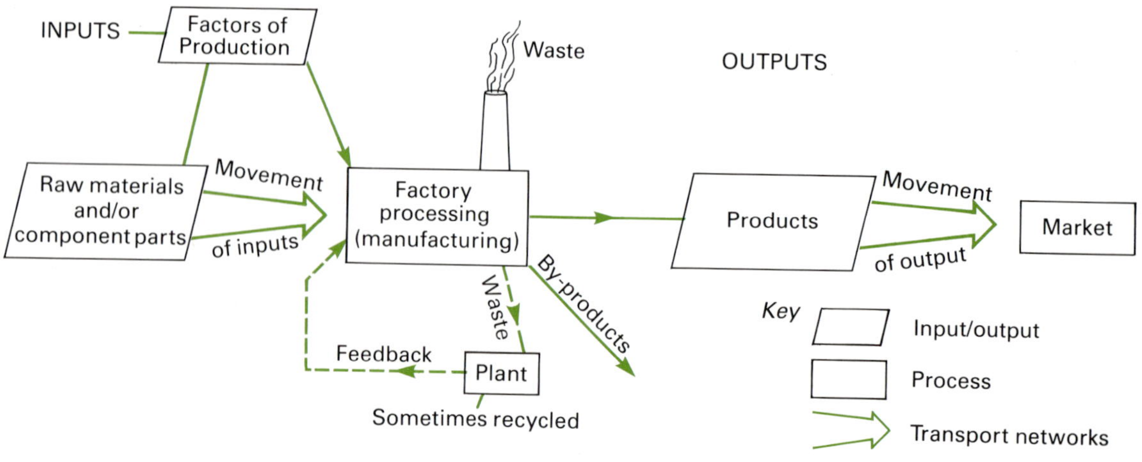

major decisions which are involved in the manufacturing process. For example, what combination of inputs should be used? How much of the money from selling the output should be ploughed back into the firm? It also introduces the idea of feedback, such as profits, which are ploughed back as inputs, eg new machinery.

The various stages in the manufacture of iron and steel are shown in a system flow diagram in fig 10.8. No decision-making points or feedback are included. This manufacturing increasingly takes place in large-scale, integrated steelworks on or near the coast where all the stages involved occur on the one site.

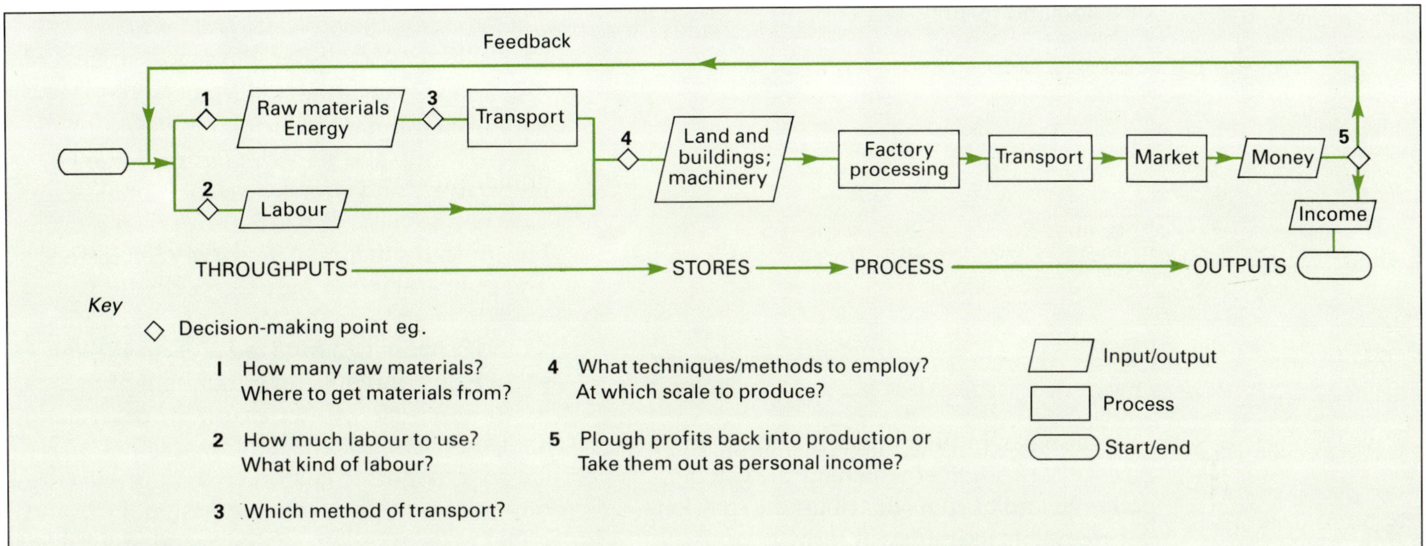

Fig. 10.7 *Manufacturing systems flow diagram showing feedback*

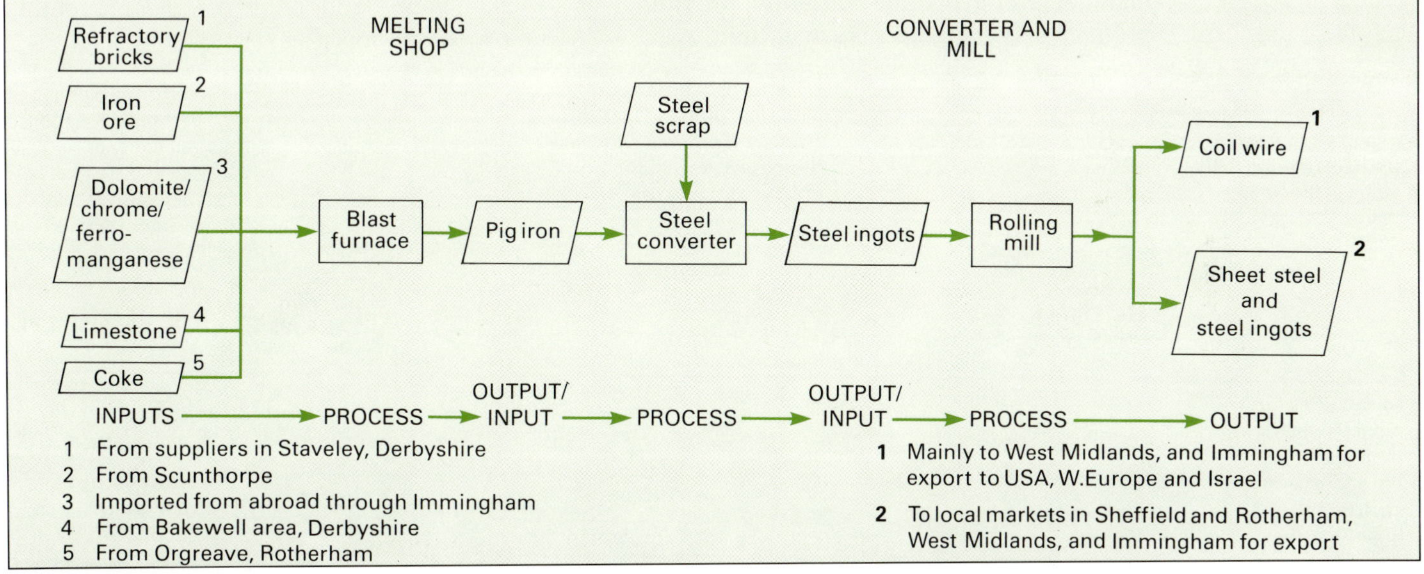

Fig. 10.8 *Systems flow diagram showing stages in iron and steel manufacture*

Activities

1 Use fig. 10.8 for an integrated steelworks. a) Why are pig iron and steel ingots shown both as an output and an input? b) Name two throughputs and two stores.

2 Draw a systems diagram to show the main inputs, processes and outputs for either a) a glassworks – main raw materials, sand, lime and soda; or b) a motor vehicle assembly plant – these plants assemble component parts such as car bodies, engine blocks, windows, steering wheels and so on. They also add oil and grease, do checks on cars and deliver completed cars to the market.

Locating manufacturing

Decision making

One of the major decisions that manufacturers have to take is where to locate a factory? This decision and its links with others is shown in fig. 10.9.

Fig. 10.9 *Manufacturing system and its three main decisions*

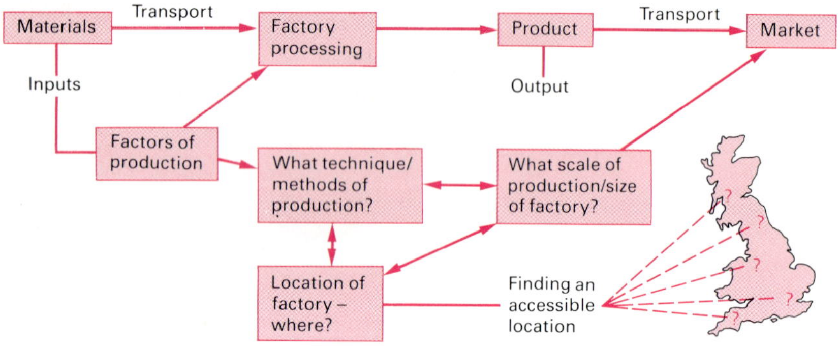

Locating an industry means finding an accessible position at which inputs can be gathered and outputs distributed to markets. An accessible location will allow a manufacturer to operate efficiently, providing profits with which there is satisfaction. A number of factors influences the location decision taken by a manufacturer (look at fig. 10.10).

Fig. 10.10 *Some factors influencing the location of manufacturing*

Decisions vary from industry to industry

The importance of each of these factors can vary from industry to industry. Figure 10.11 refers to pulp and paper mills and bakeries respectively and shows how locational factors vary between the two industries. The size of box indicates the importance of each factor. The pulp and paper industry is clearly attracted by raw materials. An ideal location would be close to a forested area and near a site which is suitable for generation of hydro-electricity. Bakeries, on the other hand, are generally market-orientated. Quick and cheap transport to customers is of prime importance in the location decision. Pulp and paper mills in Britain can be found around Fort William in Scotland. Large bakeries are found in towns and cities.

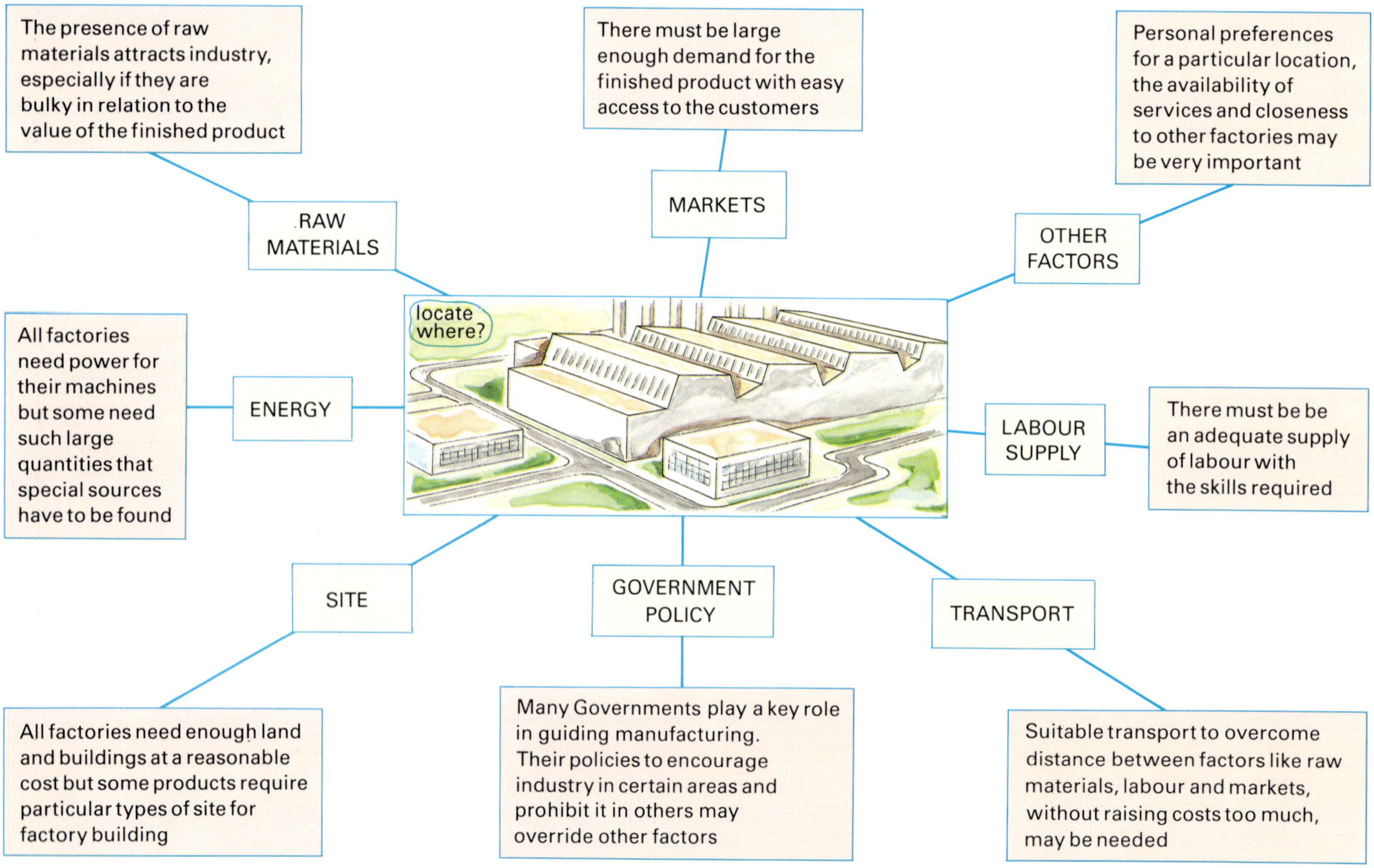

Decisions vary within industries

The importance of factors can vary within the same industry. Figure 10.12 and fig 10.13 show how the sites chosen for iron and steel making in Brazil and Japan vary. The major Brazilian plants are inland, close to the sources of iron ore and limestone in Minas Gerais (the so-called 'iron quadrilateral'). However, they are also not too far from the large markets in Sao Paulo and Rio de Janeiro. Usiminas in Minas Gerais is the largest producing plant in Latin America. The Japanese industry, on the other hand is mainly located on the coast. The Kawasaki works in fig. 10.13 is a good example. Japan has to import nearly all of the raw materials needed in the industry. So it is cheaper to use coastal sites.

Fig. 10.11 *Relative importance of five locating factors to two industries*

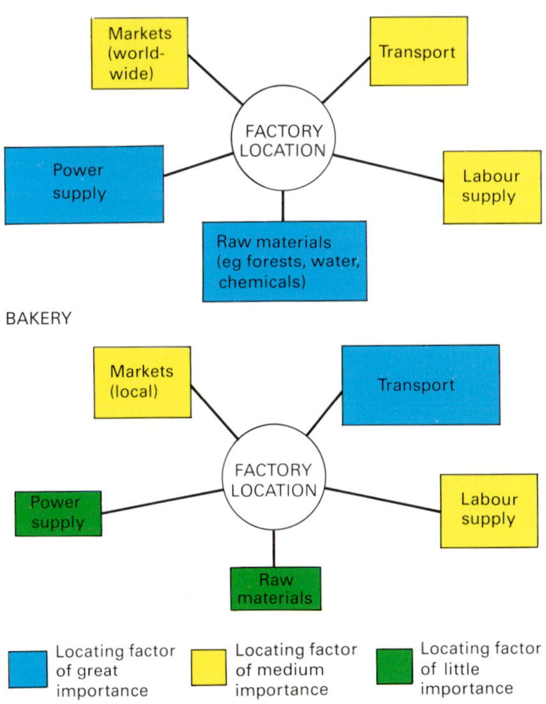

Decisions vary in time

The iron and steel industry in Britain was originally located inland near supplies of iron ore, like Corby, or on coalfields like Sheffield. When British ore supplies ran out and imports became more important, steel production was concentrated on coastal sites like Port Talbot and Redcar.

Fig. 10.12 *Brazilian iron and steel industry*

Key
- Main iron and steel plants
- Iron ore
- Coal

1 Volta Redonda
2 Cosipa
3 Usiminas
4 Belo Horizonte Group

Fig. 10.13 *Location of steelworks in Japan*

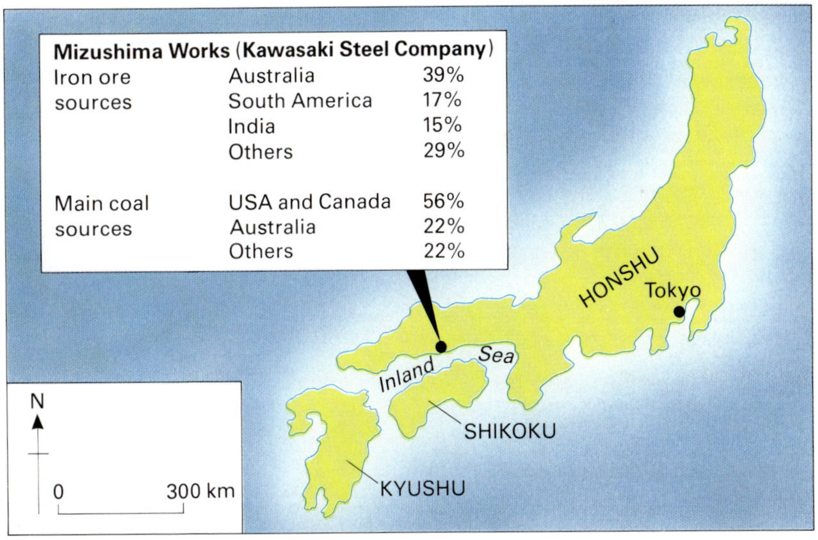

Activities

1 The location of factories is usually explained by the economic factors shown in fig. 10.10. Sometimes the personal preferences of the owners are the main influence. Carry out a group brainstorm to list these personal factors.

2 Some manufacturing industries employ male labour whereas others employ mainly female labour. Give an example of each of these kinds of industry. Suggest how labour requirements might affect the location chosen.

Concentrations of manufacturing

Localisation

Localisation is the concentration of firms in an area. Manufacturers concerned with similar types of work may come to similar decisions about where to locate their plants. They may, for example, consider closeness to those factories producing component materials an important locational factor. Manufacturing firms and similar types of manufacturing work often group together in certain areas, in ports, near raw materials and, increasingly today, in the main market regions close to customers. Manufacturers specialise in producing those goods and services for which they have either a comparative advantage (ie can produce better or cheaper than a competitor) or an absolute advantage (ie can produce better or cheaper than any other area). This concentration of firms and specialisation of areas is known as industrial agglomeration or localisation. It occurs at a variety of scales. Regional and national scales are shown in figs 10.14 and 10.15. There are often clear economic benefits to a firm when it locates in a manufacturing area close to a number of other firms. External economies of scale (reduced costs resulting from larger scale production) due to local concentration of firms encourage manufacturers to cluster together. External economies are of two main types:

1 *Linked process*. The production process might be divided up with individual plants specialising on a limited number of stages. There may be marketing links between firms such as the sharing of a lorry's load. Firms might 'sub-contract' work to others.

2 *The local infrastructure of services*. This includes availability of services such as water supply, banking, transport and of a pool of skilled labour.

Fig. 10.14 *Manufacturing in the regions of Brazil*

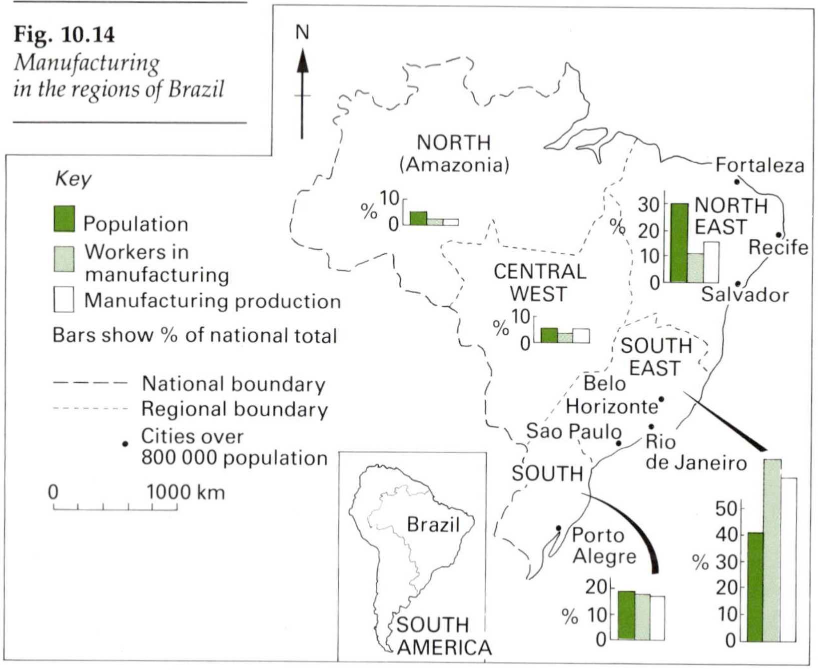

Fig. 10.15 *Location of Metal Box plants in England and Wales.*

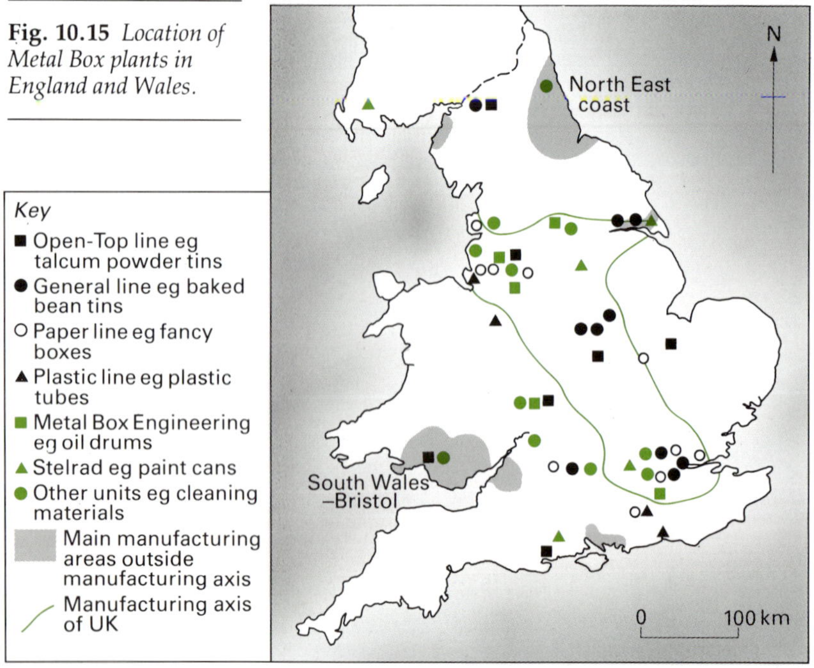

Fig. 10.16 *Metal Box PLC (since 1988, CMB Promotional Packaging), Mansfield, Nottinghamshire*

There are advantages for a firm to operate in an area where there are strong links with other firms and a good local infrastructure. Total production costs can be reduced. Capital can be borrowed more easily. Services and facilities such as advanced technology and research, that each firm could not provide for itself, can be attracted. These sorts of links enable firms to act as if they were larger. Multi-plant firms often consider such linkages important when deciding upon plant location. Metal Box Group PLC is an international company with many plants in England and Wales. Each plant specialises in one of the seven lines given in the key to fig. 10.15. Linked factories and easy access between them is important to Metal Box, and helps to account for the pattern of distribution of their factories.

Location quotient

A localised industry is one which concentrates its firms in one area. The extent to which an industry is localised and the extent to which a region specialises in a particular type of industrial production can be measured using the following simple formula:

$$\frac{\text{\% of workers in the region employed in the industry}}{\text{\% of the country's workers employed in the industry}}$$

The number produced is known as the location quotient (LQ). It is useful for studying the distribution of industry. Figure 10.17 shows the LQ for two industries in the regions of the USA – printing and publishing, and petroleum and coal products. The national average for each industry equals 1.0 so that a regional LQ of greater than 1.0 shows the industry to be concentrated/localised and that region to have more than its 'fair share'. A 4.8 LQ for petroleum and coal products in the South Central States of the USA means it has 4.8 times the national average of that industry in the region.

Light industries tend to be less localised than heavy industry and more widely dispersed. For example, food, drink and tobacco manufacturing in Britain (light industry) has regional LQs which range from 0.6 in Wales to 2.2 in East Anglia. The LQs for metal manufacturing (heavy industry) range from 0.1 in East Anglia to 3.8 in Wales.

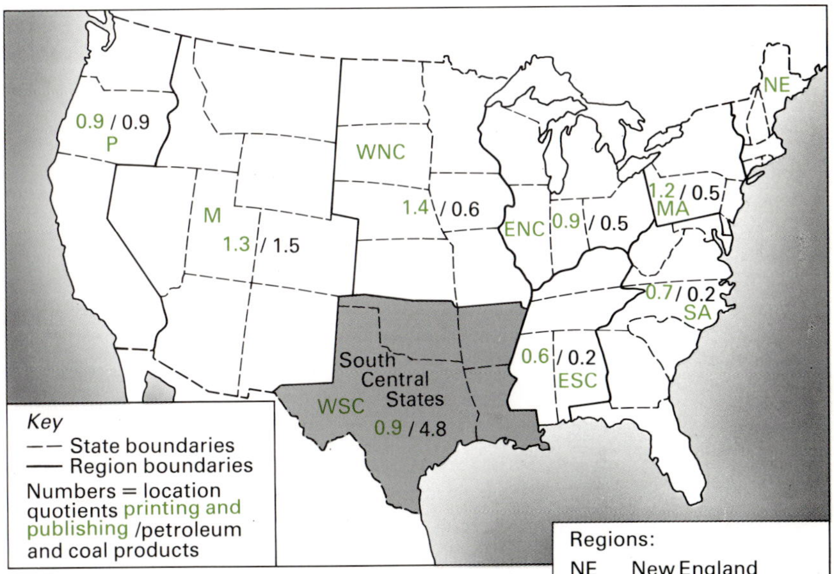

Fig. 10.17 *Regional location quotients for two industries in the USA*

Activities

1 In your discussion groups, discuss possible linkages in the motor vehicle industry between Lucas, Goodyear, Triplex and Ford.

2 Use the percentages below. Calculate the location quotients for a) the motor vehicle industry in both the West Midlands and the East Midlands; b) the chemical industry in both the South East and North West of England.

Industry	Percentage of workers employed in the industry				
	West Midlands	East Midlands	South East	North West	GB
Motor vehicles	19.5	8.9	10.4	10.3	10.3
Chemicals	1.9	4.4	6.4	8.7	5.6

What do the LQs tell you about the localisation of these industries?

Choosing particular locations

Influence of human geography

Study the 'Why did you locate in Wisconsin' survey in fig. 10.18. Transport is clearly important. Many firms in Britain would also say that access to a motorway and/or to a freightliner depot are important to them. However, interviews with manufacturers often show that decisions about factory locations are as much influenced by personal, social and political reasons as by the pure economic reasons of transport, materials and markets.

In many long-industrialised countries like those in the European Community, not only does the government encourage industries to locate in certain regions, but towns, cities and regions also try to attract developments. Look at the advertisements and articles from newspapers shown in figs 10.19 to 10.22. Some actions by local governments can also discourage firms from expanding or locating in their area. The high rates in some British cities make it more expensive for industry to develop there, and this is sometimes blamed for forcing businesses to set up elsewhere (look at fig. 10.21). One of the reasons for the growth of industrial development in East Anglia has been the relatively low price of land compared to the rest of southern England. One hectare of industrial land in Harlow, Essex costs about one quarter the price of a similar piece of land in Slough, Berkshire.

Fig. 10.18 *Survey of 2000 firms of all types in Wisconsin and the whole of USA*

State of Wisconsin, USA		*USA*	
Rank	*Reasons behind location choice*	*Rank*	*Reasons behind location choice*
1	Available road transport	1	Personal reasons (eg home town of manufacturer)
2	Reasonable cost of property	2	Close to markets
3	Reasonable or low local taxes	3	Access to other plants (ie trade links and production relationships)
4	Ample area for expansion	4	Suitable buildings and/or site at favourable price
5	Favourable labour climate (no labour problems or trade union pressure)	5	Close to raw materials
6	Favourable local attitude to industry	6	Suitable labour at favourable wage rates
7	Nearness to large market	7	Assistance or encouragement by local groups
8	Reasonable cost of factory construction	8	Suitable transport facilities

Fig. 10.19 *Advert for Mid Glamorgan*

Closeness to the market does seem to be more important to firms today than closeness to raw materials. Two examples illustrate this:

1. IBM, the world's largest computer company, decided to locate its British headquarters in Portsmouth. After looking at 22 possible locations around the country, it was decided to locate near London.
2. 'There is a population bigger than that of the USA and Canada within 2 day's truck journey of here', said the managing-director of one new plant which opened on the coast of south-east England.

The personal reasons of the founders are often the key location factor. In fact, the decision facing new firms may actually be – 'What shall we produce here?' rather than, 'Where do we produce this?'. It may help to explain why many manufacturers seem to be located in an area in which satisfactory profits can be made rather than at the ideal, most profitable location.

Fig. 10.20 *Advert for Swindon*

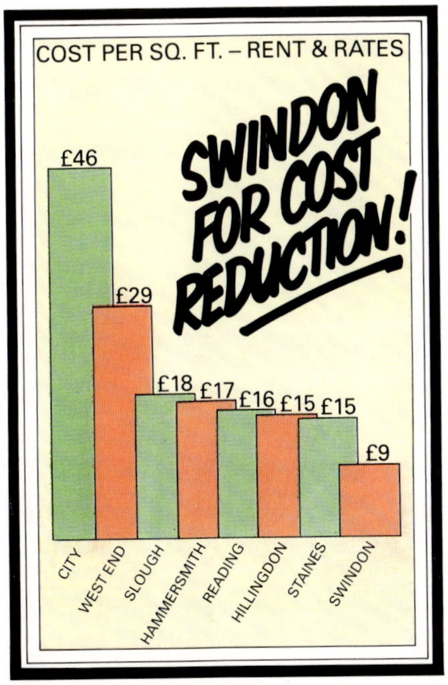

Fig. 10.21 *Location influences*

High Rates Bill Drives Out Business And Industry From City

Fig. 10.22 *Flanders in Belgium*

FLANDERS

The Heart of the European Community The Centre of a Rich Consumer Market of more than 200 Million People

- Flanders has the most dense road and rail network in the world.
- Flanders has an international airport – Brussels National airport.
- Flanders has four large seaports – Antwerp, Ghent, Zeebrugge and Ostend – linked by a waterway network.
- Flanders has one of the most specialised and productive labour forces in the world.
- Flanders has numerous scientific research centres and univesities.
- Flanders has about 120 completely equipped industrial parks.

Activities

1 What are the similarities and differences between the two American surveys shown in fig. 10.18?

2 Make a summary of the various local authority advertisements in figs 10.19, 10.20 and 10.22. How does each authority try to sell its area to potential industrialists?

3 Find out why the business rate varies between local authorities in Britain.

Importance of transport

The location of manufacturing activities is influenced by a range of factors which include raw materials, markets, energy, labour supplies and sites with specific qualities. It is possible to use these factors to develop a general explanation (or model) for the locations chosen by manufacturers. One well-known model produced by a geographer called Weber suggests that there is an ideal location for an industry. It occurs at the point where the combined costs of transporting raw materials to the plant and taking finished products to market are at their lowest. This is called the balance point. By locating the site where transport costs are at their lowest, profits will be at their highest. The triangle (fig. 10.24) shows a possible ideal location for a factory at the balance point between the market and the raw materials.

Transport costs are affected by what happens to the raw materials during

Fig. 10.23 *Peugeot-Talbot car assembly plant at Ryton near Coventry*

manufacturing. For example, they may lose or gain bulk and weight; become more or less perishable and more or less fragile. Beer, for example, gains bulk and weight during

Fig. 10.24 *Factory location triangle*

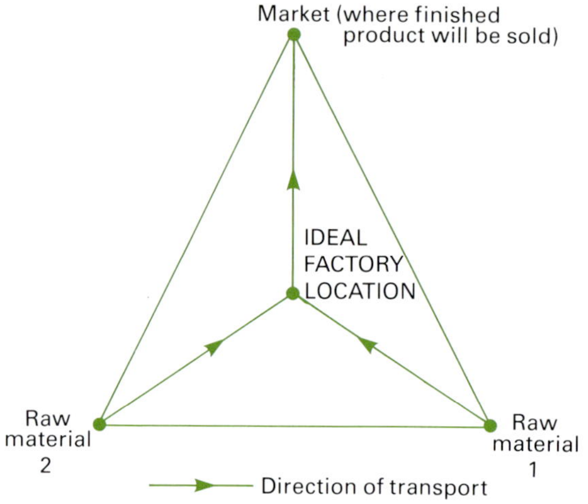

Fig. 10.25 *Where to locate a car assembly plant?*

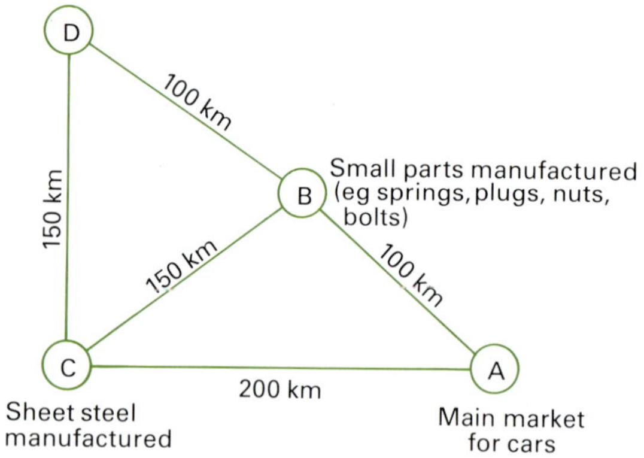

processing. Adding water makes beer heavier than the main raw materials, malt and hops. The cost of transport for brewers can be reduced by locating the brewery near the customers, that is, near the main markets for beer.

Figure 10.25 shows an area with four possible sites for a car assembly plant, A, B, C and D. The 1-ton car in question takes ½-ton of sheet steel and ½-ton of small parts to make. The cost of producing the car, excluding the costs of transporting the sheet steel, small parts and finished car, is £5000 at each of the four sites. The transport costs of the small parts are £1 per ton per km; of the sheet steel £2 per ton per km, and of the finished car £8 per ton per km. The 'best' site for the plant was chosen by using the calculations and reasoning shown in fig. 10.26. Transport costs were lowest and profits highest at site A. Where a range of sites is available, the most profitable one is often chosen.

Transport costs may not be the dominant industrial location factor and they may have been over-emphasised by Weber in his model (fig. 10.24). Policies to increase sales and revenue, and having a good share of and access to the market, even dominating it if possible, may be more important than reducing costs to a minimum, for many manufacturers. Earning sufficient profits rather than the biggest possible profits may be how some industrialists actually think. This means that they can locate and produce profitably at many places within an area. The geographical limits of this area may be wide, however, and transport will probably be an important factor.

Site	*Costs of production of one car*	*Costs of transporting raw materials for one car*		*Costs of distribution of finished car*	*Total manufacturing cost of one car*
		sheet steel	*small parts*		
A	£5000	½-ton moved 200 km ½ × 200 × £2 = £200	½-ton moved 100 km ½ × 100 × £1 = £50	0	£5250
B	£5000	½-ton moved 150 km ½ × 150 × £2 = £150	0	100 km to market 100 × £8 = £800	£5950
C	£5000	0	½-ton moved 150 km ½ × 150 × £1 = £75	200 km to market 200 × £8 = £1600	£6675
D	£5000	½-ton moved 150 km ½ × 150 × £2 = £150	½-ton moved 100 km ½ × 100 × £1 = £50	200 km to market 200 × £8 = £1600	£6800

Fig. 10.26 *Transport costs*

Activities

1 Draw a systems flow diagram for two of the factories on pages 120–21: brewery; car plant; sugar factory; coalite & chemical plant. Name two inputs, two processes and the output in each case.

2 In your groups discuss which diagram, A or B, is more likely to represent a) a 19th century manufacturing location; b) a 20th century manufacturing location.

	Inputs		Processes		Output
A	Raw Materials	———	Factory Location	———————————	Markets
B	Raw Materials	———————————	Factory Location	———	Markets

——— Transport (length of arrow indicates distance of transport)

Contrasting manufacturing locations

Most manufacturing locations fall into three groups:

1 *Material-orientated*. Production is carried out near to the source of the raw materials (primary products) which are processed. Examples include brickworks, pulp and paper mills, sugar beet factories (look at fig. 10.27). Such industries and those which are energy-orientated (ie located close to sources of fuel and power eg aluminium smelting) can be referred to as input-orientated.

2 *Market-orientated*. Production is located near to consumers, for example bread baking, brewing, televisions and motor vehicle production.

3 *Footloose industries*. Production is not tied to either raw material or market locations. A plant can be located by considerations such as transport, location of supplying-firms, local and national government incentives, and so on.

About half of the manufacturing we see around us today is footloose, although many such industries choose locations with good access to large centres of population. Market-orientation, with factories located near to markets, is a feature of twentieth century manufacturing. Figures 10.28 and 10.29 referring to Mansfield Brewery, Nottinghamshire and the Volkswagen car plant in Sao Paulo, Brazil respectively, provide examples of market-orientation. Material-orientated industries, more typical of older industries, do still remain today. The British Sugar Corporation plant at Kelham, Newark (fig. 10.30) and the Coalite Fuel and Chemical plant at Bolsover, Derbyshire (fig. 10.31) are examples.

Fig. 10.27 *Sugar beet cultivation in the British Isles*

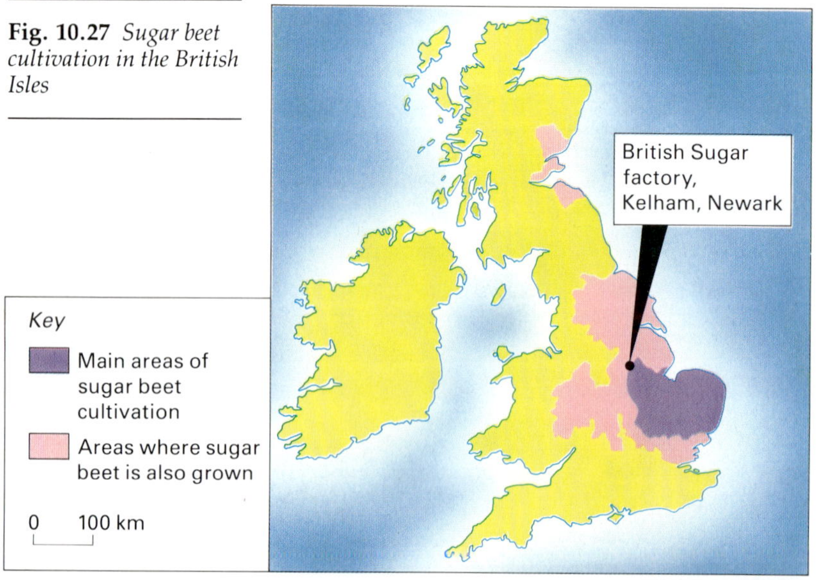

Activities

In your groups, discuss the main advantages to firms moving to a new location in North east England. What are the main costs/losses to the firm resulting from the move?

Fig. 10.28 *Mansfield Brewery, Nottinghamshire*

Brewing is a market-orientated industry. Beer is made from barley (malt), water, hops and yeast, close to where it will be sold. This brewery uses locally-grown barley, converted nearby into malt, and hops from Worcestershire, Herefordshire and abroad.

Fig. 10.29 *Volkswagen car plant, Sao Paulo*

Motor vehicle plants are assembly industries involving either thousands of workers or computer-and-robot automation. Brazil is the world's eighth largest vehicle producer though two-thirds of the industry is foreign-owned. Most of the transnational companies operate in and around the city of Sao Paulo with its population of nearly 9 millions. The motor vehicle industry is market-orientated.

Fig. 10.30 *British Sugar factory, Newark*

Sugar production is a material-orientated industry. Most sugar beet processing factories are located within the area where sugar beet is grown (fig. 10.31) because it is bulky and costly to transport over unnecessarily long distances.

Fig. 10.31 *Coalite fuel and chemical plant, Derbyshire*

The need for large coal supplies has influenced the Coalite Fuel and Chemical plant to locate next to two Derbyshire coalfield collieries, Bolsover and Markham. The plant today has an acquired advantage; the M1 runs within half-a-mile of the plant. NB *the coal stocks in the foreground of the photograph.*

Government policies

Governments are an important factor in the location of industry. Since 1934 the British government has tried to encourage industry in those parts of the country known as 'Areas for Expansion'. This is part of a regional economic policy to ensure a reasonable spread of economic activity across the country.

Fig. 10.32 *Areas for Expansion and Enterprise Zones in Britain*

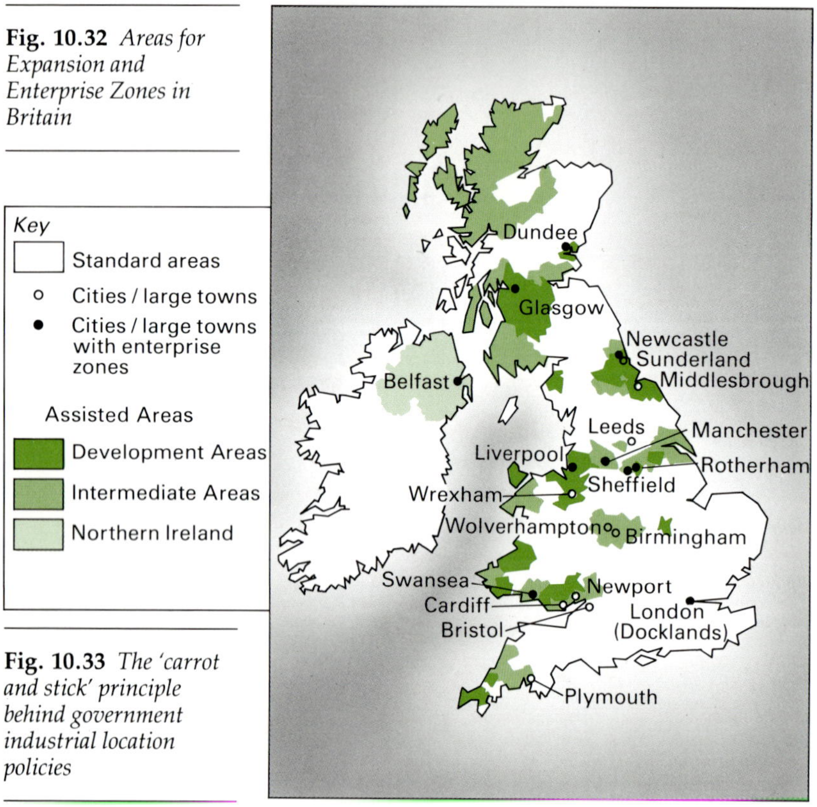

Fig. 10.33 *The 'carrot and stick' principle behind government industrial location policies*

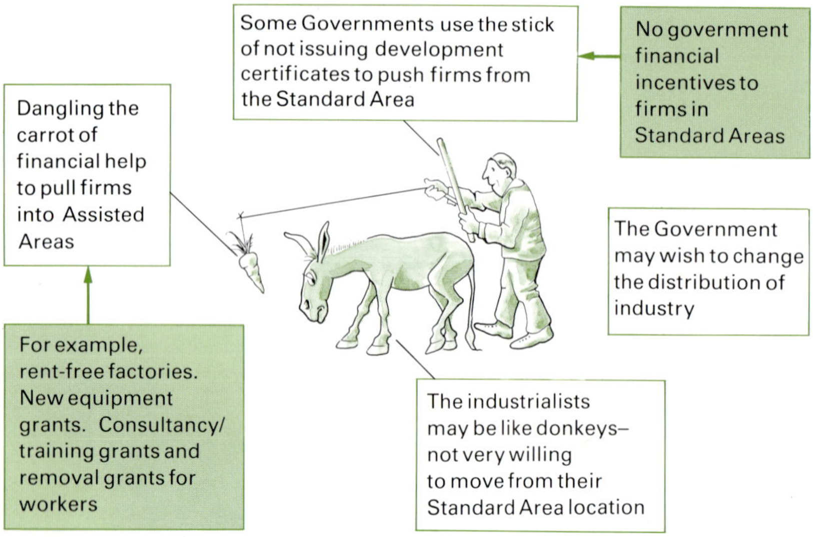

Employment and income should be more equally shared out between the various regions. Those areas with a lack of industrial development, with higher unemployment and lower wage rates can become 'Areas for Expansion'. In any industrialised country, regional economic differences occur naturally, as some industries grow rapidly, others more slowly, and others actually decline. Figure 10.32 shows the location of the 'Areas for Expansion' (or 'Assisted Areas', split into Special Development, Development and Intermediate Areas). The 'Areas for Expansion' are either:

1. Regions suffering from economic depression because of the decline of past industries such as the heavy industries of North East England

or

2. Regions with little industrial tradition eg Cornwall.

They all have under-used resources, especially labour. This can lead to stresses in community life in the region. At the same time, in the Standard Areas (fig. 10.32) industry may be growing so that there is congestion, over-crowding and housing shortages. There may even be a need to restrict the number of new factories being opened. Government policy has tried to 'take work to the workers' in the 'Areas for Expansion' rather than 'move workers to the work' in the Standard Areas through a 'carrot-and-stick' policy. Study fig 10.33 carefully which outlines the principles behind this policy.

European Economic Community

Grants from European Community funds have also been made available in 'Areas for Expansion'. These are usually intended to improve the infrastructure for industry as shown in fig. 10.34. The Kielder Reservoir project in Northumberland for example received £37 million from the European Regional Development fund.

Enterprise zones

A more recent development has been the introduction of Enterprise Zones (EZs), shown in fig. 10.32. These encourage industrial enterprise in particular areas, especially inner cities within the 'Areas for Expansion'. 'Areas for Expansion' policy focuses on the region as a whole and supports, equally, firms setting up on edge-of-town sites and inner-city sites. Assistance through the EZ scheme does create some unfairness for firms located just outside the EZ boundary. It may also encourage firms to move into the zone from close by, simply to pick up the financial assistance. The Tayside Enterprise Zone (fig. 10.35) covers 100 hectares of industrial land in Dundee and Arbroath on seven sites. For an initial 10-year period from 1984, the following are some of the benefits available to firms already operating or setting up in the Tayside zone:

1. Free from paying local rates
2. Tax relief on spending on new industrial buildings
3. Grants because the EZ is in an 'Area for Expansion' eg Regional Development Grant to help firms starting up; training grants to cover the cost of retraining.

Brazil

Many governments offer assistance to manufacturing industry in order to develop the country economically. These actions may affect the location of industry although policies to encourage industrial development in specific regions are rare. The Brazilian government has tried to spread industrial development away from the South and South East. Regional Development Agencies (fig. 10.36) have been established. Tax incentives, loans and subsidies are available to companies willing to develop in the North, Amazonia, North East and Centre West regions. The building of Brasilia, as the country's new capital city in the Centre West region was a special regional development programme.

Fig. 10.34 *Chesterfield Industrial Estate*

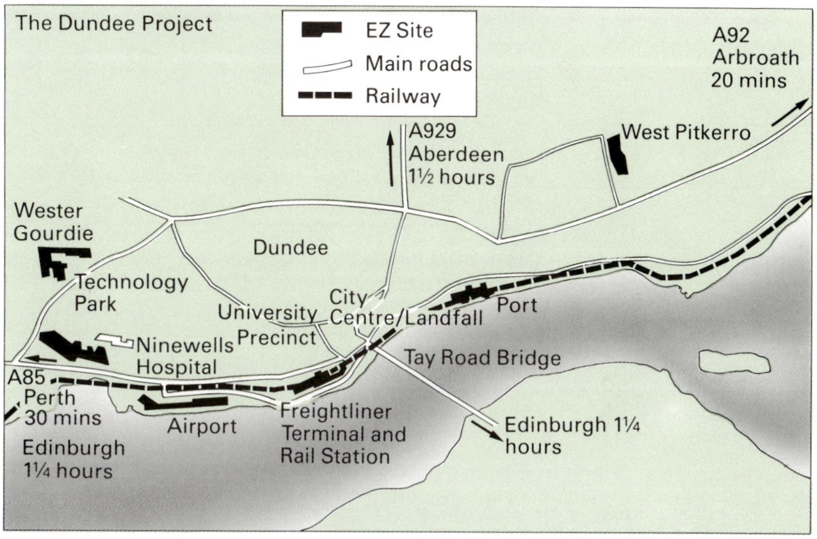

Fig. 10.35 *The six Enterprise Zone sites within Dundee*

Fig. 10.36 *Brazil's four regional development agencies*

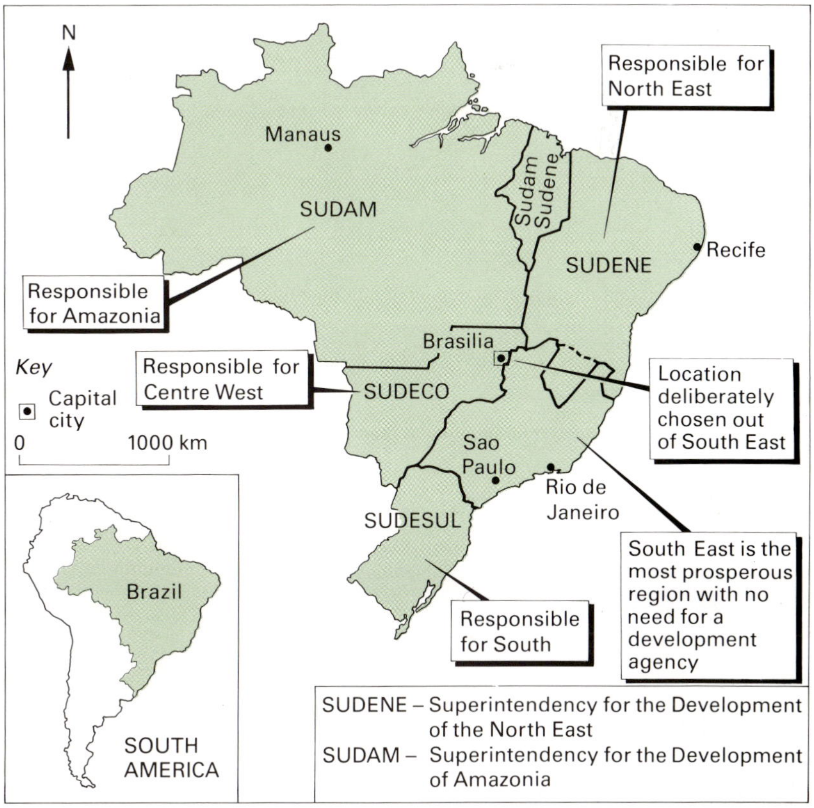

Footloose manufacturing

Fig. 10.37 *Types of Manufacturing Area in Leicester*

Type	*Main features*
1 *Backyard*	– isolated pockets throughout older residential areas – small-scale firms of house size – cheap rents
2 *Neighbourhood*	– medium-large plants surrounded by housing – typical of inner city areas drawing labour from immediate locality
3 *Concentrated*	– old firms (19th and early 20th century) – separated from residential areas – directly accessible to major transport routes
4 *Estate*	– large, modern and landscaped – planned with services provided (water supply, electricity, gas, telecommunications, off-street car parking . . .) – located close to major transport routes

Industrial (trading) estates

Footloose industries can often be found on industrial estates. There are four types of manufacturing area in most towns, as shown in fig. 10.37 for Leicester. It is policy in Leicester to concentrate new industrial development mainly on industrial estates. This keeps manufacturing away from residential areas. Permission to develop new manufacturing on sites other than on industrial estates may be refused by the city council.

Figure 10.38 shows the location in Sheffield of thirty major industrial estates. The map shows:

1. The importance of road transport
2. The clustering of estates in the old industrial areas of the Lower Don Valley.
3. The edge-of-city location of most estates.

Fig. 10.38 *Major industrial estates in Sheffield*

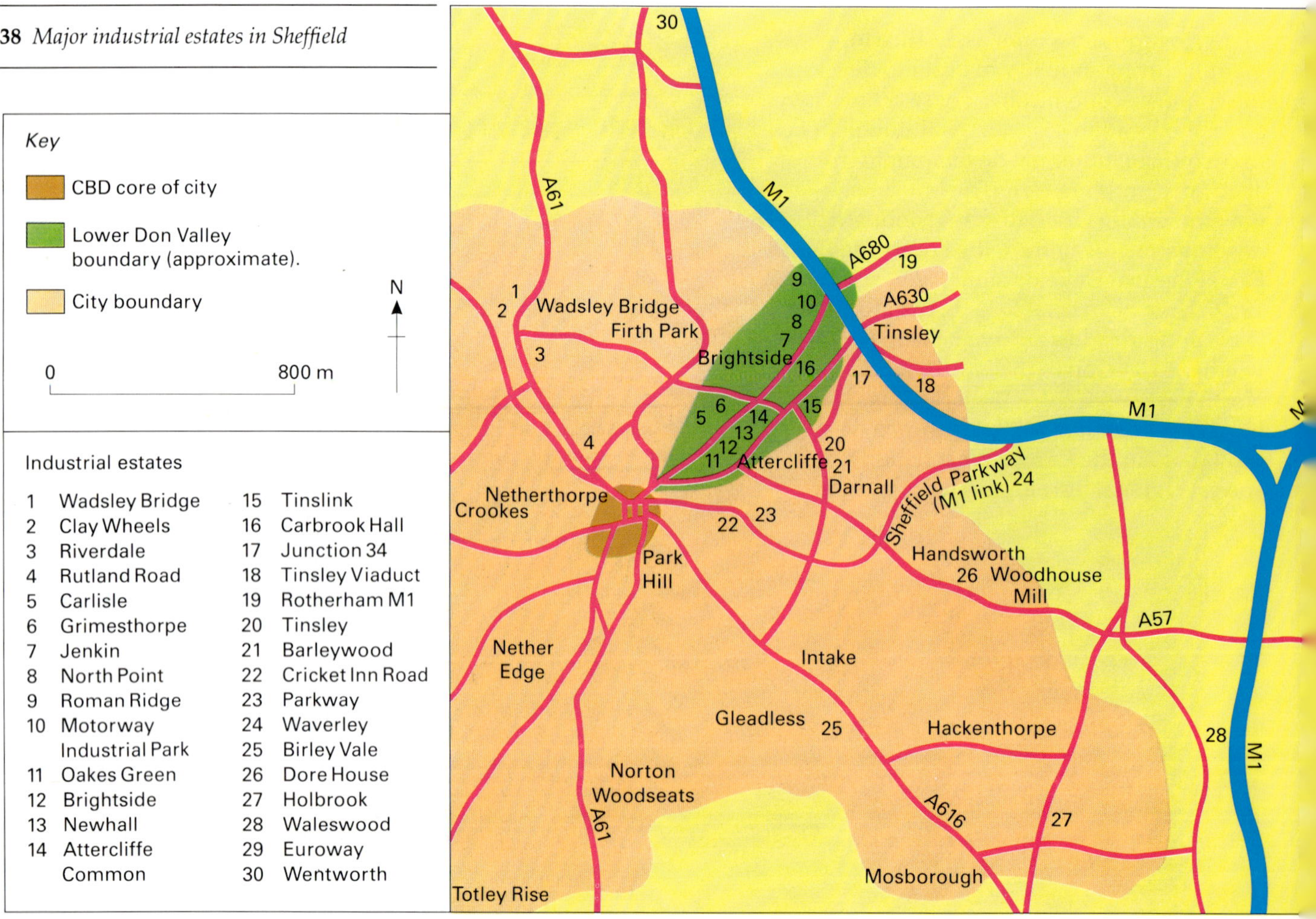

The results of a survey carried out on the Chesterfield Trading Estate, are shown in fig. 10.39. This is an industrial estate built on a green-field site next to the Sheffield-Chesterfield dual carriageway road, which has dual carriageway access to the M1 motorway. This estate is similar to many others in Britain in that:

1. Industries are light and 'footloose'. They are not tied to materials, specific markets or Chesterfield and its trading estate. Modern transport improvements have reduced the importance of these old locating factors.
2. Industries are concerned with services and direct consumer products which depend on road transport, especially for their distribution.
3. Firms are small- or medium-sized and employ relatively few people. In recent years industrial estates have been established in some developing countries. Figure 10.41 shows areas of industrial estate in Singapore. Do you notice any similarities between the urban lay-out of Jurong and that of a New Town in Britain?

Activities

1 For an industrial estate near your home/school, a) draw a plan to show each factory unit; b) name each firm and its product(s).

2 In your groups, discuss the advantages that industrial estates have for manufacturers.

Fig. 10.40 *The Chesterfield Trading Estate*

Fig. 10.41 *Industrial estates at Jurong in Singapore*

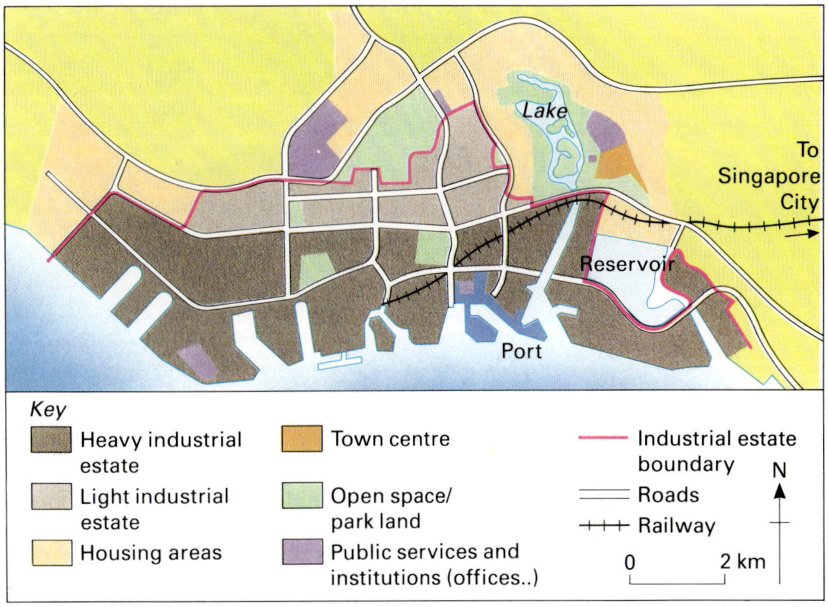

Fig. 10.39 *Survey of firms on the Chesterfield Trading Estate.*

Types of industry	*Number of factory units occupied*	*Total number of employees*	*Example*
General Engineering and Metal	25	453	precision tools
Plastics	6	43	window systems
Food Processing	10	131	frozen foods; soft drinks
Timber and Paper	4	19	woodwares
Warehousing, Packaging and Distribution	6	76	Pickfords (National Freight Consortium)
Others including service industries and unoccupied	13	164	florist; car accident damage repairers; contractor; petrol pump servicing . . .
TOTAL	64	886	

Changing energy consumption

The importance of energy

Energy describes fuel and power sources such as oil, natural gas, coal and running water on which our whole way of life largely depends. Energy is of interest to geographers in a number of ways:

1. It is a major input to the industrial system, especially manufacturing, and can influence both its success and its location.
2. It is characterised by primary (extractive) industry eg coal mining.
3. It is the basis of secondary (manufacturing) industries. For example, petroleum is the major raw material for the oil refining and petro-chemical industry.

Fig. 10.42 *Energy consumption in Kenya*

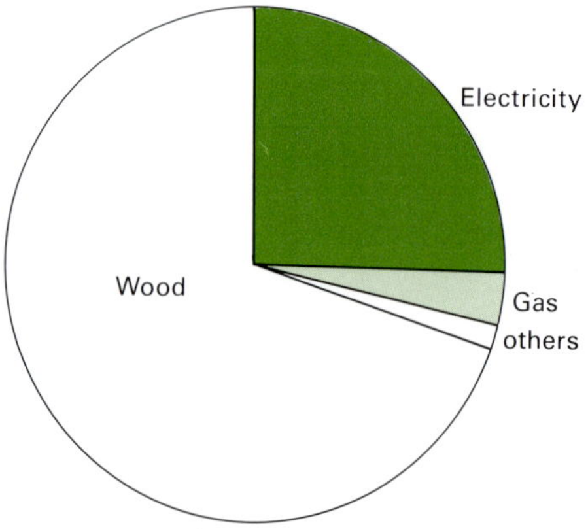

Fig. 10.43 *The development of energy production around the world*

Area	*Tonnes of oil equivalent per person per year* Potential energy production (estimated)	Actual energy production (1986)	GNP per person (US $ 1986)
North America	44	9.3	14 335
Europe	20	7.4	8 091
USSR	79	2.5	N/A
Asia	12	0.3	4 051
Africa	62	0.2	786
Oceania (Australasia)	28	6.3	6 726
South America	58	0.7	1 650

One of the main reasons for the growth of the heavily populated, industrialised areas of the developed world has been the availability of energy sources. However, it has been estimated that nearly half of the world's population relies heavily on firewood and farm waste like dried dung, straw, crop stalks, cobs and husks for their fuel, for cooking and heating. The single most important fuel in Kenya is wood (fig. 10.42) and in Bangladesh and China they use straw and crop stalks. Figure 10.43 shows that the more wealthy an area is, the greater is its production and consumption of energy. So, there are clear differences in the sources of energy used between developed and developing countries. One reason for the lower level of economic development of countries like India and Ethiopia is either that they do not have the quantity of energy necessary to begin genuine industrialisation or they have not developed the sources they do have.

Fig. 10.44 *Wood is the major energy source in Africa*

Classifying energy sources

One way of classifying energy sources is to regard them as renewable or non-renewable:
Renewable. These are sources which cannot be exhausted so that their use does not reduce their supply eg hydro-electricity; wind; solar; tidal.
Non-renewable. These are exhaustible sources whose supply is fixed in quantity. Oil, natural gas, and coal, once burned, are lost to people.

The 'energy crisis' which could face the world is partly a result of the dependency on fossil fuels, especially oil and natural gas. Figure 10.46 shows the changing consumption of energy in the world, especially the gradual switch from fossil fuels. These made up 93 per cent of world consumption in 1973 falling to a predicted 86 per cent in 1990.

Energy consumption can also be classified. Primary energy consumption deals with the original sources of supply of fuel and power such as coal and oil deposits. Figure 10.47 shows Britain's primary energy consumption. Secondary energy consumption is concerned with the users of the primary sources, industry, transport and domestic consumers. Look at fig. 10.45.

Fig. 10.45 *Secondary energy consumption in Britain*

Types of secondary consumption	*Percentage of total consumption*
Industry (including manufacturing)	40
Domestic	25
Transport	22
Others	13

Power stations

Industry is the single most important secondary consumer in Britain today, and electrical energy the principal form in which it is consumed. Coal burning power stations are located in clusters near water supplies and coalfields, such as the Trent Valley. Others are found around important urban areas. Nuclear power has different location factors. They are mainly coastal, away from urban areas, near water supplies. People's attitudes towards the expansion of the nuclear power station programme vary. What is your opinion? Remember that some countries, like France, depend much more on nuclear energy, over 50% of total consumption.

Fig. 10.46 *Changing world primary energy consumption, 1970–90*

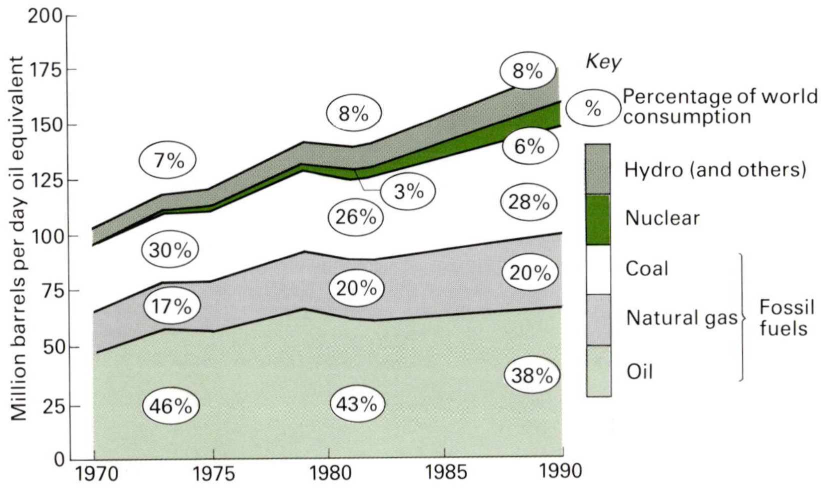

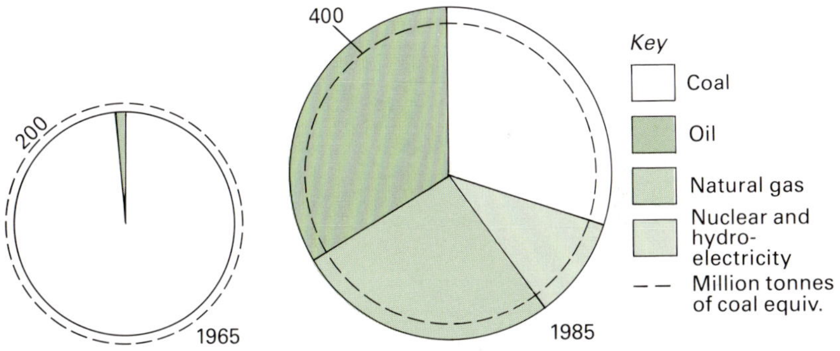

Fig. 10.47 *Primary energy consumption in Britain*

Activities

1. Find out where oil fired power stations are located in Britain. Try to give some reasons for this pattern.
2. Coal, oil and natural gas discoveries are increasingly important as the world realises that fossil fuels have a limited life. Choose one of the following:
   a) the new Selby or Vale of Belvoir coalfield.
   b) the North Sea oil and gasfields or the Morecambe Bay gasfield.
   Collect as much information as you can by writing letters, searching newspapers and magazines, etc. What are the arguments for and against the development of the energy source(s) you have chosen?
3. In your groups, discuss the arguments for and against the development of nuclear power stations.

Energy-orientated manufacturing

Fig. 10.48 *High Marnham power station, Trent Valley*

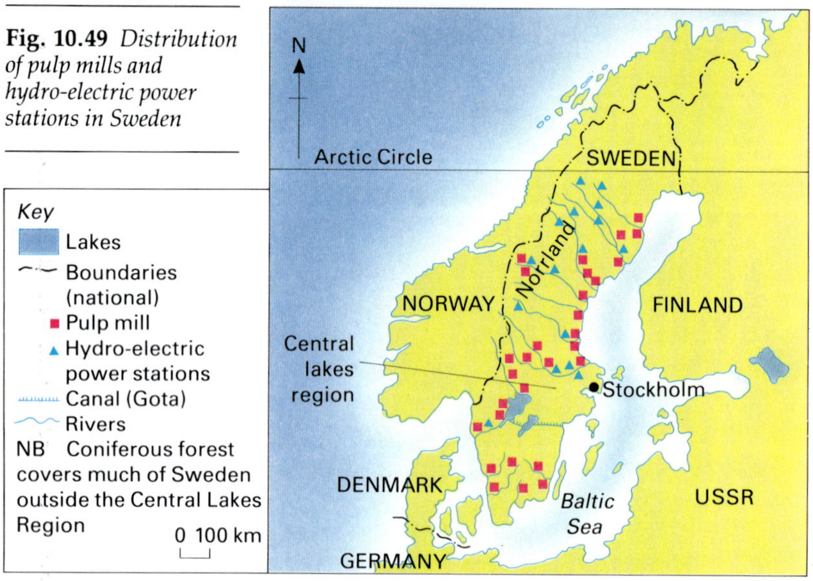

Fig. 10.49 *Distribution of pulp mills and hydro-electric power stations in Sweden*

Many industries locate factories near energy supplies. Factories need power to drive their machinery. In some present-day industries and in most manufacturing industry in the past, energy was such an important input that the location of the factory was largely determined by the location of energy sources. During the Industrial Revolution of 18th and 19th century Britain, energy was the most powerful factor effecting the location of industry. Factories were opened mainly on the coalfields. Coal is a heavy and bulky commodity which is expensive to transport. Industrial locations close to the coal kept transport costs low. The development of an iron and steel industry in the river valleys of Sheffield owed much to local water power and later coal from the nearby Yorkshire-Derbyshire-Nottinghamshire coalfield. The National Grid for electricity, fed by the Central Electricity Generating Board's (split into two divisions in 1989: PowerGen and the National Power Company) power stations, makes energy available almost everywhere in Britain. So, energy no longer has the locational pull on manufacturing that it once did. However, although energy sources are now less likely to influence the location of industry, there are still examples of industries and industrial areas which are highly dependent on nearby abundant energy supplies as can be seen in figs. 10.49 and 10.50.

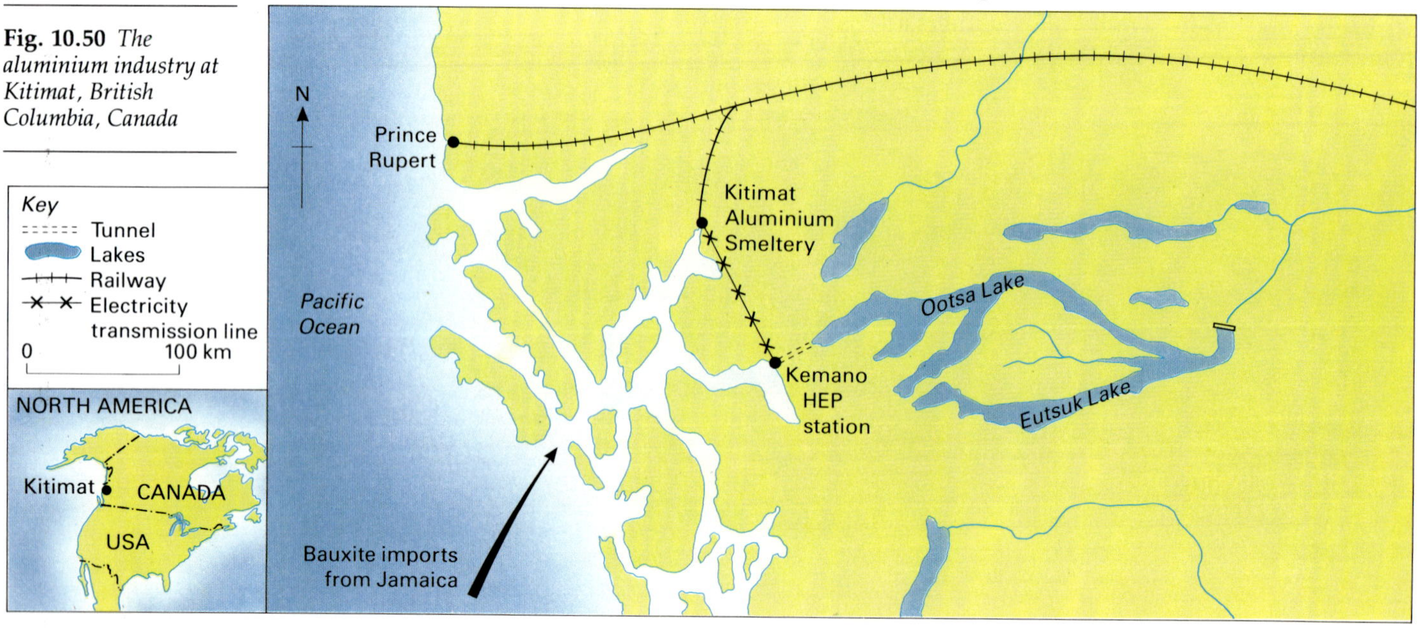

Fig. 10.50 *The aluminium industry at Kitimat, British Columbia, Canada*

Figure 10.49 shows how wood pulp mills in Sweden, producing the main raw material for paper-making, are located alongside rivers with the potential for generating hydro-electricity. Large quantities of water are used in the pulping process, and the rivers are used to transport timber from the forests to the mills.

Aluminium smelting requires very large quantities of energy. Figure 10.50 shows the Kitimat-Kemano area of British Columbia, Canada, where a large aluminium smelter was built in the 1960s. The area was very suitable for producing hydro-electricity, with steep slopes, heavy rainful year-round and natural lakes. The Kitimat smelter is heavily dependent on the abundant supply of locally-generated hydro-electric power.

Northern Italy is one of Europe's great manufacturing zones. The so-called 'industrial triangle', formed by the three cities of Milan, Turin and Genoa, has iron and steel, heavy engineering, motor vehicle, textile, chemical and shipbuilding industries. This area, near the Alps has cheap and abundant hydro-electric power.

There have been schemes to generate large quantities of HEP in some 'developing' countries, for example the Volta Scheme in Ghana (look at fig. 10.80) and the Damodar Valley Scheme in North East India. These have tended to attract many of the countries' largest industrial plants. However, advances in electricity transmission and the easier distribution of energy make energy-orientated industrial locations less likely. The Polonoroeste project in Upper Amazonia, Brazil and the Narmada River project in India will increase energy supply to these countries as a whole.

Oil is perhaps the source of energy which has had the most impact in the 20th century. Its extraction and refining has produced a modern primary industry (see fig. 10.51). It has also become the basic raw material for the chemical (petro-chemical) industry. The coastal and linked locations of oil terminals, refineries and petro-chemical plants in Britain are shown in fig. 10.52.

Fig. 10.51 *Oil refinery, Fawley, Southampton*

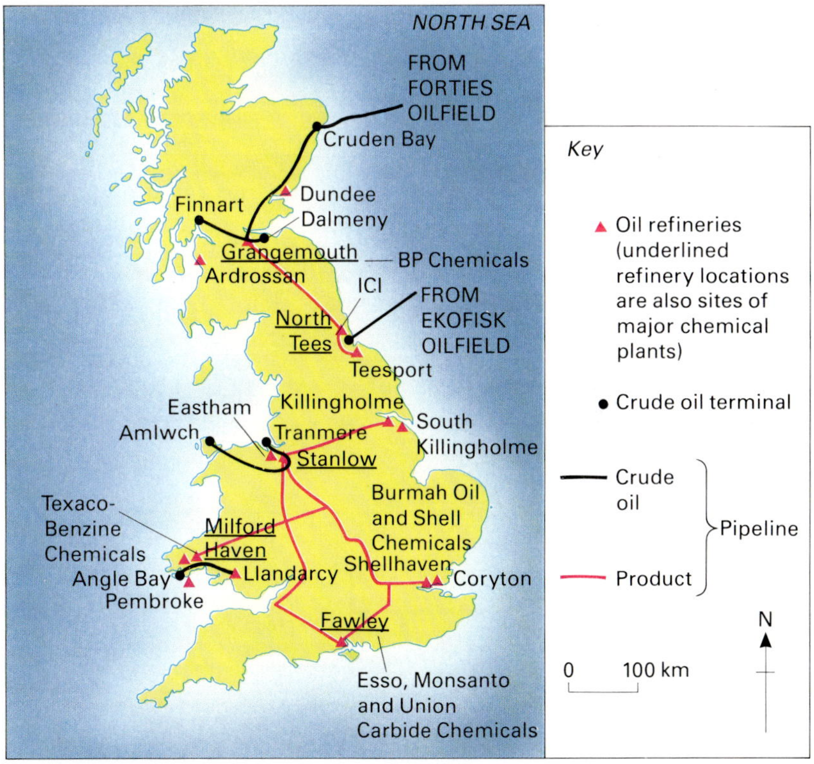

Fig. 10.52 *Location of oil terminals and refineries, and major petro-chemical plants in Britain*

Activities

1 For one manufacturing industry that developed during the 18th and 19th century Industrial Revolution in Britain, for example textiles, in Lancashire/Yorkshire; iron and steel making in Sheffield, etc, find out how energy resources influenced location of factories.

2 In your groups, discuss why tertiary industries are less influenced by energy supplies than manufacturing.

New manufacturing areas

'Sunbelts'

High-tech industries develop often near attractive residential areas. 'Sunbelt' has been used to describe these areas where industry is booming and where there is the growing prosperity. This can occur at a number of scales; regions within countries, countries, and groups of countries. In Britain the so-called M4 'silicon corridor' to the west of London; in the USA California's Silicon Valley south of San Francisco towards San Jose, and the area around Atlanta, Georgia have been described as 'sunbelts'. The shaded area in fig. 10.53 is developing into an important area of advanced industrial activity; a 'sunbelt' in Britain. Modern high-tech industries and large service industries are being attracted to areas surrounding the London-Cambridge motorway (M11). The development of nearly 400 new small science- and technology-based firms in Cambridge, including the opening of the Cambridge Science Park, during the past decade, has been called the 'Cambridge Phenomenon'. It is transforming this area which once had little manufacturing. The links with the city's university and links between firms are very strong. Other reasons for this successful development are:

1. The combined attractions of the M11 and M25 (London Orbital) motorways.
2. The expansion of Stansted airport into a major international airport.
3. The availability of land for industrial purposes at prices lower than elsewhere in South-east England. Industrial land in East Anglia is about a quarter of the price of that along the so-called M4 corridor west of London.

Fig. 10.53 *An area full of manufacturing promise*

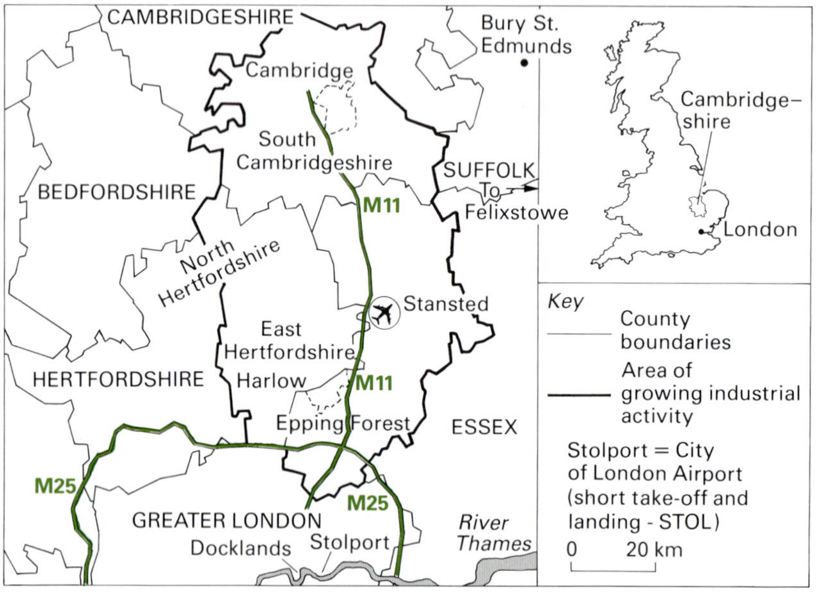

Fig. 10.54 *London Docklands area*

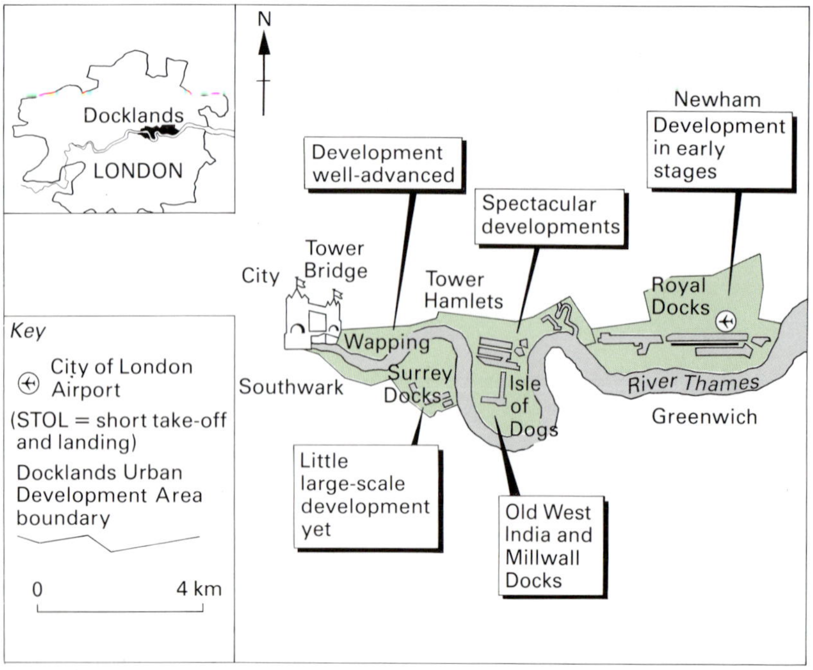

London Docklands

Inner city redevelopment schemes can attract new industries. One such area is London Docklands. Look at fig. 10.54. Since the 1960s, the London Docks and dock-related industries have closed down leaving a large area of land near the city centre suitable for redevelopment. The government formed the London Docklands Development Corporation to be responsibile for the redevelopment by spending the Government money given to the project and by attracting private property developers. One spectacular plan is to build 80-storey office towers at Canary Wharf on the Isle of Dogs and to try to persuade some of the financial institutions in the 'City' of London to move to them. There will be office space for thousands of new or transferred jobs.

Developing countries

New manufacturing areas may grow fast enough to take a whole country forward. Brazil and Mexico are now recognised as 'newly industrialised' countries. Brazil's 'economic miracle' of the 1970s, when the economy grew four times in the 10 years from 1968, was geographically very selective (look at fig. 10.55). Industrialisation including motor vehicles, footwear, aircraft, iron and steel, and shipbuilding, has been limited to the south east and south of the country, especially the cities. These regions today are quite developed, economically. North east Brazil, on the other hand, where about one-third of Brazilians live, has only about 5 per cent of the country's manufacturing and is still in the early stages of economic development.

Fig. 10.55 *Numbers of factories in the regions of Brazil*

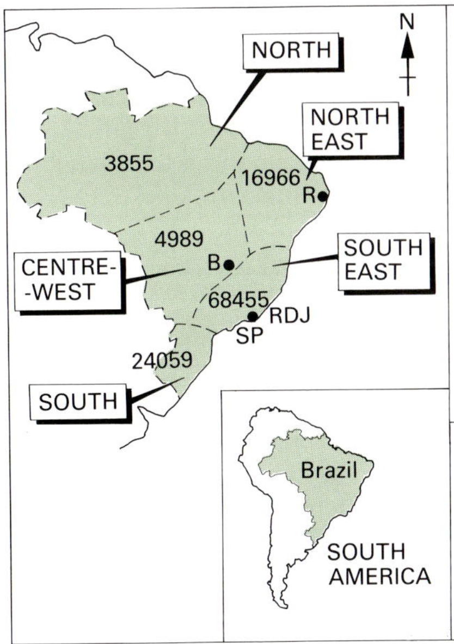

Sao Paulo is the most industrialised area in Latin America with shipbuilding, motor car, metal, aircraft, textile, chemical and food processing industries.

Many countries around the Pacific Ocean in Eastern Asia such as Japan, South Korea, Taiwan, Hong Kong, Singapore and Malaysia, have been increasing their manufacturing sectors in recent years. Japan is now a highly industrialised country whose manufacturing industry has been growing at a very fast rate for over a quarter of a century. Its output is now exceeded only by those of the USA and USSR, and it leads the world in automated technology. Shipbuilding, steel-making, machine tools, electronics and computers (highly-advanced manufacturing), motor cars, telecommunications, financial services have been the industries on which rapid development has been based. Many of these Pacific countries rely heavily upon imported raw materials and are highly dependent on exporting their products to the developed industrial countries.

Fig. 10.56 *Main manufacturing areas of the world's newest industrial giant, Japan*

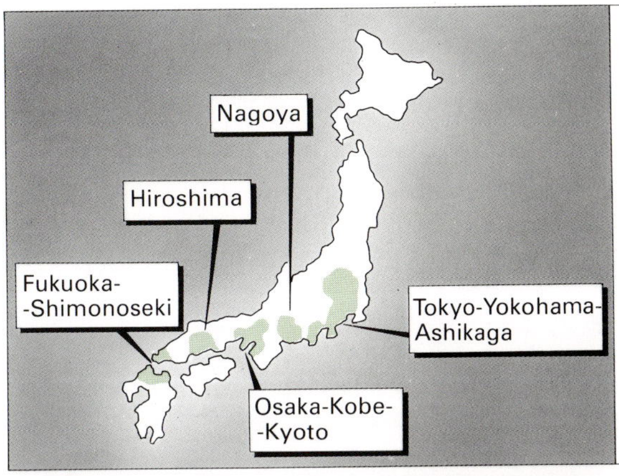

Nearly half of Japanese manufacturing output comes from the Tokyo Bay area though new coastal areas are being developed for industry.

Fig. 10.57 *Seoul, South Korea, rapidly becoming an industrialised country*

Activities

1 Draw a map to show the following Pacific Ocean countries. Plot on the map the figures given in brackets which are percentages showing the rate at which industrial output grew between 1975 and 1985.
Japan (3.3); Singapore (6.5); Hong Kong (6.8); Taiwan (5.5); South Korea (5.6); Malaysia (4.9); Thailand (4.0); Philippines (2.9); Indonesia (4.6); Canada (1.1); Australia (0.9); New Zealand (−0.3); Mexico (3.2); Chile (1.4); Colombia (2.7); Peru (−0.3); USA (1.5); Nicaragua (−5.3); USSR (2.0); China (No figures available)

2 Draw a bar chart to show the growth of industrial output in these countries.

High-technology manufacturing industry

> 'a £5 million project to create a Science Park in a run-down area of Sheffield which would attract vital hi-tech industry to the city and create hundreds of jobs.'

Fig. 10.58 *Extract from Sheffield Star, March 1987*

Business parks

The idea of locating industries in a park-like setting has grown during recent years in developed countries. They are known by various names – business parks, research parks, technology parks, science parks, office parks – and are most common in the USA. In Britain they are either on university sites (eg the Cambridge Science Park), in New Towns (eg Llantarnam Park, Cwmbran), in Enterprise Zones (eg Dundee Technology Park) or in a few forward-thinking towns and cities with access to airports and motorways (eg Bristol, Swindon and Birmingham). These are high-tech (high technology) or 'sunrise' industries producing computers, micro-electronics and telecommunication equipment. They use techniques involving micro-electronics rather than old-style heavy manufacturing or low-tech industries. In these industries no special inputs or facilities are needed and neither the raw materials nor the finished products are bulky or heavy. The industries are footloose and the availability of good modern transport facilities is important. Road and air is used to transport the small raw materials and products. Factories are usually single-storey as well as modern, and may be automated. Industries are attracted to industrial parks for several reasons. These include:

1. The immediate environment is attractive with fully-grown trees and lakes, attractively designed buildings with open spaces between them and plenty of facilities like restaurants and tennis courts. They normally occupy 'greenfield' sites which have a high amenity value.
2. They are close to universities and colleges where there is expertise in science and computer research. Industry and business working closely with university departments is a major feature of many industrial parks.
3. They have been developed on sites with good communications, close to motorways and/or airports.
4. They are often close to other established high-tech firms. Links with other firms are seen as important.

One of the earliest, and best known British business parks is the Cambridge Science Park, opened in 1973 on 53 hectares on the northern edge of the city close to major roads (fig. 10.59). Sixty-eight science-based firms and research institutes have located in this attractive, well-landscaped park. It is

Fig. 10.59 *OS map extract, Cambridge Science Park*

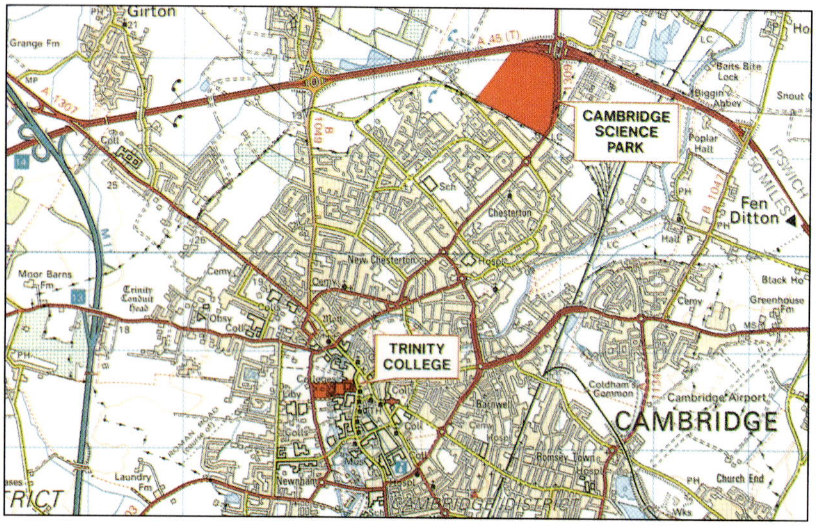

Fig. 10.60 *Plan – Cambridge Science Park*

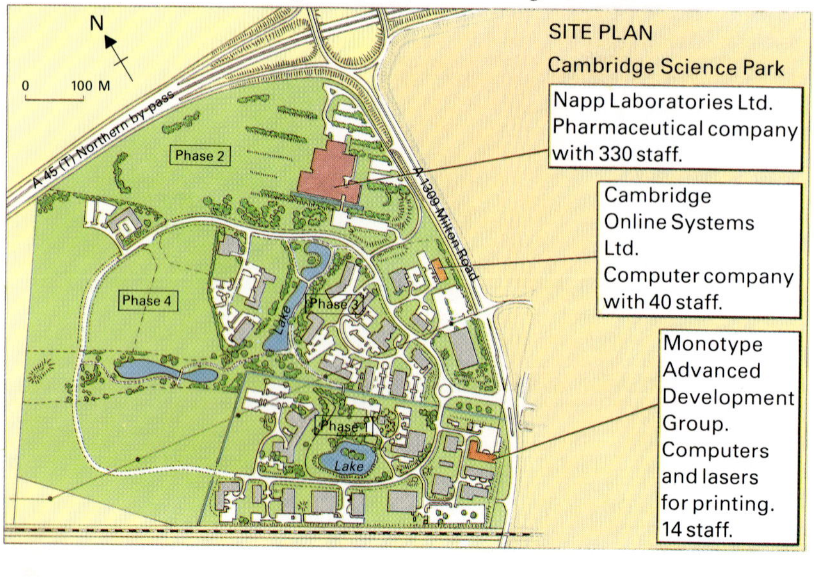

developed to a very low density with only about one-sixth of the total area being building floor space. One condition of locating in the Park is that firms must be involved in the research and development of products rather than their large-scale manufacture. They must also take advantage of links with the University. University-linked industry, marrying scientific brains and business is the basis of the Science Park. Most firms are small and are mainly involved in laser, telecommunication, precision electronics and pharmaceutical production.

The Dundee Technology Park, recently developed by the Scottish Development Agency for high-technology manufacturing industry, also offers financial benefits to firms opening up there. It is an Enterprise Zone site within a Special Development Area and so some suitable projects can enjoy benefits such as 40% of start-up costs as a grant or no rates to pay for 10 years. In recent years, central Scotland has developed into an important area of high-tech manufacturing (the so-called 'silicon glen'). The Dundee Technology Park is planned to become the centrepiece of these Scottish developments. Characteristics of its site will include:

1. 50 hectare greenfield site, extensively landscaped,
2. Proximity to Dundee University and teaching hospital, Dundee airport, and rail and harbour facilities,
3. Access to roads of motorway standard,
4. Specifically designed for high-tech businesses, both large and small, with a low-density of development.

Figures 10.61 and 10.62 show the location of this developing industrial park.

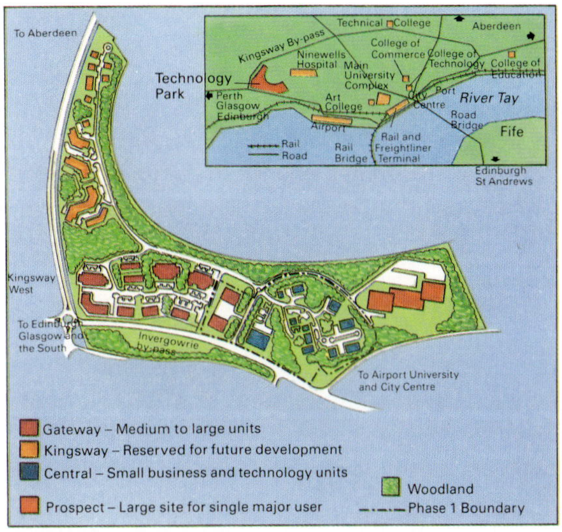

Fig. 10.61 *Map – Dundee Technology Park*

Fig. 10.62 *Dundee Technology Park site*

Activities

1 Write down the main features of a business park and suggest why they might provide suitable sites for industrial development.
2 Using fig. 10.59 draw a sketchmap to show the location of the Cambridge Science Park.

Unemployment and changing manufacturing

The decline of employment

Unemployment and underemployment (part-time and occasionally employed people who may work for only a few hours a week and so not have a full week's earnings) are problems in both developed and developing countries. Along with its partners in the European Community, Britain has experienced a sharp rise in unemployment during recent years. In 1962 unemployment in Britain stood at 432 000 (4% of those working). In 1987 over 3 millions were unemployed (13%). The idea of a 'job for life', for all those willing and able to work, no longer applies, with unemployment as high as 28% in parts of the country. Youth unemployment is a particular problem. Figure 10.63 shows that three-quarters of Sheffield's school-leavers go on to Youth Training Schemes and only 13% go straight into employment. Large-scale unemployment can be said to have split the jobs market into two. There are secure, usually salaried, skilled workers and there are less secure, often unskilled or seasonal workers, the unemployed and the underemployed. Two million jobs have been lost since the late-1970s. The number of jobs lost or gained in the ten main regions of Britain is shown in fig. 10.64.

Fig. 10.63 *School-leavers looking for work in Sheffield*

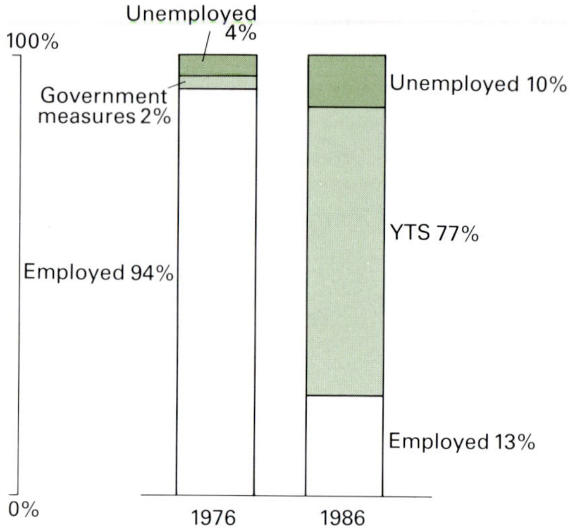

Figure 10.65 shows the pattern of unemployment in Britain in 1987. It has been suggested that unemployment shows a North-South divide in the country. It is

Fig. 10.64 *Job losses and gains in the regions of Britain, 1979 to 1987*

Region	*1979–83 ('000s)*	*1984–87 ('000s)*	*Type of jobs lost or gained*	
Scotland	− 204	− 12	*Lost*	*Gained*
North	− 191	+ 20	Mining	Clothing and
Yorkshire & Humberside	− 240	+ 5	Steel	Footwear
North West	− 374	− 41	Shipbuilding	Insurance
Wales	− 145	− 30	Railways	Electronics
West Midlands	− 298	+ 78	Agriculture	Electrical Engineering
East Midlands	− 132	+ 91		Health Service
South West	− 84	+ 54		Light Industries
South East	− 391	+269		
East Anglia	− 15	+ 74		
British Total	−2074	+508		

generally higher in the North and people find it more difficult to get a job there. Figure 10.65 does show, however, that parts of the South East also had a very large growth in unemployment between 1979 and 1983. The Severn-Humber line can be misleading. There is more poverty, decay and unemployment in the North and more prosperity and employment in the South. However, there are pockets of higher and lower development in all regions.

Rising unemployment has been associated with changes in manufacturing industry. The switch from a manufacturing to a service society, sometimes called de-industrialisation, is partly responsible for the higher unemployment. Look at fig. 10.66. Many of the new industries do not employ large numbers of people. Despite the growth of high-tech manufacturing, only 10% of new jobs in the USA are in this type of industry. Cambridge, with many high-tech industries still has a 10.1% unemployment rate. It is the changes in the structure of industry and techniques of manufacturing that cause most unemployment. Heavy, 'smokestack' industries like shipbuilding, steel making and textile manufacture have declined to produce unemployment 'blackspots' in areas which once over-specialised. Labour saving automation has caused much unemployment. It is predicted that by the 1990s manufacturing industry will employ no more than 20% of Britain's workers. Unemployment is also affected by a variety of other causes as well as changes in industry. These include general trade recessions, government economic policy, and reluctance of people to migrate to areas with job vacancies.

In developing countries unemployment and underemployment are extremely high and in parts of Africa have been estimated at averaging well over 35%. Unemployment from a lack of money for investment in tools and equipment is common in developing countries. Figure 10.67 shows the populations of the developing and the developed worlds in 1980 and predicted for the year 2000 divided into those employed and those unemployed and economically inactive. Underemployment or disguised employment is a particular feature of developing countries. There are many part-time or unofficial workers in the informal sector. It must also be said that the informal sector is growing in many developed countries.

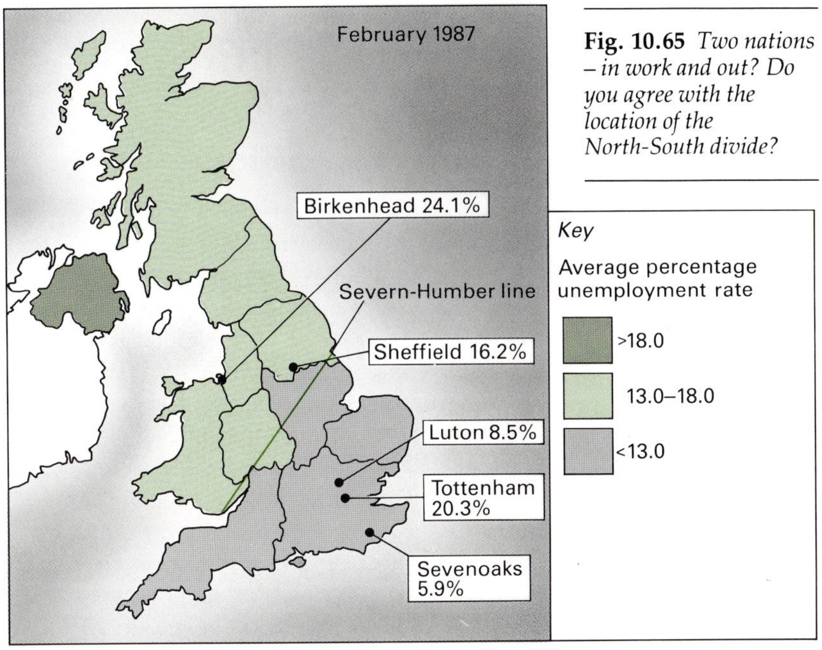

Fig. 10.65 *Two nations – in work and out? Do you agree with the location of the North-South divide?*

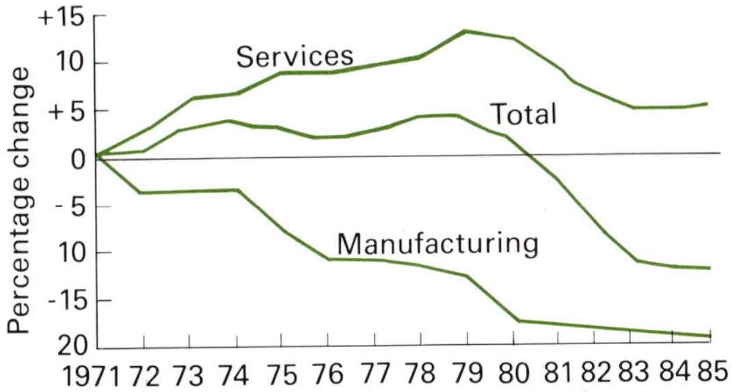

Fig. 10.66 *Employment changes in Britain, 1971 to 1985*

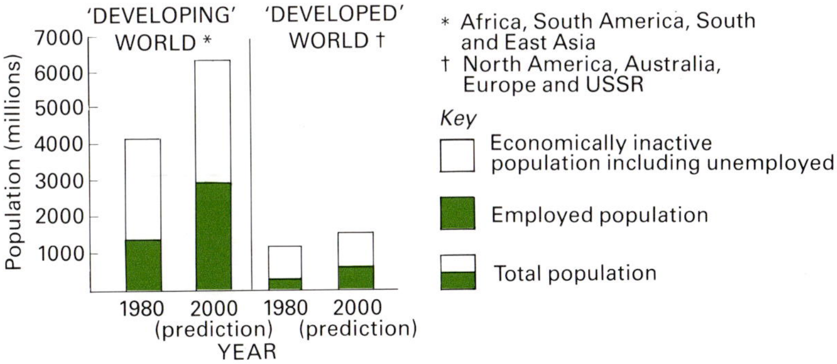

Fig. 10.67 *The employed and the economically inactive parts of the populations of developed and developing regions*

Activities

1 Study fig. 10.65 which shows Britain divided into North and South. In your groups, discuss a) your images of the North; b) your images of the South.
Then discuss whether there is a North-South divide.

2 Write a paragraph to explain why modern industrial development is increasing unemployment.

Old manufacturing areas

Regions decline industrially

Some regions grow economically. Others decline. Despite government regional policies, imbalance between regions is common. In Britain unemployment, incomes and living standards vary between the regions. Decline is most noticeable in the old industrial areas which developed in the North, the Midlands and Wales during the Industrial Revolution. These regions tended to specialise in heavy, smokestack industries such as steel, cotton and shipbuilding. They were very vulnerable to changes affecting those industries. Areas which did not 'have all their eggs in one basket', had more diversified industry. They were less vulnerable to change.

Fig. 10.68 *Industrial decline*

There are various changes that can cause an old industrial area to experience economic problems:

1. The resources that attracted industry to the area in the first place can become exhausted eg iron ore in Cleveland.
2. The introduction of new techniques, equipment and ways of industrial organisation which require fewer employees causes unemployment.
3. Demand for traditional products may fall.
4. Production costs may become higher than those in other areas, so a region becomes less competitive.
5. There is a lack of money for investment in modern developments.

Industrial inertia

Sheffield was a largely single-industry city, heavily dependent on its world famous steel industry. It has suffered from the decline of its former staple activity of steel-making. About 50 000 jobs that existed in steel and engineering before 1980 have since been lost, as whole plants closed down. The British steel industry has had to lose two-thirds of its jobs and to concentrate production at its five big modern integrated works at Port Talbot, Llanwern, Ravenscraig, Redcar and Scunthorpe. Steel, especially Sheffield steel, had become more expensive than steel produced elsewhere. Sheffield had long since declined as an ideal site for making steel. The industry had begun there during the Middle Ages and had developed during the Industrial Revolution. Iron ore, timber, fast-flowing streams, and later coal, limestone and hard gritstone had all been available. However, none of these resources saved the modern Sheffield steel industry. The local iron ore was used up long ago. The furnaces began to use electricity instead of coal or timber. Nevertheless, the industry stayed in its original site, even though the original attractions no longer applied. This is known as *industrial* or *geographical inertia*. There were better places to make steel by the twentieth century but relocation was costly and inconvenient. Specialised buildings and

Fig. 10.69 *The Lower Don Valley, Sheffield*

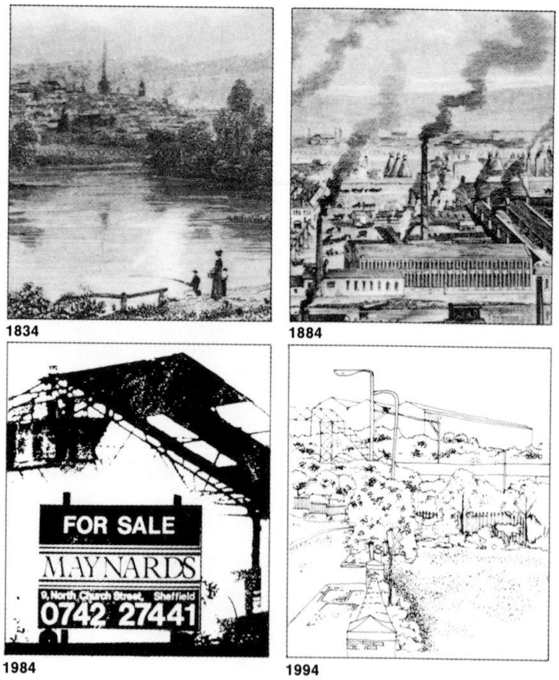

Sheffield City Council

machinery, and skilled, experienced labour were still available in Sheffield so, for some years the industry remained.

Figure 10.69 shows the changes in the Lower Don Valley at various dates as the steel industry has risen and fallen. Figure 10.70 shows the valley in 1986. In the 1960s it was one of the most heavily industrialised landscapes in the world. By 1984 some of Sheffield's traditional industrial area had become part of Britain's 'rustbelt' of old, declining industries. Often these areas were amongst the poorest places in Britain, even though they had been prosperous in the past.

Fig. 10.70 *The Lower Don Valley, Sheffield in 1986*

The closure of industry has effects on the economic welfare of whole regions. This is sometimes known as cumulative causation i.e. a vicious circle and is shown in fig. 10.72. The introduction of new industry to an area is likely to mean an opposite set of effects, and the development of a 'growth pole' or core, an area of growing industry and prosperity. Government industrial location policies tend to benefit these core areas where new industry is attracted. In some economic fringe areas like Sheffield, industry may be closing down.

Sheffield City Council has imaginative plans for the future of the Lower Don Valley, the now 'rundown' former home of its traditional steel industry. These plans involve using the land for leisure, recreation, retail developments and new industrial parkland. Some of the leisure and recreation facilities are being built for the 1991 World Student games, as is a 'City' airport and new light rail transit system.

Sheffield Urban Development Corporation set up in 1988 by the Government will now be responsible for developing this inner city area. Figure 10.71 shows how it is hoped that the valley will look in the 1990s.

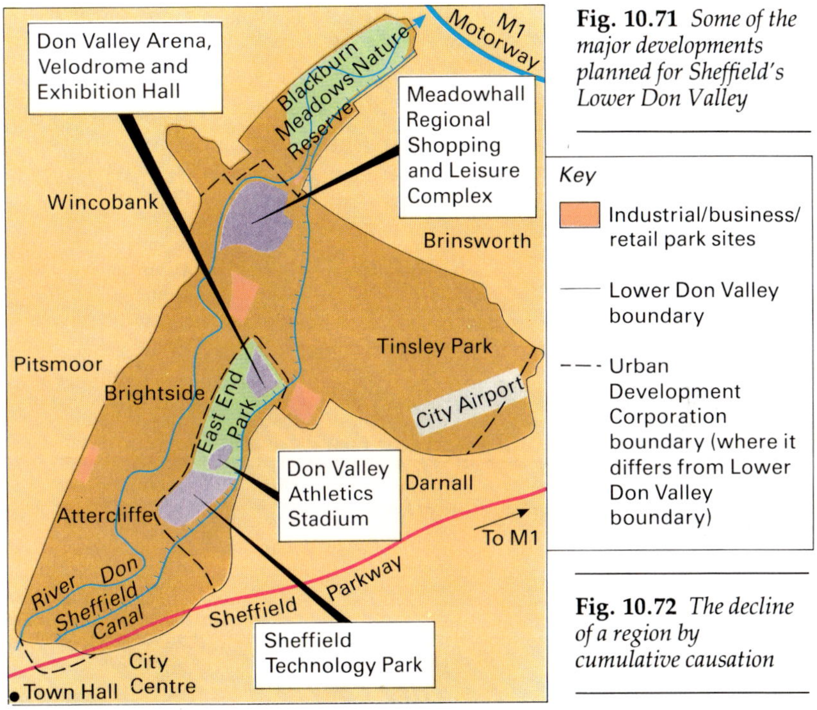

Fig. 10.71 *Some of the major developments planned for Sheffield's Lower Don Valley*

Fig. 10.72 *The decline of a region by cumulative causation*

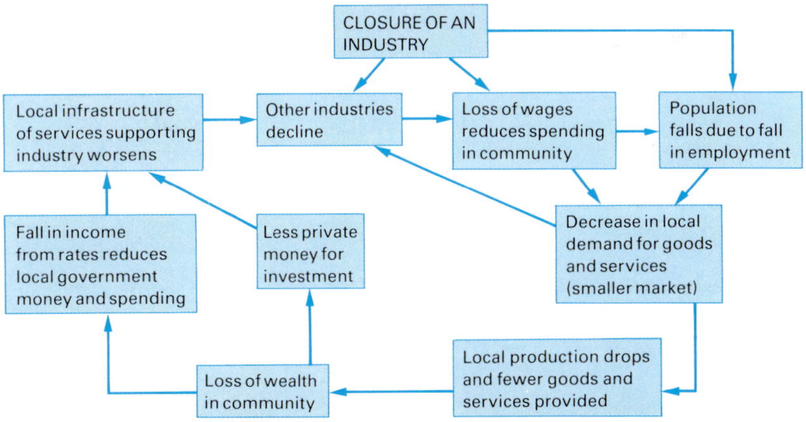

Activities

1 Use fig. 10.72 as a guide and draw a diagram to show the effects of a new industry on a region's welfare.
2 How will Sheffield City Council's plans for the environment of the Lower Don Valley be attractive to new industry?

Transnational companies

Some companies are richer than countries

Transnational companies are large, international firms operating across national boundaries, often in dozens of countries, and exerting enormous influence over people's lives. Those in charge of these transnational companies may have more influence on the shape of society than many of the elected politicians. Figure 10.73 shows the fifteen largest of these companies, listed in rank order of their sales turnover in US dollars. These fifteen companies, plus a further thirty-two, added to fifty-three countries make up the one hundred most financially powerful organisations in the world. Transnational companies have grown very quickly since the 1960s.

There are now more companies than countries with incomes greater than the GNP of Ireland. In 1985 the sales turnover of the Royal Dutch/Shell Group of Companies was £73 000 million; the GNP's of Argentina, Norway and Bangladesh were £67 000 million, £57 000 million and £13 000 million respectively. Figure 10.74 illustrates this point that the turnover of some transnational companies is greater than the GNP of some countries. The largest transnationals have turnovers greater than the combined GNP's of large groups of African countries.

Fig. 10.73 *The world's 15 largest companies in 1983*

Turnover ranking (in US $)	*Company*	*Headquarters*	*Main industries*
1	Exxon (Esso)	New York	Oil, Chemicals
2	Royal Dutch/Shell Group	London/The Hague	Oil, Chemicals
3	General Motors	Detroit	Cars, Trucks
4	Ford Motors	Dearborn, Michigan	Cars, Trucks
5	Texaco	New York	Oil
6	Mobil Oil	New York	Oil
7	British Petroleum	London	Oil, Chemicals
8	Standard Oil of California	San Francisco	Oil, Chemicals
9	National Iranian Oil	Tehran	Oil
10	Gulf Oil	Pittsburgh	Oil, Coal
11	Unilever	London	Food, Detergents
12	General Electric	Fairfield, Connecticutt	Electrical Products
13	International Business Machines (IBM)	Armonk, New York	Computers
14	International Tel. & Tel.	New York	Telecommunications
15	Chrysler	Highland Park, Michigan	Cars, Trucks

Fig. 10.74 *Total annual sales turnover of 5 transnational companies and the GNP of five countries in 1985*

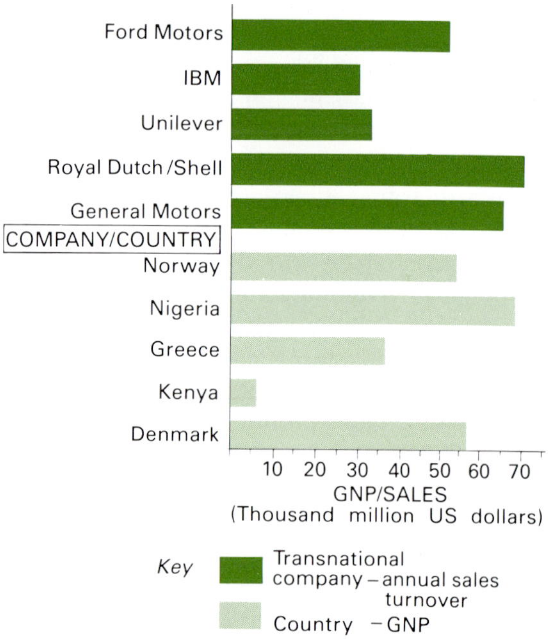

Fig. 10.75 *The countries in which Unilever has plants*

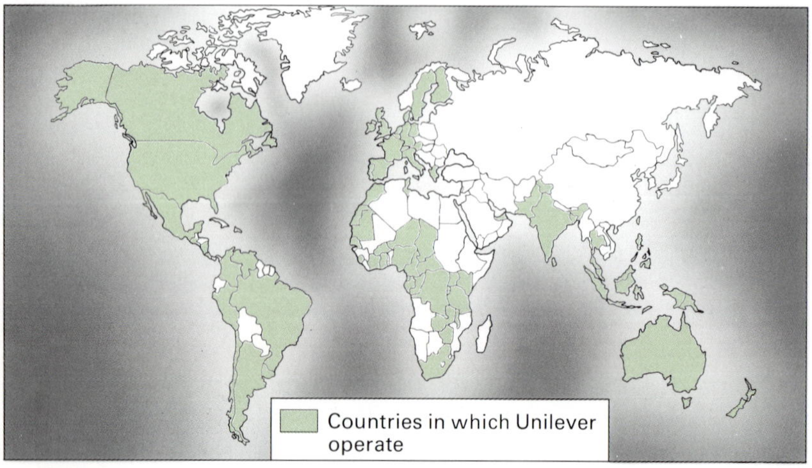

Unilever PLC (UK) and Unilever NV (Holland) is a transnational corporation composed of 8000 firms. Many of these are multi-plant and multi-industry, making 1200 different products and operating in all five continents and seventy-five countries (fig. 10.75). It is a truly world-wide company whose products sold in Britain include Wall's Ice Cream, Bird's Eye frozen goods, Lux, Lifebuoy and Pears soaps, Vesta foods, Stork margarine, Lipton's tea, Crisp N' Dry cooking oil, Signal toothpaste, Batchelor's Cup-a-Soup and many others.

Are transnationals too powerful?

Transnational companies have an important influence upon the organisation of both manufacturing and agriculture in developing countries. However they have brought both advantages and disadvantages to the countries in which they have located. The table in fig. 10.76 shows the main advantages and disadvantages of the build-up of foreign companies in developing countries. It is clear that the factories, farms and jobs of a transnational company in a country will be part of a larger organisation. So, they may depend on processes and workers elsewhere. They will also depend on decisions made elsewhere. The transnationals play a major part in developing world agriculture. In many countries which were formerly colonies, plantation commodities like tea and coffee are grown for export to developed countries. This can dominate agriculture and the whole economy of the country. For example in Sri Lanka such products, especially tea, take up twice the land area used for growing local food crops and account for 76 per cent of the country's foreign earnings.

Because transnational companies are so powerful, decisions about what is grown and about prices are made outside the developing countries. The Brandt Report of 1980 suggested that the governments of both 'North' and 'South' should develop a 'code of conduct' to control the actions of these massive companies. Decisions made at the company's headquarters (see fig. 10.73) can vitally affect the countries in which they operate. Decisions made in the interests of the company may be against the interests of these countries.

Fig. 10.76 *Profits made by 3 transnational companies in Brazil, 1960 to 1980*

Transnational company	*Profits made as a percentage of original capital investment*	*Percentage of profits sent back to home country*
Volkswagen (of West Germany)	+ 300%	80%
Pirelli (of Italy)	+ 350%	70%
Exxon (of USA)	+ 1875%	40%

Transnationals
eg Unilever, Brooke-Bond Liebig ...... sell 85% of world tea exports
eg Nestle; General Foods .... sell 85% of world coffee exports
eg Geest; Del Monte.............. sell 70% of world banana exports
eg Tate and Lyle .... sell 60% of world sugar exports

General Motors, with subsidiaries around the world like Vauxhall and Opel, are able to switch production from one country to another and so affect the livelihoods of working people.

Fig. 10.77 *Advantages and disadvantages that transnational companies may create for developing countries*

Advantages	*Disadvantage*
Provide money (both capital and foreign money) for development	Make profits in developing countries often sending more of them back home than they invest locally
Provide jobs for local people	Can undercut local prices and drive local firms out of business so causing some job losses
Introduce new technology	Hire mostly unskilled local people with many skilled and management jobs being held by foreigners
Produce useful products for the local market which might otherwise have to be imported eg oil, cars	May produce goods not appropriate to developing countries, but being foreign carry appeal especially with the rich eg Nestle's powdered baby milk . . .
Often pay higher wages than local firms	Attracted by cheap, controllable labour, especially female and pay less than workers doing same job in 'developed' countries
Are a cause of change, and progress (economic growth)	Often borrow local capital rather than import it and so perhaps reduce local industry's supply of finance
	Technology is often imported with Research and Development work staying in the developed countries

Activities

1 In your groups, discuss the following: Are products like Guinness, powdered baby milk, Lux soap, Coca-cola, and 7-Up, which are produced by transnational companies, appropriate for sale in developing countries?
2 How are the livelihoods of working people in some developing countries linked to the profits and policies of transnational companies? Write a paragraph.
3 Write a paragraph, using fig. 10.76, to show how profits from transnational companies in Brazil are used.

The need for manufacturing

Developing countries

The 140 developing countries of the world together produce less than 10 per cent of the world's manufacturing production yet they had about 75 per cent of the world's population in 1985. The whole of Africa produces only about 1 per cent of the world's manufactured goods. There have been increases in production in some African countries especially Ivory Coast, Cameroon and Nigeria, but throughout most of Africa, production is either falling or not changing. This very low rate of manufacturing industrialisation helps to explain the fact that they are developing rather than developed countries. Africa is not naturally poor in an economic sense. It has many raw materials needed in industry such as chrome, manganese, uranium, oil, natural gas and platinum. However it remains mainly a producer of primary products rather than a manufacturer of goods. These products are mainly exported to the developed industrial countries for processing. The world trade of India in fig. 10.78 demonstrates this imbalance between developed and developing countries. Japan, for example, depends on imports of iron ore from India, wood and rubber from Malaysia, copper from the Philippines and Papua New Guinea, petroleum from Indonesia and cotton from Mexico. This pattern is even more striking in those developing countries which were formerly colonies for European countries. They supplied raw materials for the manufacturing industries of the developed colonising countries and provided a market for their manufactured products.

There is another problem for the primary producers of the developing world. World trade is arranged so that their primary products sell at comparatively cheap prices in the developed countries. This helps to explain the situation shown by fig. 10.78. Developing countries have an import bill greater than the export bill. Most developing countries are in debt, especially those in South America. Chile's foreign debts amount to 88 per cent of its GNP. In Argentina it would take more than a full year of annual exports (114%) to pay off its foreign debt. Some developing countries borrowed large amounts of money in the 1970s for spending on major, industrial projects which carried a bit of prestige. In the 1980s they have faced a crisis in trying to pay for the interest on the loans, let alone repaying the original capital loan.

Many developing countries are keen to develop manufacturing industries. Most of them depend too heavily on agriculture and have less than a quarter of their workers in manufacturing. Kenya, for example, is mainly an agricultural country in which manufacturing contributes 13 per cent to the GNP, which is quite a high figure in Africa. Small-scale and cottage industries, often located in villages, make up a large part of this manufacturing output. This kind of small-scale manufacturing employs large numbers of people and is encouraged by governments in many developing countries. Figure 10.79 shows Nepalis spinning and carding wool in Danabari, Bhutan. The cottage industry or domestic system existed in early eighteenth century Britain and still exists in many developing countries today. It involves craftsmen working in their own homes or in small workshops. Raw materials are supplied by a merchant who also collects the finished goods and makes arrangements for their sale.

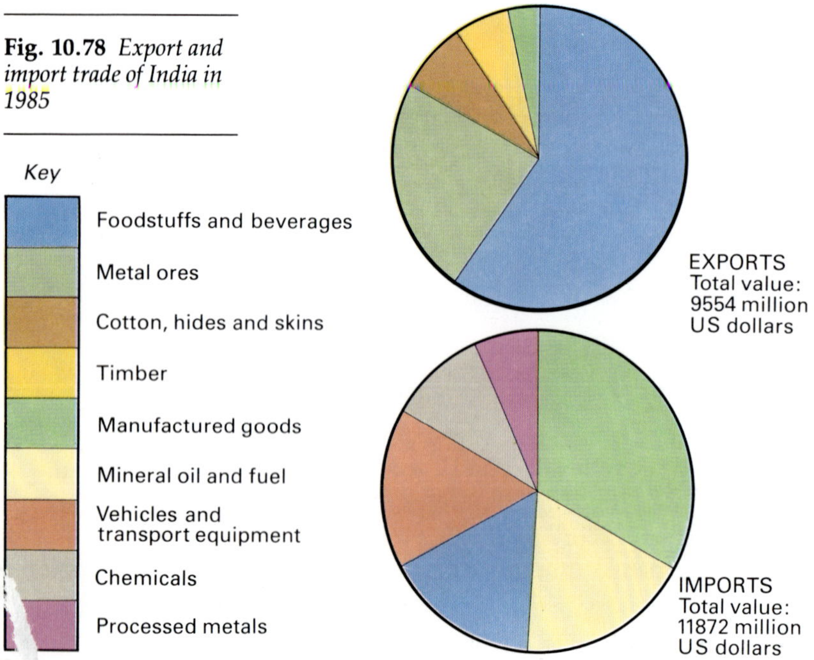

Fig. 10.78 *Export and import trade of India in 1985*

Fig. 10.79 *Spinners and wool carders, Danabari, Bhutan*

Most developing countries have been trying to develop manufacturing industry in order to increase the level of economic welfare of their people. They have faced problems in doing this. Many of these countries have produced a series of national development plans. For example, the Fourth National Development Plan for Nigeria, 1981–85, recognised the importance of using the money from oil exports to encourage industrial development. Nigeria is potentially the most economically developed country in tropical Africa, but its industry has been dominated by foreign companies and foreign capital. Cheap labour has attracted a number of multi-national companies to its ports and large cities.

Large-scale industrial projects have been carried out in other developing countries, for example, Ghana's Volta Scheme (known by Ghanaians in the 1970s as the 'big project'). Figure 10.80 shows Ghana's attempt to produce a large supply of cheap electricity in order to encourage industry. The Akosombo dam, generates hydro-electricity both for the aluminium smelter at Tema and for the rest of Ghana. However, the building of the dam and flooding of the river Volta to produce Lake Volta resulted in a loss of agricultural land and the rehousing of 80 000 people. Despite such grand industrial projects like the Volta Scheme and the recent encouragement of small-scale enterprises, most developing countries still believe they are under-industrialised.

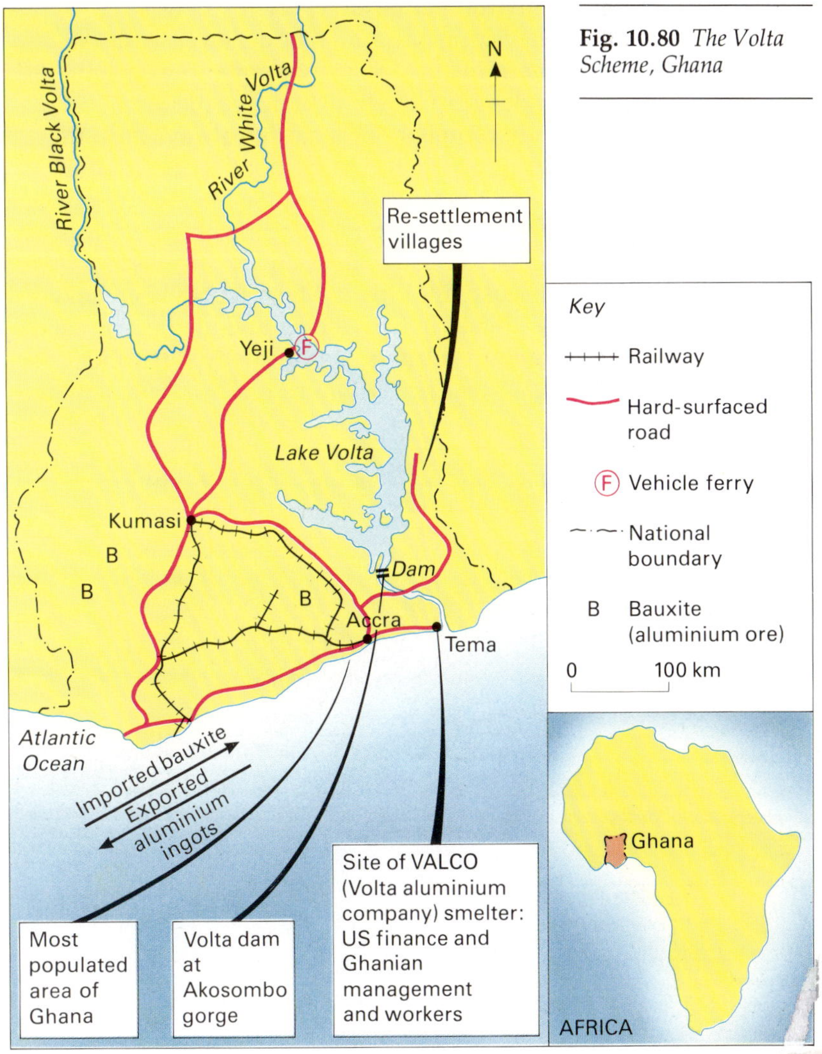

Fig. 10.80 *The Volta Scheme, Ghana*

Manufacturing and the environment

Manufacturing can cause conflicts between industrialists and people. Along with many other local authorities, Leicester City Council now tries to prevent further mixing of housing and manufacturing. However, housing does occur in some existing industrial areas. It is recognised that manufacturing has three unfavourable effects on the local environment:

1. Traffic and parking problems
2. Noise and air pollution
3. Poor appearance

These effects can give rise to conflicts between industrialists and residents. For example, the cars of factory workers parked on a street may prevent residents from parking their own cars in front of their homes and may be a source of danger to children. Local authority planners today consider the environmental effects of any new development. Can it be achieved without harming the local environment? To what extent can it help to improve the local environment? This has not always been the attitude taken and it is not the case in some developing countries today where air pollution from factories and dumping of factory wastes into rivers often goes on uncontrolled. Industrialisation in Malaysia has been linked with falls in fish catches and medical problems among villagers, such as body sores and gastro-enteritis. Figure 10.82 shows a familiar sight in the industrial areas of developing countries. These effects of manufacturing, are known as social costs or externalities. They are costs borne not by the manufacturer but paid for outside by society, in many forms such as illness, dirty washing and traffic congestion.

In the nineteenth century, Sheffield became a major centre for iron and steel-making, and was once described as the 'foulest and most disgusting of places'. The work of Sanitary Inspectors, Environmental Health Officers, Planning Officers, Industrial Air Pollution inspectors and regulations by the local Council and Water Authority have enabled Sheffield to describe itself by 1970 as the 'cleanest industrial city in Europe'. Figure 10.81 shows how the level of sulphur dioxide in the air in Attercliffe, part of the Lower Don Valley steel-making and engineering area of Sheffield, has fallen over the past 25 years.

Fig. 10.82 *Air pollution from a cement factory, South Korea*

Fig. 10.81 *Airborne sulphur dioxide in Attercliffe*

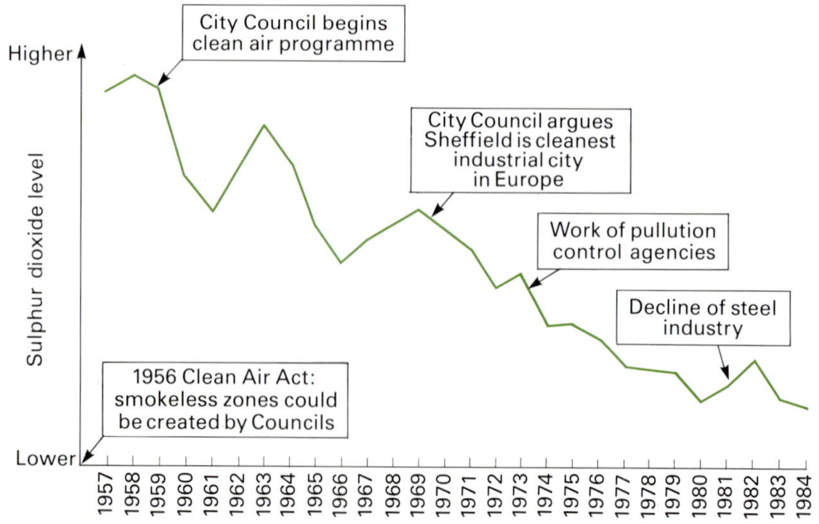

The decline of heavy industry in Britain, like the collapse of the Sheffield steel industry, has helped to reduce pollution. The chief air pollutants are smoke from industrial chimneys and domestic fires, sulphur dioxide from power stations and factories, and vehicle exhaust gases (look at fig. 10.83). Smoke is less of a problem today than the other two. In many urban areas the main sources of air pollution today are exhaust gases, especially nitrogen oxide, from very large numbers of motor vehicles. This causes the 'smog' of Los Angeles and the wearing of masks by pedestrians on the streets of Tokyo. British people living and working close to busy roads and motorways are worried about being exposed to high lead and carbon monoxide levels which come from high vehicle exhaust pollution.

Acid rain

Sulphur dioxide is produced in the air from the burning of coal and oil. This gas and nitrogen oxide from car exhausts mixes with water vapour in the atmosphere. The rain therefore contains nitric and sulphuric acids ('acid rain'). Power station chimneys are built tall to reduce the pollution around the station but it spreads further afield. Acid rain damages the environment in many ways. It corrodes buildings, paints and metals in British cities. It destroys forests and lakes in Norway, Sweden and Germany. Scandinavian countries complain that the acidic rain falling on them is largely caused by the sulphur dioxide put into the atmosphere by British power stations and carried by the westerly winds. Figure 10.83 shows how the amount of pollution from power stations has fallen since 1970, and how a further clean-up is planned for the future.

Fig. 10.83 *Fall in pollution levels from power stations in Britain*

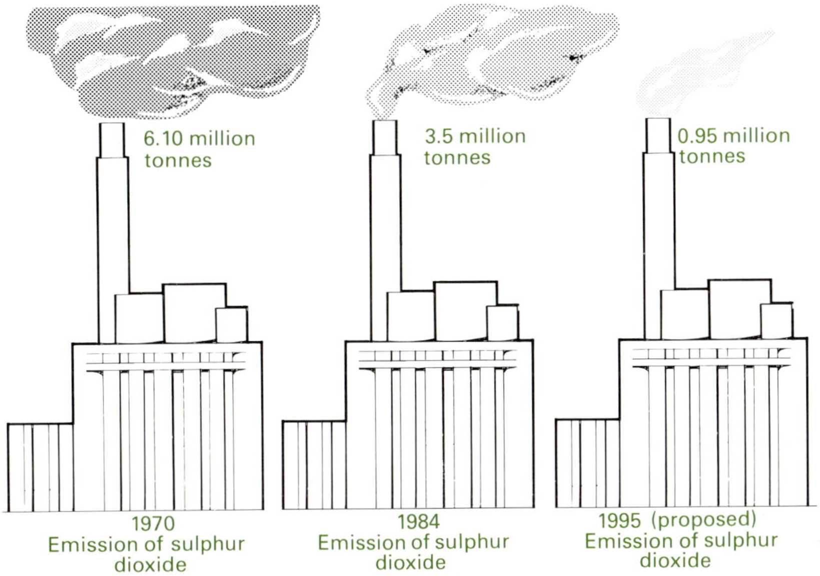

Economic gain/environmental loss

Manufacturing results in both gains and losses for people. It may have been that people in nineteenth century Sheffield thought the economic/social gains from heavy industrialisation were worth the environmental losses. Many of these losses were accidental and accepted by people at the time. But over time people's values change. Today, they may consider that the environmental losses resulting from industrialisation are not being balanced out by the economic/social gains. Modern, high-tech industries are less-polluting, and business parks do not allow activities which produce pollution to be located there. The conflicts between manufacturing and the environment which occur when a company wishes to extend limestone quarrying in the Peak District National Park can be seen in fig. 11.23 and illustrate the present concern that future generations should be protected.

11 SERVICES

The swing to service industries

A large proportion of the working population in developed countries is no longer employed in agriculture or manufacturing but in services. Figure 11.2 shows this for five countries and fig. 11.3 shows the importance of tertiary activities in London. These include wholesale and retail distribution, government and administration. The structure of the service sector is shown in fig. 11.1. Remember that service jobs can be split into tertiary and quaternary activities (look at page 82). Employment in shops, hotels, offices and other establishments providing services has grown rapidly in recent years, especially in developed countries. There are many reasons for this:

1. As the needs and demands of people have become more complex, the supply and range of services has increased.

Fig. 11.1 *The service sector*

Group	*Type*	*Examples of extablishments*
Trade	Retail	superstore, launderette, used-car dealer
	Wholesale	warehouse
Financial	Banking	building society, local bank
	Insurance	insurance broker's office
	Real Estate	estate agency
Other Services	Recreation	theatre, sports stadium, restaurant
	Vacation	hotel, camp site
	Transport and communications	petrol station, airport, bus depot
	Medical	hospital, surgery.
	Research and teaching	school, college, university, research laboratory
	Public administration	government offices, Town Hall
	Business and repair	advertising agencies, accountants, TV repair premises, computer consultancy

Fig. 11.2 *The size of the service sector in 5 countries*

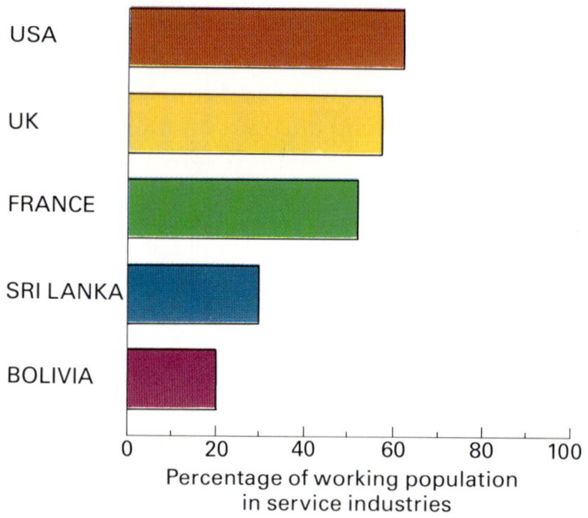

Fig. 11.3 *London's jobs in 1985*

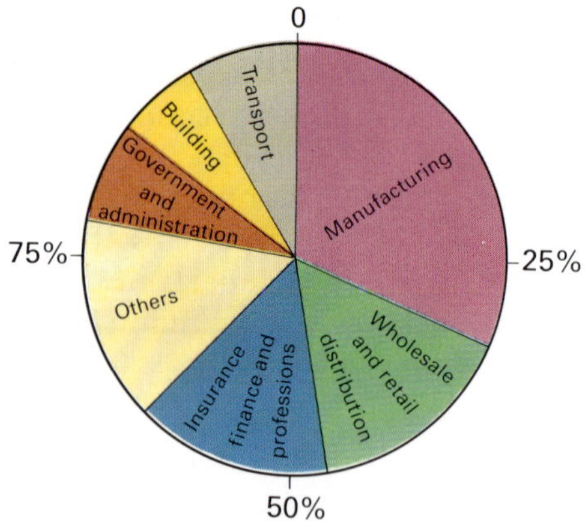

2. The length of the working day has fallen and the amount of leisure time has increased. The importance of leisure activities has grown tremendously.
3. Economic growth has raised income levels per head so that people can afford more leisure activities.
4. Manufacturing, especially heavy manufacturing such as textiles and mining has declined as an employer of labour. More people are taking jobs in tertiary activities.

The influence of transport

Service activities are strongly attracted to large urban centres. They are located near to demand, so they are said to be customer-, or market-oriented. City centres are where government and commercial offices, shops, entertainment, hotels and public services like libraries are found (look at fig. 11.4). For many people, 'city centre' means shopping. Out-of-town shopping and service industries in the suburbs such as wholesale warehouses and offices have been made possible by improvements in their accessibility. This is the result of developments in transport and communication. A 'transport revolution' has occurred mainly because the number of cars has greatly increased. There were about 2 million cars in Britain in 1950. Today there are over 14 million. Rapid transit systems such as the Tyneside Metro, urban and intercity motorways and regional airports have made suburban sites attractive for tertiary activities. The result has been an explosion in the movement and mobility of people and goods. This has led to a reduction in time-distance (ie the length of time a journey takes) between places. Such developments produce even more economic activities. Transport improvements lead to the better distribution of goods and so a manufacturing industry may be able to supply a bigger market.

Fig. 11.4 *Sheffield City centre.*

The influence of leisure

Transport and leisure services are major employers of people and an important part of the service sector. The travel industry is one of Britain's four main earners of foreign money, along with banking, insurance and shipping. Invisible earnings which come from services rather than goods, are very important to the British economy. Leisure activities and the social environment are now important resources in many areas. They strongly influence economic growth. Figure 11.5 shows details of three recently developed and contrasting leisure facilities in the borough of Rotherham. These amenities are now regarded as a basic need in many communities.

Fig. 11.5 *Three contrasting, modern leisure facilities in Rotherham*

Site	*Location*	*Leisure activities*
Herringthorpe Leisure Centre	Close to town centre with high accessibility on large open space.	Athletics stadium; playing fields, including all-weather surface; tennis courts; swimming pool with wave machine, slide and large shallow water area and teaching pool; two 3-level sports halls for badminton, basketball, volleyball, indoor tennis, netball, cricket, five-a-side football, archery, rifle shooting, golf, fencing, martial arts, keep-fit and gymnasium activities. Suitable for public meetings, concerts, dances and exhibitions. Bar and restaurant. Community centre and sports centre.
Ulley Reservoir	30-acre reservoir in a rural area outside built-up area	Sailing, canoeing, fishing and nature study on 20 acres of water. Toilet and car parking.
Valley Park	70-acre park between two large housing developments in town suburbs	Tennis courts; bowling greens; putting green; pitch-and-putt course; landscaped and woodland footpaths.

Activities

1 Copy fig. 11.1 into your books and add a fourth column, headed 'Examples of jobs'. Name examples of each type of job in this column, eg medical – doctors.
2 For a town or city you know, give examples of specific service activities under the headings: a) Government offices; b) Commercial offices; c) Entertainment; (d) Hotels; e) Retailing; f) Public services.
3 In a small group, plan a new suburban leisure park/shopping centre. It should include a theme park, a golf course, a lake for water sports as well as half a million square metres for shops and car parks. Use a 1:25 000 Ordnance Survey map which contains a large town and plan your location. Your group should produce an illustrated report of the plan.

Retailing

Traditional retailing

The selling of goods directly to the public is known as retailing. It employs around 10 per cent of the working population in Britain and is strongly attracted to CBDs. Figure 11.6 shows that in five Derbyshire settlements there is a relationship between the size of the population and the number of shops found in main shopping centres.

Fig. 11.6 *Shops in main shopping centres either CBD or suburban in Derbyshire settlements*

Town/City	*Population*	*Number of shops*
Derby	214 900	549
Chesterfield	70 546	385
Ilkeston	33 031	230
Ripley	18 900	150
Matlock	19 684	85

There are different types of shopping centre, at different locations in most towns. The main types are:

1. *City centre (CBD)* – this is usually the largest and most important shopping centre and serves the whole settlement. It may include under-cover shopping complexes or precincts eg the Arndale Centre in Wandsworth, London and the Victoria and Broad Marsh Centres in Nottingham.
2. *Suburban high street* – these centres serve large areas of towns and are located along main roads, often at cross-roads in the suburbs. Figure 11.7 shows 14 large shopping centres in the suburbs of Sheffield, most of them representing old villages which were absorbed as the city grew. They are sometimes called OBDs (Ordinary Business Districts).
3. *Neighbourhood shopping centre* – these are smaller shopping areas scattered throughout the housing areas of towns and are often little more than a few local/corner shops.

Fig. 11.7 *Shopping centres and superstores in Sheffield*

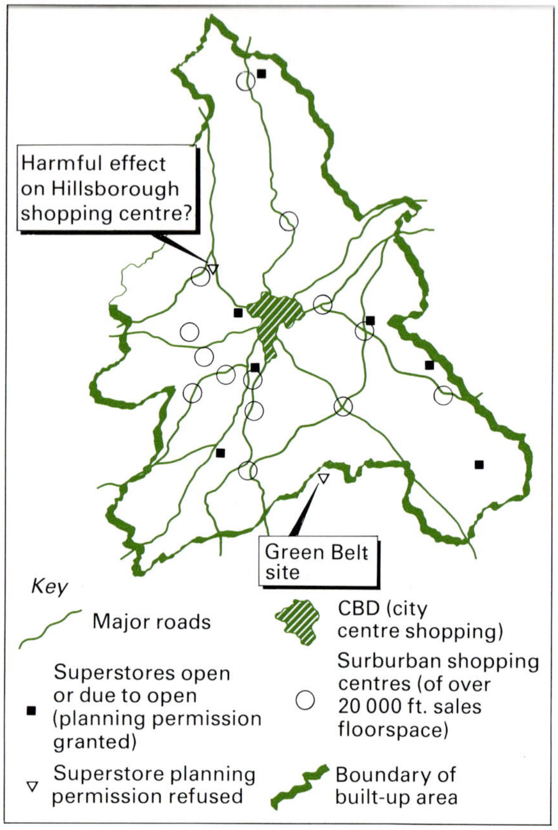

Changes in retailing

Retailing is a fast changing industry in many countries. Recent changes include
- a decline in the number of small independent shops
- a general decrease in the number of shops
- a general increase in the size of shops
- an increase in the importance of multiples or chain stores
- the construction of new shopping centres and superstores where most shopping can be done in the one centre or one shop
- more out-of-town shopping.

In the USA huge shopping schemes, which include hypermarkets, have been built on the outskirts of many towns and cities. They are accompanied by facilities such as cinemas, restaurants, swimming pools and playgrounds. Brent Cross in North London and the Metro Centre in Gateshead are examples of the move towards the American locational pattern of out-of-town shopping (see fig. 11.8). Out-of-town superstores owned by a few leading retailers such as Asda, Tesco and Sainsbury's have been replacing small independent shops. It is said that one new supermarket replaces 10–15 small shops.

Fig. 11.8 *The UK superstore revolution*

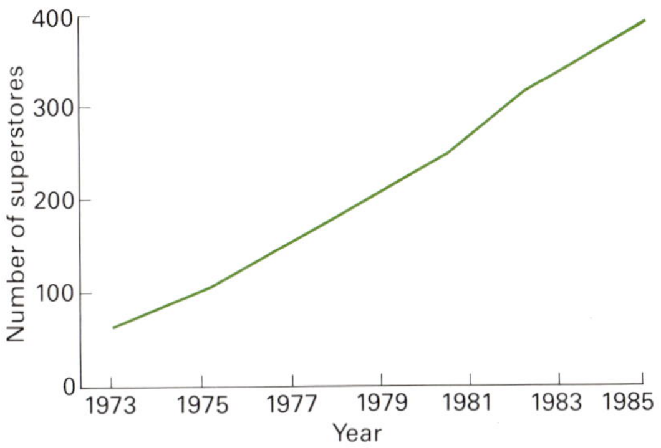

There are many different effects of the superstore revolution in Britain.

1. Some people have further to travel to shop. This is a problem for the old and infirm; for those without their own transport and those living where public transport is inconvenient or unreliable.
2. Congestion and pollution occur in suburbs due to the increased use of the car for shopping.
3. Large areas of countryside have been used for purpose-built superstores and their car parks.
4. There are fewer shops in villages and suburbs.
5. 'One-stop' shopping (a wide range of goods under one roof), using the car and free on-site parking has made shopping more convenient.
6. People buy their own storage facilities (eg freezers) so they shop less often.
7. Lower prices can be charged because often there has been an increase in bulk-buying.

The development of out-of-town shopping centres is threatening to kill town centre trade in many towns. There is a growing conflict between established town centre shopping and new out-of-town shopping centres like that in fig. 11.9. Local Authority Planning Departments faced with this conflict consider the following points when deciding whether to grant planning permission for new superstores:

- Will it harm the future of shops in established shopping centres?
- Will it be readily served by public transport?
- Will it cause traffic congestion?
- Will it harm the amenities of the surrounding area?

Fig. 11.9 *Artist's impression of an out-of-town food superstore in Chesterfield, Derbyshire*

Chesterfield Council were in the first place opposed to shopping development outside the town centre as they believed it would damage existing businesses in the town centre.

The property developers believe that food shopping patterns are changing and the public require easy access and level parking for their weekly main shopping trips. Town centres can no longer provide for car-borne shoppers because of traffic congestion and difficulties of parking, particularly in multi-storey car parks which are unsuitable for shopping trolleys and unpopular with women because of the danger of muggers.

Activities

1 Write down the effects of the superstore revolution in two lists:
a) Advantages to the community. b) Disadvantages to the community.

2 Write to the planning office of a city authority in which there is a large city-centre shopping complex (eg the Victoria and Broad Marsh Centres in Nottingham; the Eagle centre in Derby or the Arndale Centre in Wandsworth, London). Ask for a plan of the complex then make a classification of the shops. What are the advantages of using this type of centre?

Offices in the modern industrial landscape

Around one-third of the British workforce is employed in offices in large towns. The landscape of the CBD in the towns of most developed countries is dominated by office blocks. Figure 11.10 shows the recent increase in office jobs in five developed countries. These figures have to be estimated because it is difficult to find out the exact number of people employed in offices. Manufacturing for example requires office staff, yet an office worker employed by an engineering firm would be counted as a worker in manufacturing industry. Office work involves the collecting, processing and exchanging of information, and includes such workers as lawyers, typists, estate agents and government officials. Figure 11.11 shows a systems diagram for an office. Compare it to fig. 9.6.

Fig. 11.10 *Office jobs in five developed countries*

Country	*Office jobs as percentage of total number of jobs*	
	1960	*1980*
France	20.2	31.7
New Zealand	27.9	32.2
Sweden	23.5	40.9
UK	24.0	34.1
USA	31.7	41.1

Fig. 11.11 *An office system*

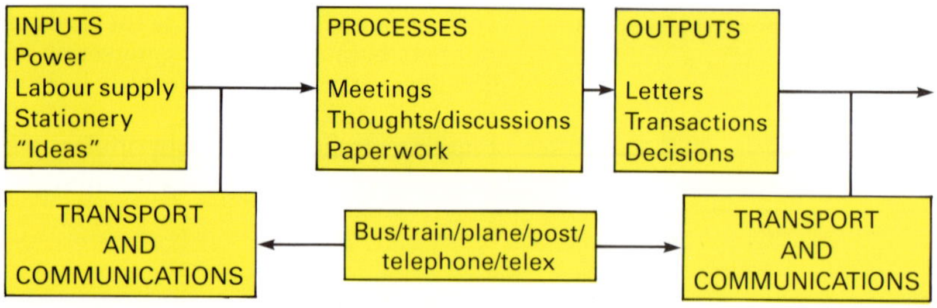

Office work in towns

Most office jobs are located in large cities, especially capital cities. This centralisation of offices in capital cities is as noticeable in developing countries as in developed ones. Offices are an important part of the landscape of cities, usually clustering in the Central Business Districts where land values (rents) are at their highest. In Nottingham 78% of the total government office floorspace and 34% of the local government office floorspace are in the CBD of the city.

Clustering in city centres is also common amongst commercial offices (eg insurance companies, solicitors). There are several reasons for this:

1. They need strong links with other offices and associated businesses such as estate agents, solicitors, banks and building societies. It is convenient to be close together so that 'face-to-face contact' is possible. However, modern telecommunications like telephone calls, telex machines and computer terminals have reduced the need for offices to cluster around other offices.
2. They are the most accessible sites for both staff and customers.
3. The traditional office area in the CBD carries prestige. It is very visible to the public and has access to business contacts and other services for the staff. There are usually office premises available.

Fig. 11.12 *An advertisement placed by the location of offices bureau during the 1970s*

High-rise offices are a common feature of the centre of towns. Because of the competition for land, sky-scrapers are no longer restricted to New York. Figure 11.13 could apply to any city centre in the developed world. London has a major role in office location and employment in Britain; over half of all office jobs in the country are located in Central London. Over half of the thousand largest companies in Britain have their head offices there. Office employment is clearly very important for London's prosperity. Between 1981 and 1984, London lost 90 000 manufacturing jobs but gained 45 000 jobs in the offices of financial institutions. Many of these are in the Square Mile around the Bank of England known as 'The City'.

Decentralisation of offices

The concentration of offices in the CBD of large cities has disadvantages. London for example has become congested. There is great pressure for car parking space as people commute to work by car and as central land values soar. This has led to office relocation to suburban sites or out-of-London locations. This policy of office decentralisation has applied to both the public sector (eg government) and private sector (ie companies). The government has moved many of its own offices away from London:

- the DVLC (Vehicle Licencing headquarters) to Swansea
- the Manpower Services Commission to Sheffield
- the Health and Safety Executive to Bootle
- the DHSS (Health and Social Security) to Newcastle

Between 1977 and 1989, 36% of the Civil Service headquarters jobs are planned to be moved from London. Of these 31 000 jobs, about 28 000 will have gone to 'Assisted Areas'* (eg the Manpower Services Commission took 1 500 jobs to Sheffield between 1979 and 1982) and the remainder to 'Non Assisted Areas'.†

In the private sector government policy has encouraged companies to move their offices out of London, especially to 'Assisted Areas' through the Location of Offices Bureau set up in 1963 (but now closed). The policy has also been effective in moving private sector office jobs away from Central London. It has been estimated that over 150 000 jobs have moved since 1963 to London suburbs, locations close to London (eg Croydon), and to 'Assisted Areas' further afield. However, movement has still been mainly to the 'Non Assisted Areas' of south-east England. Despite all the efforts, most office jobs remain in London.

(*also known as Areas for Expansion)
(†also known as Standard Regions)

Fig. 11.13 *City centre office tower blocks in Toronto*

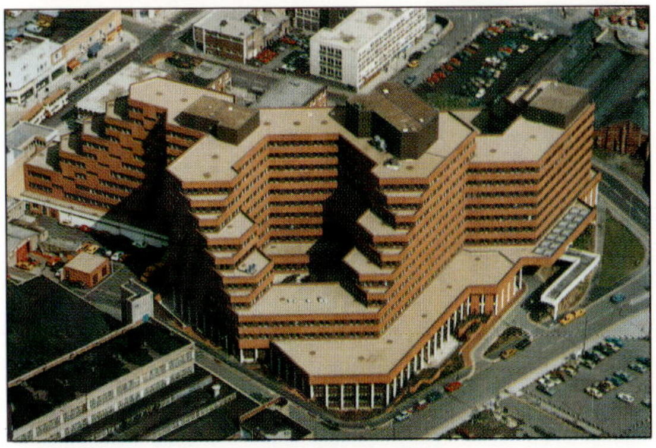

Fig. 11.14 *Manpower Services Commission Head Office, Sheffield*

Activities

1 Write down six examples of jobs regarded as office work.
2 Carry out a class/year group survey. How many of their parents work in offices? Show the proportions in a bar-graph.
3 Imagine you are the director of a major company which is considering moving its headquarters out of London to a northern town. You support the move and see many advantages of relocation in the north. You are also aware of some of the problems that will occur in carrying out the move. Make a list of the advantages and another list of the problems the company might face.

Service industries in developing countries

The main difference between the service industries of developed countries and developing countries is that the former have a much higher proportion of workers in this area. There are professional workers and office workers in both government and commercial companies in towns in developing countries, but not as many as in developed ones. The centres of towns, especially capital cities, in developing countries are not unlike those in developed countries. Mombasa, in Kenya, is a good example of such a city. Look at figs 11.15 and 11.16 both of which suggest the presence of a Central Business District and employment in service industries.

Fig. 11.15 *Mombasa, Kenya*

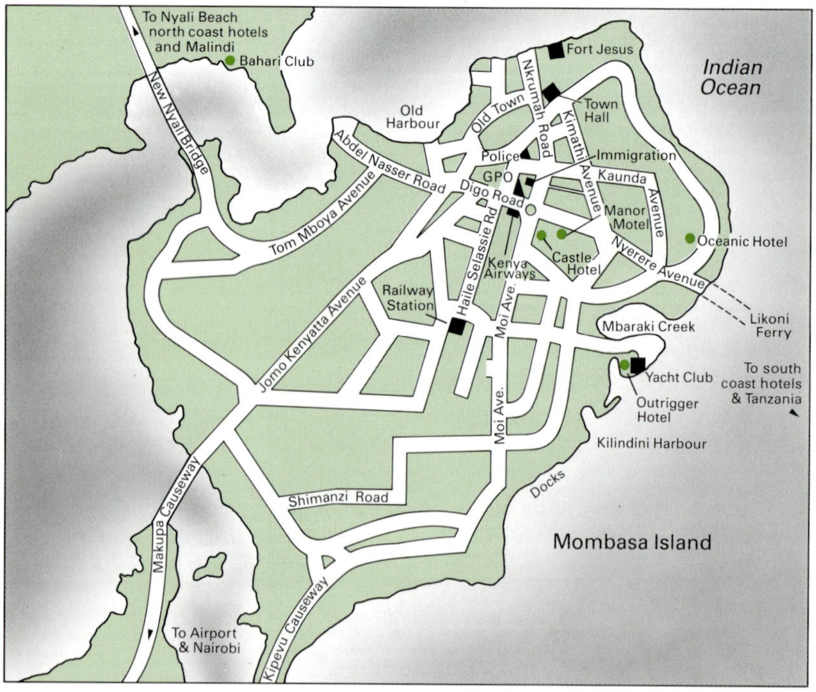

Activities

1 Study fig 11.15. Try and locate the CBD in Mombasa. What evidence is there of a tourist industry in and around Mombasa?
2 Since the 1950s, the government of Brazil has built a new capital city, Brasilia, in the shape of an aeroplane (look at fig. 7.51). Draw a simplified sketch map of Brasilia and locate on it the service industries.
3 Write a paragraph to explain why capital cities should have a higher proportion of service industries than other settlements.

Fig. 11.16 *City centre, Mombasa, Kenya. How does this compare with city centres in developed countries?*

The informal sector

In all countries there is work which does not fit into the official classification by sectors. This includes irregular employment in usually small-scale enterprises, some of which may not be strictly legal. A common name for this in European countries is 'the black economy'. Such irregular work is sometimes referred to as the informal sector.

Fig. 11.17 *The market, Marrakesh, Morocco*

It is also an important type of employment in developing countries. It can include up to 40% of all workers and includes street traders, taxi-drivers, rickshaw-men, carters, shoe-repairers, market stall-holders, and the like. Figure 11.17 shows Marrakesh in Morocco where street trading and roadside stalls are common features of retailing.

Services and service occupations grow in response to people's needs. Settlements which have large numbers of people with high living standards develop many and complex service activities. In most developing countries the proportion of the population which is wealthy is fairly small. So, service activities are usually less extensive than in developed countries.

However, the highest living standards are still found in the towns so it is there that service industries are best developed (Remind yourself of this by studying South-east Brazil on Page 31).

Leisure and tourism

The importance to the economy

Leisure and tourist industries are important sources of income in many countries. In some, like Barbados, it is the main source. In Britain, although its overall importance is less, it is the biggest growth industry. It is a very labour intensive industry which employs directly and indirectly, in Britain, 1.5 million people, in hotels, restaurants, travel, transport and leisure activities. The size of the workforce has increased by 22% over last ten years to 1987. It is at present creating jobs at a rate of 50 000 per year.

Leisure and tourism in Britain contribute 3 to 4% of the Gross National Product. They bring in billions of £'s of foreign currency each year. They are London's second biggest money earner. Since 1960, income from tourism has grown faster in Britain than in any other European country. The number of tourist visitors to Britain has increased enormously, from less than one million in 1960 to over 7 millions in 1985. Figure 11.18 shows the main countries of origin of these visitors in 1985. The main destinations of tourists in Britain, for both British holiday-makers and foreign tourists, are shown in fig. 11.19. Notice the popularity of London for foreign visitors. Which are the popular areas for British holiday-makers?

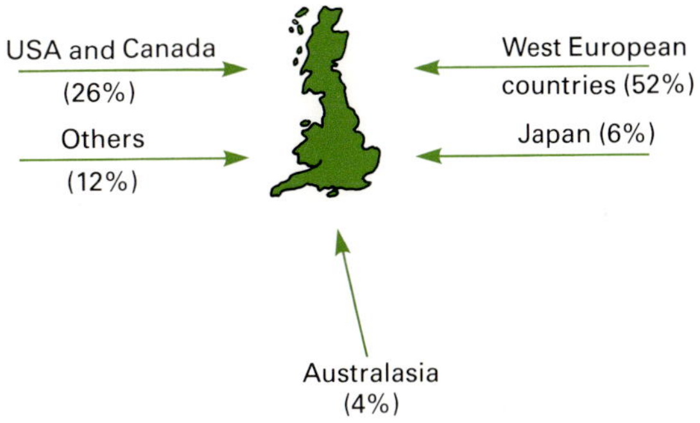

Fig. 11.18 *Country of origin of tourist visitors to Britain*

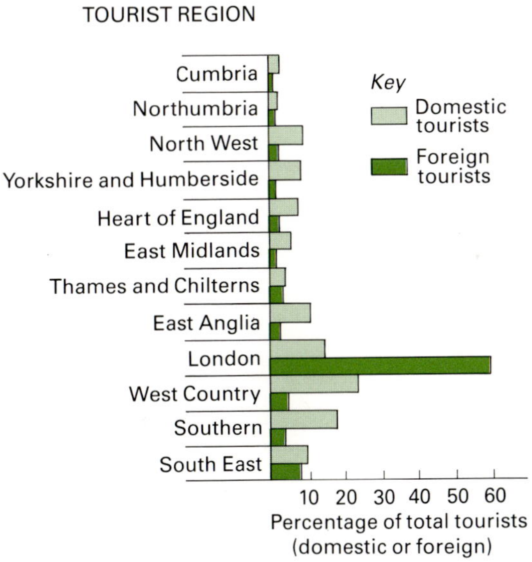

Fig. 11.19 *Visitors to the tourist regions of England*

Activities

1 Use advertising information for a National Park in Britain, a major seaside resort or a country park. Carry out a geographical enquiry either individually or in small groups to answer the following:
Why is your chosen park or resort popular with visitors?
What problems does this popularity create for other people?

2 Study fig. 11.23 on page 153. List the groups of people or organisations whose interests are in conflict. Which one(s) would you support? The class could divide into several groups and carry out a simulated public ènquiry from your studies.

Fig. 11.20 *Torquay*

Holiday resorts

Figure 11.21 shows that Torquay is sunnier and warmer than most other British seaside resorts. Variations from place to place in the natural environment, the weather and the landscape have important effects upon tourism. The British tourist industry is more dependent upon these, especially the weather, than most other countries. This causes it to be a very seasonal activity. Many British resorts have little attraction to people in the winter months. This can be a problem for people working in the industry in the resorts. For example, the population of Weymouth rises from 60 000 to over 200 000 during the months of July and August. Good communications and easy access to tourist centres for people living in large urban areas are secondary factors upon which the success of tourism depends. Figure 11.21 also shows the location of National Parks and some of the major resorts in relation to motorways.

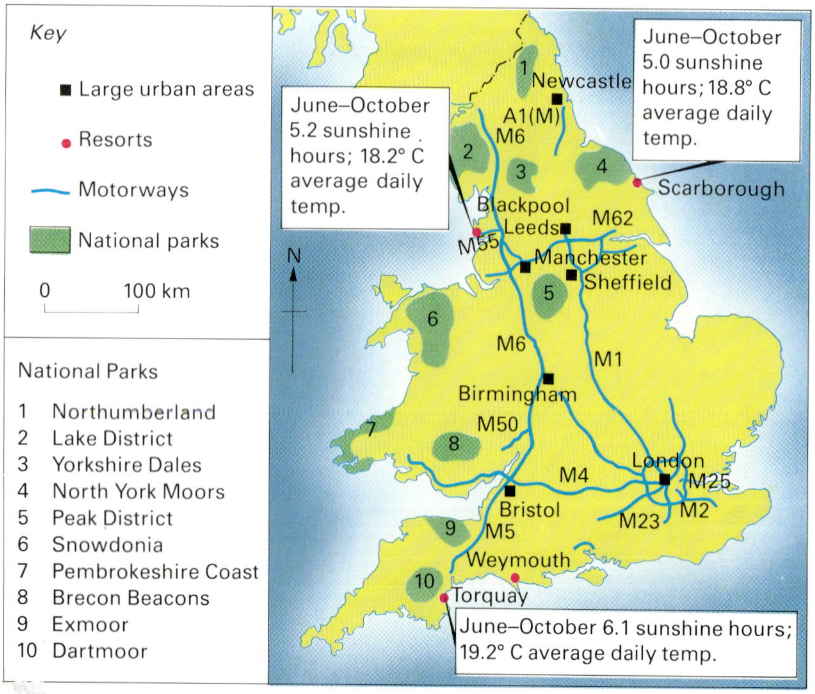

Fig. 11.21 *Tourist resorts and National Parks in England and Wales*

Leisure activities

Increased tourism, which involves travel out of the home area, is only one aspect of the leisure industry. There has also been an explosion in the recreational and leisure facilities in many areas to cater for local people. The upland areas of Britain, those over 240 metres above sea level, are particularly attractive to tourism and recreation, and attract many visitors. Figure 11.21 shows the ten National Parks of Britain. 80% of upland England and 30% of upland Wales have been designated either as National Parks or as 'areas of outstanding beauty'.

There is another side to the growth of tourism. Over the last 40 years, the British countryside has been increasingly threatened by people's activities. Nature conservation and protection of certain natural environments is now regarded by many people as a priority (look at fig. 11.22). However, the wish to conserve areas of beauty can become a major conflict of interests. Other people may wish to use the land in other ways. One conflict of interests which occurred was the proposal of Thos. W. Ward (Roadstone) Ltd. to extend a limestone quarry at Eldon Hill in the Peak District National Park (fig 11.23). The decision required careful judgement, trying to balance all the issues. If it could be proved that the country needed the mineral and that it could not be obtained elsewhere, then permission to quarry might be given.

Tourists themselves are a source of conflict inside National Parks. They create litter problems and cause fire hazards. Large numbers of walkers can erode footpaths. Gates to fields are left open and livestock escape. Town-bred dogs are a danger to farm animals. Car parks in the National Parks are increasingly needed and they can create 'eyesores'.

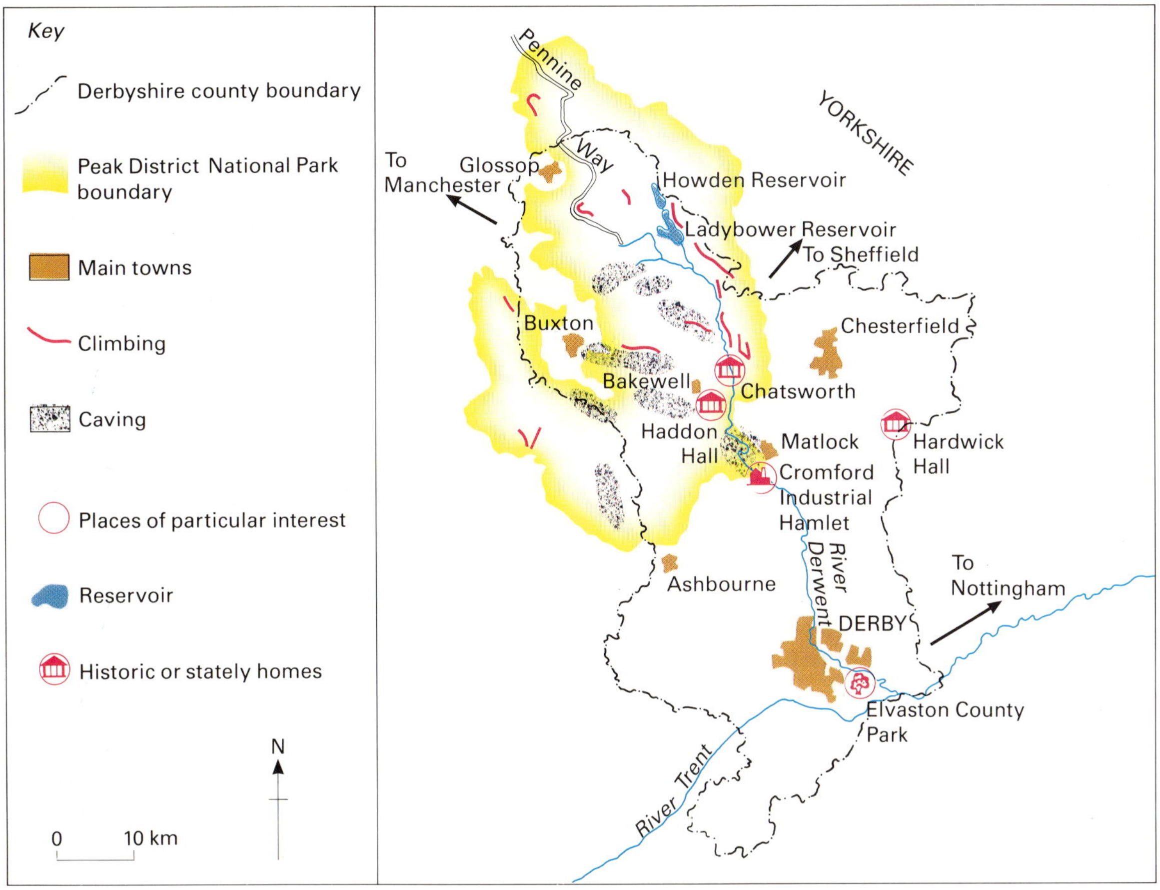

Fig. 11.22 *Some leisure and recreational facilities in Derbyshire*

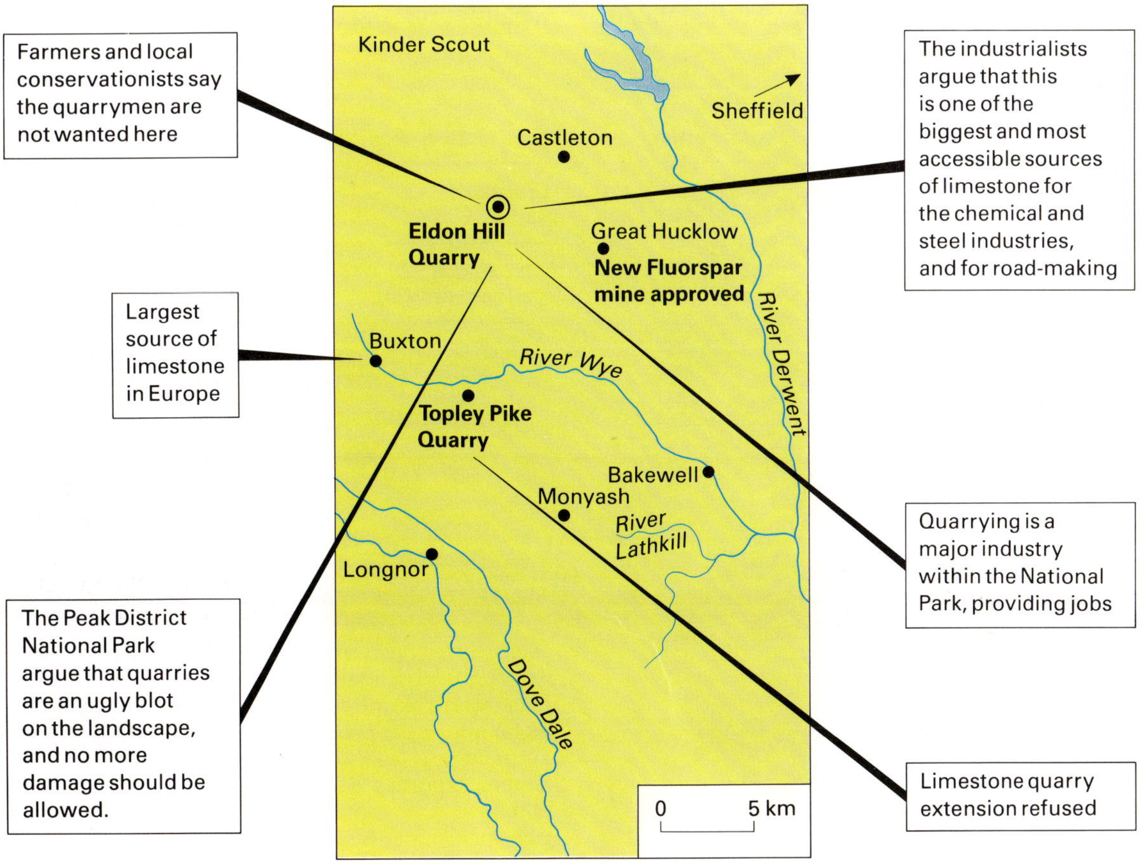

Fig. 11.23 *A proposal to extend Eldon Hill limestone quarry, Derbyshire*

International tourism

The pattern of tourist movement becomes increasingly complex. About one quarter of French tourists take their holidays abroad, mainly in Spain, Italy, West Germany, Switzerland and Britain. Since the 1950s, the international migration of tourists has become both more hectic and more complicated. British people holiday mainly in Spain. Germans holiday in Italy and Yugoslavia. Italians holiday in Switzerland. Americans holiday in Britain, Greece and Italy. The pattern becomes more complex as more countries become destinations for tourists and as tourism becomes more of an all-year-round activity.

Figure 11.24 shows the growth in the number of tourists visiting Spain since 1964. Tourism has become Spain's most important industry and its biggest earner of foreign currency. A 'sun-rush' is largely responsible for this as in Jamaica, Fig. 11.25. Two modern developments have made it possible. Air travel has become relatively cheap and 'package holiday' arrangements have combined travel and accommodation in one deal. Most tourist centres attracting foreign visitors are serviced by a nearby airport. Alicante serves the Benidorm area: Malaga allows access to the Costa del Sol and Palma airport allows millions of people to visit Majorca. An efficient airport has become essential for modern tourism.

The income from tourism is vital in the economy of developing countries like Jamaica and Kenya (see fig. 11.27 and 11.28). It is intended that the money earned will help to broaden the industrial base of the country. However, tourist developments bring both benefits and problems to Kenya. Tourist

Fig. 11.25 *Origin of tourist visitors to Jamaica 1985*

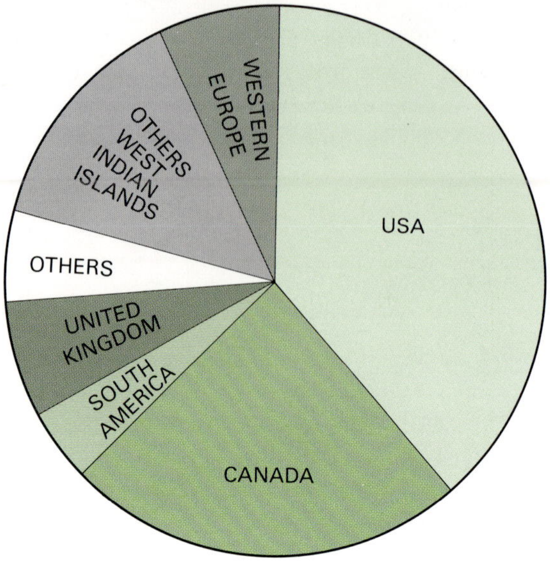

Fig. 11.24 *Number of foreign tourists visiting Spain*

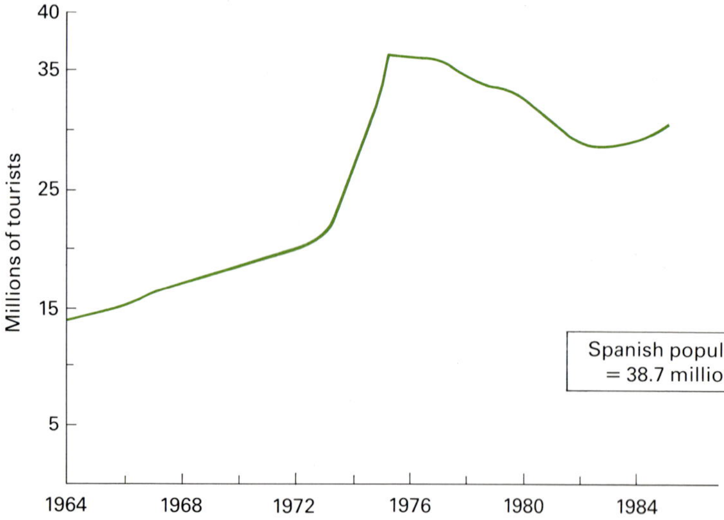

Fig. 11.26 *Climatic information for Kingston, Jamaica*

Climatic Factor	*January*	*July*	*Annual Average*
Average day temperature (°C)	24.4	27.2	26.1
Rainfall (mm)	22.9	38.1	800.1
Daily sunshine (hours)	7.9	7.9	7.4

Fig. 11.27 *Sources of foreign income in Jamaica*

Sources of foreign earnings	*1965*	*1985*
Bauxite and aluminium exports	39%	48%
Sugar and sugar product exports	29%	10%
Tourism	17%	26%
Banana exports	6%	4%
Others	9%	12%

spending may provide more jobs but they tend to be seasonal. They also tend to attract too many people to the popular tourist areas. The foreign currency does produce a general increase in the standards of economic welfare of the whole country but real and lasting benefits tend to apply to only a small number.

Fig. 11.28 *Tourist centres in Kenya*

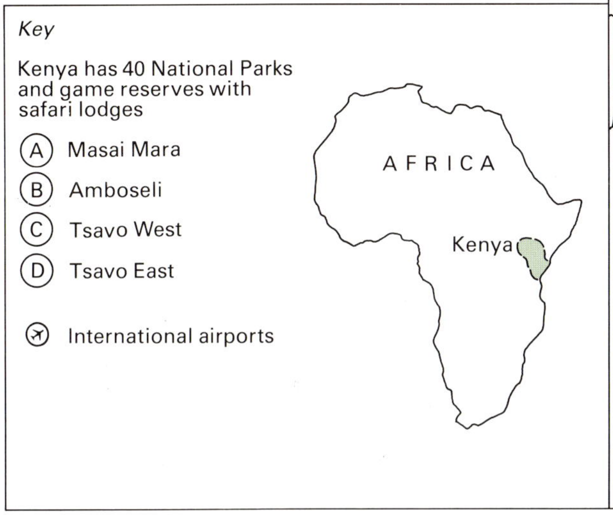

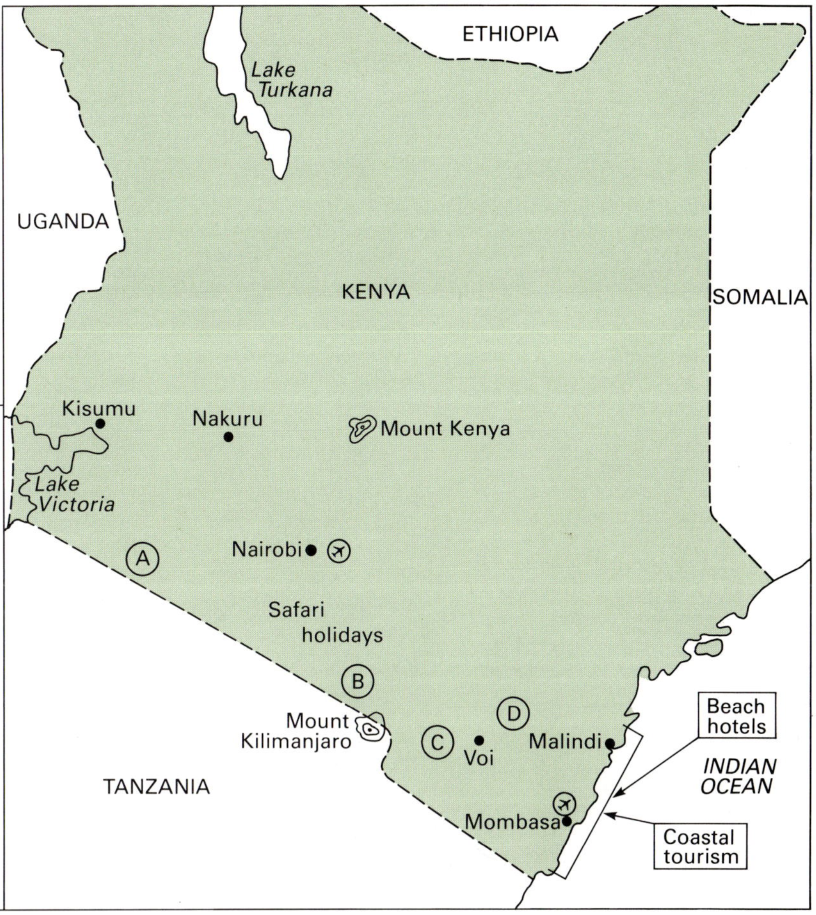

Activities

1. Draw a bar-chart to show the relative importance of the various sources of foreign income in Jamaica in 1985 (look at fig. 11.27).
2. Draw a sketch map of the Caribbean area to locate Jamaica. Include on the map the USA, Mexico, Central American countries and those of northern South America as well as the larger Caribbean islands.
3. Compare the temperatures and daily sunshine hours of Kingston, Jamaica, (fig. 11.26) to those of English resorts (fig. 11.21). What other considerations do you have to bear in mind when choosing a holiday?
4. Use information and illustrations from a holiday brochure.
   a) Draw a map to locate your airport of departure and airport of arrival.
   b) Draw a more detailed map of your chosen resort area, locating the airport and showing the main geographical features of the area.
   c) Draw a graph to show the hours of sunshine and temperatures of your resort area.
   d) Describe and illustrate the attractions for you in your chosen resort.

INDEX